A Lady of Anglesey

A BIOGRAPHY

Sophia Pari-Jones

Grosvenor House
Publishing Limited

All rights reserved
Copyright © Sophia Pari-Jones, 2025

The right of Sophia Pari-Jones to be identified as the author of this
work has been asserted in accordance with Section 78
of the Copyright, Designs and Patents Act 1988

The book cover is copyright to Sophia Pari-Jones

This book is published by
Grosvenor House Publishing Ltd
Link House
140 The Broadway, Tolworth, Surrey, KT6 7HT.
www.grosvenorhousepublishing.co.uk

This book is sold subject to the conditions that it shall not, by way of
trade or otherwise, be lent, resold, hired out or otherwise circulated
without the author's or publisher's prior consent in any form of
binding or cover other than that in which it is published and
without a similar condition including this condition being
imposed on the subsequent purchaser.

A CIP record for this book
is available from the British Library

Paperback ISBN 978-1-83615-106-7
Hardback ISBN 978-1-83615-107-4
eBook ISBN 978-1-83615-108-1

I dedicate this book to Jenny Moles, née Addison-Smith, a true friend and supporter. A genuine person who lost her life to cancer when they stopped her treatment due to COVID. She is sadly missed.

Introduction

Emma

I first encountered Emma when writing a book on the history of the mill, Felin Faesog, in Tai'n Lon, Clynnogfawr, Gwynedd, and an account of its the owners, the millers, and people who lived there. It began in the archives at Caernarvon, where I discovered an Indenture from 1760 between Thomas Rowlands and Robert Price (the Miller) for a two-hundred-year lease on the mill—referred to then as a water corn grist mill.

The Rowlands name caught my interest, so I went and I paid a visit to Bangor University Archive, where I met a very nice lady called Mrs Helen Ramage, who used to arrange bus trips around Anglesey, including to a place called Caerau in Llanfairynghornwy. Mrs Ramage is well known especially in Anglesey as the writer of *Portraits of an Island*. She encouraged me to find out more about Emma, and to go and look in the National Library of Wales in Aberystwyth. And so, the long days of research began.

I stayed in Aberystwyth for a week, studying various books and papers including one collection called 'Llanfair & Brynodol' and another called 'Garthewin'. Here, I came across letters from Emma to Mrs Owen of Porkington who was married to Thomas Rowlands's cousin William Owen. I had copies made of all the letters I found, so I could have time to read them and decide how they would be used in the book.

I found letters from Emma's father, Thomas, to his cousin which were a great contribution to her life story. And so, with her letters, those of her father's, and some from her aunt, Mrs Margaret Griffiths of Llanfairisgaer, Caernarvonshire to Mrs Owen of Porkington, I felt an interesting story emerging. There was one obstacle and that was, there were no records of Emma's childhood. I sat and contemplated what to do. At the Bangor University Archive, I found a collection of William Bulkeley's diaries, and amongst them descriptions by William

Bulkeley of various court actions with frequent mentions of Thomas Rowlands of Caerau.

Over the winter months, I would visit regularly, sitting there nice and warm. The archivist, Thomas Roberts, was very helpful, and allowed me to have copies of pages containing information helpful to my story. I spent hours reading them. They were so interesting and gave me a vivid picture of what life was like in the eighteenth century: the hardships, the poverty, and the constant deaths from influenza, when you would find eight or ten coffins outside a Church ready for burial.

As a second visit to Aberystwyth had not been as fruitful, and as I still had many questions in my head that needed answers, I went to the archives in Llangefni. Here I found the book that Thomas Rowlands had presented to the Church at Llanfairynghornwy on his marriage to Elen Roberts of Caerau. In the parish records, I found the birth dates of Thomas and Elen's children—of which Emma was one. I was now able to give dates to events and—with the information from William Bulkeley's diaries—things began to take shape.

One day, on yet another visit to the Bangor Archive, I was going through the papers of a solicitor to the Bulkeley's when I found a map which the archivist Mr Einion Thomas had never seen before. He helped me lay it on the floor and placed weights on the corners, so that I could photograph Caerau, which was then called 'Caerau Hall'. In the Bulkeley collection, I was excited to find letters from Emma to her second husband, Sir Hugh Williams, as well as letters from Sir Hugh to Emma during his time in Gibraltar. At long last I felt I had enough material on Emma to write an account of her life.

Like most young women, Emma had her fancies, such as a crush on Thomas Pennant, a well-known naturalist, and another on Owen Merrick of Bodorgan, Anglesey. While it was Lord Bulkeley who became her first husband, her real love affair was with Sir Hugh Williams.

She was lucky that Lord Bulkeley had a house in London, as she loved London with its fashion not only in dress but also in hairstyles. She met very interesting people, including Clive of India. She was also a very good businesswoman, and despite having lavish taste, saw to the accounts every Michaelmas and settled quite a lot of Lord

Bulkeley's debts when they were married. She also had a keen interest in the political situation and was determined to keep the Bulkeley seat in Parliament for her son Thomas James, who became the last Lord Bulkeley.

The most difficult part of the book was deciding where to begin and how to describe her life right up to the end, with her burial at Llanfairynghornwy Church, where there is a tablet dedicated to her, as well as one for Sir Hugh Williams and another for her grandfather, William Roberts.

There were many letters from Emma to Sir Hugh but were indecipherable, so I decided to use his letters. I have not translated the letters into modern English, as I felt that to do so would take away their magic. I have also kept to the village names as they were three hundred years ago, as many of the modern translations are incorrect.

I realise that someone else could come along and write a much better story, but what I have done is prove that Emma existed and described the difficult times in which she lived. I can only pray that I have done her justice.

Sophia Pari-Jones.

Places Names

Baron Hill	Home of the Bulkeley family
Boderwyd	Home of Chancellor Edward Wynn
Bodfior	Home of Emma's cousin also called Emma
Bryn Du	Home of William Bulkeley
Caerau	Home of Mrs Emma Roberts and of Emma
Friars	Home of Sir Hugh Williams
Gwyndy	The Old Coach House was where many stopped for refreshments. It was situated on the Old Post Road. Emma was one of the first people to give a large donation towards the building of Gwyndy. It was opened by the granddaughter of Jane Williams, who was matchmaker to the love affair between Emma and Sir Hugh Williams.
Hen Blas	Home of Mr Morgan, a relation of William Bulkeley
Llwydiarth	Home of Mr Lloyd
Mynachdy	Home of Mr Robinson, who drowned off the Skerries
Penrhos	Near Holyhead, home of the Owen family
Plas Newydd	Home of Mr Bayley
Presaddfed	Home of John Owen MP, a nephew to Mrs Roberts of Caerau
Rectory	Home of the vicar
Rhosbeirio	Home of Francis Lloyd, acting medical doctor.

List of Characters

B

William Bevan of Croes Fechan, Mold	Horse Dealer
Nicholas Bayley of Plas Newydd	Parliamentary candidate
James, Lord Bulkeley	Emma's first husband
Mr John Bulkeley	Owner of a school at Llanfechell
Richard, Lord Bulkeley	James Bulkeley's brother
William Bulkeley of Glanalaw	John Owen of Presaddfed's agent
William Bulkeley of Brynddu	18th Century Diarist of Anglesey
Mr William Bulkeley	Third son of Robert and Catherine Bulkeley of Dronwy, married to Ann Warmingham

C

Charles	Friend of Emma's brother William
Hugh Charles of Voyle	Sheep breeder

D

Lady Dalkeith	A friend
John Davies	A miller from Frogwy, accused of killing his maid
Joseph Davies of Cheshire	On trial for killing his comrade

Elizabeth Davies	Thomas Rowlands's sister
Richard Davies	Apprentice to Hugh Williams, glazier of Llannerchymedd
John Douglas	Robert Owen's father-in-law
John Downing of Mold	Horse breeder

E

John Edwards of Llanfechell	Boat owner
William Edwards	Bailiff of Caerau
Ella	Emma's Maid
Richard Evans	Surgeon from Llannerchymedd
Shadrach Evans	Butcher

F

Robert Foulkes	Boat owner
John Fowles of Dublin	John Owen's brother-in-law
Lady Prendergast	Sir Hugh William's cousin

G

George	Farm hand at Caerau
William George of Llanfwrog	Basket Maker
Grace	Cousin to Thomas
John Griffith of Brynodol	Margaret's husband and Thomas's brother-in-law
John Griffith of Dyffryn & Margaret Whyte of Neugwl Ucha	Mother and Father of John Griffith of Llanfairisgaer, husband of Margaret Griffiths, Thomas Rowland's sister

Margaret Griffith, Llanfairisgaer, Caernarvon	Thomas Rowland's sister
William Griffith	Owner of a boat called 'Cloxan' carrying coal
Captain William Griffith of Cefnamwlch	Grandfather to Hugh, William and Frances Griffith
William Griffith	Emma's cousin

H

Mr Herbert	Ministry Man
Mr Roger Holland	Judge
Mr Host	Potato specialist
Mr Hughes of Denbighshire	Curate of Beaumaris
Mrs Hughes	Elizabeth's Mother
Elizabeth Hughes	Emma's friend
Jane Hughes	Housekeeper's Mynachdy
John Hughes of Gwredog	Stallion's owner
Owen Hughes	Chancellor of Bangor
Richard Hughes	Tenant of Thomas's living at Castellior

I

Robert ab Ifan & his wife Margaret	Lived at Caerau
Iris	Kitchen Maid

J

Richard Johnson	Merchant
Mr Jones of Plas Gwyn	Juror
Gabriel Jones carrying coal	Joint-owner of a boat called the 'Cloxan'

John Jones of Penhesgin	Apprentice
Rev John Jones	Cousin of Thomas
Owen Jones	Relative of Thomas
Morgan Jones	Skerries lighthouse keeper
Rev Rowland Jones	Cousin to Thomas
Tom Jones	Teacher from Llanfechell
Nicholas Jourdin	Silk Mercer

L

Simon Langford	Brother-in-law to Mother Roberts
Sina Langford	Sister to Mother Roberts and wife of Simon Langford
Robert Lawrence	Owner of the Maesincla estate, which he sold to John Rowlands
Lettice	Mrs Emme Roberts's sister
Mr Lewis	Artist from Shrewsbury
Richard Lewis	Vicar of Llanidan
Thomas Lewis of Trefeibion Meyrig	A well-known drover who did many favours for people
Lady Longerville	William Owen's sister
Mr Lloyd	Bailiff at Plas-y-Nant
Mr Lloyd of Llwydiarth	A friend
Betty Lloyd of Llanfechell	Dressmaker
Catherine Lloyd	William Bulkeley's sister
Mr & Mrs Francis Lloyd	Settled in Rhosbeirio
John Lloyd	Son of R. Lloyd of Ireland

Gruffydd Llwyd	Bought the land and built Caera
Richard Lyster	Electoral Candidate
Lumely	Daughter to William Bulkeley's uncle

M

Margaret	Daughter of William Owen
Mrs Meyrick	Wife of Owen Meyrick of Bodorgan
Mrs Ann Meyrick	Wife of William Hughes, parson of Llantrisant
Owen Meyrick	Son Of Owen Meyrick Bodorgan
Owen Meyrick of Bodorgan	A well-known Whig and father of Owain Bravura
Mr Morgan of Henblas	A relative of William Bulkeley
Rowland Morgan	Son of the Parson of Llanfairynghornwy
William Morgan	Vicar of Llanfairynghornwy
Morris Brothers	18th Century Recorders of Anglesey and its people
Thomas Morris of Rhydygroes	Wildlife searcher

O

Nicholas Oughton	Choir Master
Mr Owen	Horse keeper at Caerau
Mr Owen of Penrhos	Juror
Ann Owen	John Fowler's wife

Emma Owen	married William Owen of Presaddfed and Emma's cousin
Hugh Owen of Penrhos	Nephew of Mrs Roberts
Hugh Owen	Son of William Owen of Bodean
Jane Owen of Llanfechell	A farmer's wife
John Owen of Presaddfed	Mrs Roberts's nephew and Emma's uncle
Lewis Owen	Cousin of Thomas
Margaret Owen	Daughter and sole heiress to John Owen of Bodior
Molly Owen	William Owen's daughter
Richard Owen	Butcher to Caernarvon
William Owen of Brogyntyn	Thomas's cousin
Robert Owen	Doctor
Robert Owen (Bobby)	Son of William Owen
William Owen of Porkington	Thomas's cousin

P

Mr Thomas Pennant	Traveller and Naturalist
Thomas Prendergast	Husband of Ann Williams
William Price of Rhiwlas	Parliamentary Candidate
Hugh Price	Receiver and storer of smuggled goods
Griffith Pritchard	In charge of the Court
John Pritchard	Burglar
Mr Pugh	The excise man
Mr Pugh of Moelfra	Carrier of sand to Cemaes by boat London

R

Ann	Mrs Emme Roberts's sister
Robert Roberts	Settled at Caerau
Captain Roberts	Officer in Colonel Philip Bragg's regiment
Emme Roberts	Emma's grandmother
Mrs Roberts	Now known as 'Mother Roberts'
Gabriel Roberts	Prolific businessman
Thomas Roberts of Bodior	Mother Roberts's brother-in-law
William Roberts	Saddler of Llannerchymedd
William Roberts	Mrs Emme Roberts's late husband
Elizabeth Robinson	Mr Robinson of Mynachdy's wife
Rogers of Cemaes	A well-known smuggler
William (Rowlands)	Emma's brother
Frances (Rowlands)	Emma's sister
Elin Rowlands (née Roberts)	Emma's mother
Thomas Rowlands of Caerau	Emma's father
John Rowlands	Thomas's father, a banker in London
Richard Rowlands	Thomas Rowland's brother who inherited the Plas-y-Nant estate

S

John Pritchard Samuel	Shoemaker of Llanfairynghornwy

T

Captain Tange	Officer in General Patrick's regiment
Mary Tannant	William Owen's cousin
Mr Thomas of Tre'r Gof	Treasurer to the Jury

V

Ann Vaughan	Heiress and daughter of Richard Vaughan of Rhosbeirio, married to Richard Lloyd of Hirdrefaig
Admiral Vernon	Naval commander in the Spanish War
Vincent of Llanfachraeth	Candidate for usher of Beaumaris school

W

Owen Warmingham	Carrier of corn to Caernarvon
Jane White	Only child and heiress of Mr William White of Friars Beaumaris
Mr Williams	Parson of Llanfaethlu
Mrs Williams	Housekeeper at Plas-y-Nant
Thomas Williams	Tailor
Mrs Ann Williams	Mrs Emme Roberts's mother
David Williams	Attorney who worked for most of the gentry
Sir Hugh Williams	Emma's second husband

Hugh Williams of Chester	The Baron Hill party parliamentary candidate
Hugh Williams	A joiner from Llannerchymedd
John Williams of Ty Newydd, Llansilin	Mrs Emme Roberts's brother
Owen Williams	A glazier from Llannerchymedd
Thomas Williams	Running boats
William Williams	The gardener at Caerau
Sir Watkin Williams Wynn	Electoral Candidate
Mr Hugh Woodcock	Charles's father
Mr Wright	William Bulkeley's son-in-law
Paul & John Wyatt	Cotton Traders
Catherine Wynn	Thomas Rowland's sister
Mrs Dolly Wynn of Glynllifon	Dolly Wynn's husband
Dr Edward Wynne of Boderwyd	Chancellor of Hereford Cathedral
Mrs Wynne	Chancellor Wynne's wife

Emma Bulkeley, 1727–1770

Chapter One

Emma sat gazing through the drawing room window at Baron Hill. Boats approaching from Conwy and the Lavan Sands, which she usually enjoyed seeing, went unnoticed.

Preoccupied with her new position, her greatest indignation was in having to wear a widow's outfit for at least two years. Had her husband, the 6th Viscount Bulkeley, been a kind and honourable man, she would have accepted her widowhood with the reverence expected of a well-known family, especially one as prestigious as the Bulkeleys of Baron Hill. The cruelty and brutality that she had endured from her husband had caused her to dislike him immensely. His family also had put her through so much discomfort after his death that it seemed it was their purpose to leave her in straightened financial circumstances.

Her future was made safe by the birth of her son, the 7th Viscount Bulkeley, six months after the death of her husband, which saved the Bulkeley seat. Emma was adamant that her dreary black dress would soon be put away despite the probability of objections from her husband's family and her own. Her cheeks flushed as her fury rose. There was no love lost; her husband had mistreated her many times. She stood up which brought her out of her disillusionment. Moving away from the window she caught a mirrored reflection of herself and thought how drab she looked in the mourning dress, hating it even further; besides, she was too young, she felt, to be wearing such dull attire. She reflected a while before deciding to join the children before they were put to bed.

Emma was born in 1727: a year that proved to be quite historical. King George I died; George II was crowned king; the famous painter, Thomas Gainsborough, was born, and Isaac Newton died; marriage advertisements appeared in the newspapers and the Racing Calendar was published for the first time. It was also the year that the well-known fairy tale, *The Sleeping Beauty,* was translated from French into English.

Caerau, Llanfairynghornwy, stands to the Northwest of Anglesey Island. It was the home of Mrs Emme Roberts and her daughter, Elin, after the death of her husband, William Roberts, who died on February 7th, 1715. It was her home now with her daughter and her son-in-law, Thomas Rowlands. Thomas and Elin had two children, William and Frances.

January 13th, 1727, was a cold blustery day and the swirling winds from around Ynys Fydlyn, Porth-yr-Hwch, Yr Hen Borth, Porth yr Ysgraiff and Carmel Point howled around Caerau. Mrs Roberts instructed that the doors were to be barred and battened down to keep the house warm. The kitchen staff were busy making sure that there was plenty of hot water for when the new baby arrived. Thomas was away for the day. It was his last as high sheriff. Dutifully he was attending the ceremony of the newly elected high sheriff, Henry Morgan of Henblas. The birth went well, and Elin certainly looked the picture of health when holding her new daughter for the first time. The baby's hair was of dark curly fluff and Elin thought how like her father she was.

Thomas returned home in the late afternoon and William was running towards him, trying to tell him that the new baby had arrived, but he was too excited at seeing his father, and his words fell out in a mumble. Thomas, afraid that his wife might not be well enough to see him, tried to quell William's excitement by saying that it would be better to wait until tomorrow to see the new infant. Mrs Roberts, who was carrying Frances, assured him that all was well and that he had a beautiful daughter with a mop of dark curly hair. This encouraged Thomas to visit his wife with William in tow. He entered the room and pushed back the curtain of the four-poster bed, kissed his wife gently on her forehead and congratulated her. He was not one to admire babies, but having entered the room and found his wife in such good health he peeped at Emma. He seemed to be transfixed. He had not seen such a beautiful baby. He felt the closeness of fatherhood. Little did he realise that this tiny baby and he were to be the only two left of his growing family.

When the excitement had calmed down, Thomas played with William before sending him to bed after Mrs Roberts had managed to encourage Frances to sleep. He sat alone that evening contemplating the making of a new will, a custom most educated families practised with great frequency as they expanded. William would inherit the Plas-y-Nant estate, Betws Garmon, Caernarvonshire, an estate that Thomas' father, John Rowlands, a banker in Lombard Street, London, had increased since he built the house in 1671. Caerau would have to be shared between Frances and Emma. It was his wife's inheritance from her father, William Roberts, who died when she was 16 years old.

Mother Roberts, his mother-in-law, joined him after dinner. They discussed various issues regarding a new will and agreed on matters amicably. Mrs Roberts was an astute woman. When Thomas married her daughter, Elin, she had made him agree, as part of their marriage settlement, that he would live at Caerau. Also, she advised that as one of his wedding gifts, he should present the Llanfairynghornwy Church with a register so that the parish could keep a record of children born and people who were married and died, which he agreed to do and carried out. It was, he felt, a way for the parson to have a better knowledge of his congregation. Everything was settled according to Mrs Roberts's instructions now and Thomas prepared to write another will.

Before his marriage to Elin, Thomas lived at Plas Maesincla, Caernarvon, an estate his father had bought from Robert Lawrence who had died with no issue. Thomas was living there on his return from Oxford. His elder brother, Richard, living at home in Plas-y-Nant, Betws Garmon, was suffering from consumption and died aged 23 leaving Thomas as the next heir of the estate. He was pleased to write a new will leaving the Plas-y-Nant estate to his son. He would, he hoped, as he grew up, take him to Caernarvonshire to see and stay at his old home.

The week following Emma's birth went by quickly for Thomas with all the extra work of a new baby, telling William stories before he went to bed each night, preparing the new will to safeguard them all, and making the arrangements for her christening on January 23rd, 1727.

When the christening day arrived, Thomas felt sure during the ceremony that Emma smiled at him which caused both his wife and Mrs Roberts to smile when informing him that it was probably a bout of wind. However, Thomas chose to believe otherwise, he felt a close affinity with Emma.

As was the custom in the 18th century, Thomas hurriedly wrote letters to many of his relatives – his sister, Mrs Margaret Griffith of Caernarvon, the wife of John Griffith, Brynodol, his sister, Catherine, who was married to Captain Samuel Wynn of Glanrafon Bach, and his sister, Elizabeth, married to Hugh Davies of Caerhun. He wrote to other members of his family, including his cousins at Porkington or Brogyntyn in Shropshire announcing Emma's birth. He was content that his immediate family were happy at Caerau, though he would soon have to think of enlarging the house to accommodate them all.

The year 1727 had certainly been extraordinary. Having been the high sheriff, Thomas along with John Owen of Presaddfed, Mrs Robert's nephew, had been considered as suitable candidates for the forthcoming election. This was caused by the death of King George on June 11th, 1727. Both men were known to be Tories and in great favour with the Baron Hill party. The 5th Viscount Bulkeley was not yet of age to stand in the election. What the Bulkeleys wanted was someone who would secure the seat for his lordship. Both John Owen and Thomas turned the request down. Thomas preferred to consider his family. He did not much enjoy the continued bickering of the political factions around the island; besides, the cost of an election was more than he could afford. Since the birth of Emma, all these matters were important as his finances were not great. He continued as a member of the jury at Beaumaris, where the courts were held, and busied himself in supporting Hugh Williams of Chester, who was standing for the Baron Hill party in the election. Time had to be given also to the running of both the Caerau and Plas-y-Nant estates. Money from rents of various lands was certainly going to be needed now.

William, Frances and Emma were very important to Thomas. Elin, his wife, was well enough to be up and about again. Nothing gave him more pleasure than to tell the children fairy stories before they went to bed. Elin held Frances as they listened, worried that some of the tales might keep the children awake rather than help them sleep, though Emma gurgled happily in her cradle.

Mrs Roberts was called away quite often as her mother, Mrs Ann Williams, the wife of Mr David Williams of Glanalaw, was getting weaker and on September 17th, 1727, she peacefully passed away.

The rest of the year was spent making sure that all was well with tenants of various properties on the Caerau lands and all the lands belonging to the Plas-y-Nant estate in Betws Garmon. Thomas travelled between Anglesey and Caernarvonshire several times between 1727 and 1728.

Later that year he learnt that another addition to his family was expected. Tragedy struck in 1729 when Elin, who was pregnant with her fourth child, had a very difficult time. The birth took place on April 7th, but the baby was seriously ill. The parson was called to christen her. She was named Elin after her mother but sadly she died. On April 10th, Elin also died. Thomas was devastated. All he had been working for over the last year he felt had been taken away from him. He would lock himself away each night, his only consolation was a bottle of brandy. The shock was so great that he nearly forgot to console Mrs Roberts who had lost her only child.

During this time, Anglesey was suffering from an epidemic, which was rather like influenza. Many people were dying from it, especially the poor. No one knew if it had affected Elin, who had caught a cold two months before the birth. Mrs Roberts had made sure that she had plenty of rest and the best food available. This epidemic ran for over two years. The death was a great shock to her, although Mrs Roberts knew much about death. She had lost her husband when Elin was 16 years old and was left to bring her up alone. In 1723 she had lost her eldest sister Lettice, the wife of John Owen, who had bought Presaddfed from Lord and Lady Duncannon. They had eight children and Mrs Roberts had been much in demand, being their favourite aunt. In 1724 she lost her only brother, John Williams of Ty Newydd Llansilin. On September 27th, 1727, she lost her mother, and in 1728, her sister, Ann, who was married to Hugh Owen, Cae'r Berllan, Llanfihangel-y-Pennant in Merionethshire, died. If anyone had cause to be disillusioned with the world, it was certainly Mrs Roberts, but having many other matters to think about – such as her grandchildren – had helped her to keep her composure for which she was well-known.

Thomas could not make up his mind whether to stay at Caerau or move back to Caernarvonshire, to his old home Plas-y-Nant, Betws Garmon. He felt sure that his sister, Mrs Margaret Griffith, who lived at Llanfairisgaer, in Caernarvon, would help with the upbringing of his children. Mrs Roberts, however, assured him that there was no good reason for him to move. She would help with the children as she had helped with bringing them up so far. Also, she claimed, rightly, that they were quite used to her. She had to be strong, not only for Thomas' sake but for her three grandchildren, who were all too small to understand what was going on. Most of her family considered her to be very wise – a woman who never panicked whatever situation arose. Afraid that depression might overtake Thomas, Mrs Roberts encouraged him to continue with his plans to extend Caerau, so that the children could have more room. It would be nice for William to have his own room. Frances and Emma could share, and Thomas would have a study all to himself downstairs.

In 1730 a substantial extension was added to Caerau, which made it look more like a Georgian house. Mrs Roberts continued living in the old part of the house, though she would join in with the big house when entertaining her rather large family, consisting mainly of nephews and nieces. A walled garden was included and to the west of the garden, a rectangular building was put up. One side was used as storage, the main division containing a privy which had three seats, and another built to one side at a lower level for the children.

The gate to Caerau.

Map showing Caerau.

William, Frances and bubbly Emma, with her head full of dark curls, were getting excited about the new house with William announcing that he was to be the first to choose the room he wanted; leaving what was left to the girls. He loved to tease them. Frances was like a little mother to Emma who was growing and full of fun and loved games, such as running around the room and hiding behind chairs. Everyone made a fuss of Emma and Mrs Roberts spoilt her. She had become the favourite and her father adored her.

William and Frances were now addressing Mrs Roberts as 'Mother Roberts' and Emma, of course, would soon follow suit. Having three children to look after was to be a full-time job for Mrs Roberts and she accepted it well. She was quite used to helping with her own sisters' children; she seemed to know exactly what to do. Now she would have to think not only about the right food but also about clothes. Extending Caerau would mean that they needed suitable clothes befitting the times and life in a Georgian house.

Thomas travelled to Caernarvon to visit John Griffith, his brother-in-law, to organise loans through mortgage bonds against the properties he already had, so that he could help Mrs Roberts with the costs and have enough money to build the extension to Caerau. John Griffith would know of other gentlemen who would be willing to help, and arrangements were made to hold a meeting so that Thomas could present them with all the facts regarding the lands he held, along with those of Caerau, which were held by Mrs Roberts. Many indentures were arranged. Plans for the house were meticulously put together which he showed Mrs Roberts and the children. Besides this, he had to find a builder who would start on the new foundations as soon as possible, while he made other decisions about how far the stables would be from the house, together with plans for a driveway, so that Caerau would have a front entrance as well as that for the tradesmen.

When he returned from his visit to Caernarvon, he took the children with him for walks as he examined the vista from various corners of the estate before deciding on the exact spot for the driveway. This would ensure that visitors would not see the house until they came near to it. The children scampered along and started playing games as Thomas studied charts and plans whilst he scribbled notes. He placed wooden posts on either side of the space for a gateway, before deciding what sort of pillars would have to be built. He loved to hear the three youngsters laughing, inventing stories about ghosts as he worked. He chose a good spot between two fields for the drive. On one side there were plenty of trees. He would plant another row of trees on the other side which would create a pleasance for his guests, where they would be able to meander along with the sea breeze billowing through the boughs of the trees on a warm summer evening. When the Caerau workmen had finished working in the fields, they were sent down to the seashore to collect stones suitable for cobbling the driveway. The whole thing had to be done by hand.

A mounting-block was erected on the outside boundary wall of the house so that Mother Roberts could mount her horse easily. She was well-known as a horsewoman and could tell all there was to know about the animals – whether a horse was well-trained and gentle or moody, and whether it tended to throw its head back, which meant that it might throw a rider off. The horse's eyes had to be right before she ever bought a horse. Her instructions to Thomas were that he should make sure that the horse did not have too much bow in its back, that the horse was in fine fettle, alert, and had a good, healthy, shiny coat. She taught Thomas so much about them and he could recognise a good breed some distance away thanks to her teachings.

After two more visits to Caernarvon to see his brother-in-law and two other gentlemen, he secured the loans needed. Staying the night to rest his horse after his journey, he welcomed the chance to talk with his sister and brother-in-law, catching up with news from both London and Oxford where he had been educated. He learnt that John and Charles Wesley had founded a Methodist sect at Oxford, and it would not be too long before Methodism arrived in the Island of Anglesey which caused much consternation amongst many of the gentry. His sister, Margaret, who was extremely interested in the new extension, enthused him with various ideas and the suitability of certain items which, according to her, would be beneficial for the children. Riding home to Caerau, Thomas thought of all that had been put forward. Most of the ideas he felt were more suited for a townhouse rather than a country house like Caerau, which suffered at times from buffeting and exceedingly cold winds circulating it.

Once the outer structure was in place, it was time to think of the inside layout. In the kitchen and adjoining pantry, built-in cupboards were placed, shelving and a dresser with panelled doors were fitted and arched recesses were built. A corner cupboard in the pantry had the date 1730 carved into it, with a geometrical design to declare the birth of the new extension. Each bedroom had pine panelling with moulded cornices, door architraves and pediments. Over the fireplace in each room, a panel containing a contemporary landscape painting was hung. In the east room, a double partition to the passage contained cupboards on either side of the door and a closet set against a large chimney stack. The staircase had turned balusters, panelled newels and a moulded handrail. Above the kitchen door leading to the hallway and the rest of the house, slats were fitted, so that the constant heat from the kitchen would filter through to keep the house warm. The choice of curtains and other draperies Thomas left to Mrs Roberts who, under the guidance of her nieces and other younger members of her family, made several suggestions on the suitability of various materials. She felt that they were living in a more modern society and therefore it was important for her grandchildren to be part of this new world.

Photograph of kitchen, showing over-door slats
which allowed heat to travel and warm the house.

1730 disappeared quickly with all the excitement of building the extension. Thomas rode out to Llannerchymedd to complete his order for windows with Owen Williams, the glazier. He also called to see Hugh Williams, the Llannerchymedd joiner, whose apprentice needed some pieces of oak to finish off a job in the kitchen. The children could hardly wait. It was early 1731 when they eventually moved in. Thomas was quite pleased with the gateposts that had been built. They were of stone and would help to make Caerau appear as a place of some importance. It was known as Caerau Hall.

Life continued to be as busy as ever. Emma was now able to say 'papa' clearly which pleased Thomas immensely. William was interested in the farm workers and knew all their names, especially those who led the horses to work. Frances amused herself with wooden alphabet blocks, trying to learn words. Her pallor had not been good for some time, which caused them all some anxiety.

Mrs Roberts took Emma with her on occasions, especially when she visited the market at Llannerchymedd, though Emma was only three years old. Llannerchymedd was not just a commercial centre of the island; it was famous throughout the whole of Wales. Traders from England, Ireland and France came to buy wares there. The shoes and clogs were of the highest quality possible and were the chief purchases by visiting trades people. The shoes were in such demand that more than 250 men were employed in making them. The market was known also for the best milking cows, oxen, pigs and horses. It sold the best butter, cheese, flax, wool, homespun cloth, hemp and the strongest rope to be found. People from London were keen to buy snuff from Llannerchymedd where what was called 'high dried Welsh snuff' by Bryan's was manufactured.

During the Protectorate of Cromwell, Llannerchymedd requested the establishment of a market which was granted in 1657 and confirmed by Charles II in 1665. At that time, except for Beaumaris, this was the only market on the whole island that was given royal consent. It continued until 1785. The market was held on Wednesdays. Besides the market, five annual fairs were held, on January 1st, March 10th, April 4th, May 6th, and June 23rd. There had been a market at Llannerchymedd in much earlier times, which diminished as other markets opened. Besides the importance of its markets, Llannerchymedd was used when the quarter sessions at Beaumaris were adjourned, the meetings would be held at Llannerchymedd. Many decisions were completed there before attending the main court at Beaumaris.

The town was also the home of the most important harpists of the day. They excelled in penillion singing which had originated in Ireland and had crossed the sea to become part of Anglesey's tradition. Every tavern in Llannerchymedd had a harpist and horn pipes who entertained the customers. As Mrs Roberts examined goods at various stalls, the penillion singing, along with the harp, could be heard from every corner of the market. Many of the gentry employed a harpist to entertain their friends when they visited, many having a night of singing old Welsh songs which had been introduced to the gentry of Anglesey by the Morris brothers, who recorded many events in connection with Anglesey and its life during the 18th century. Therefore, visiting Llannerchymedd market was an entertaining day out. Mrs Roberts was very proud of the market and loved visiting it. Here she bought cloth to make dresses for Frances, Emma, and a new jacket for William. He was growing so quickly that nothing fitted him for long. Emma was taken with all the colours and loved nothing more than to be taken to see the horses. Often Mrs Roberts' maid, Elizabeth, would look after Emma so that Mrs Roberts could have a few hours to herself with plenty of time to buy all the necessities.

When she returned home, she found that Thomas was out. He had gone over to Presaddfed, the home of her nephew, John Owen. He spent the late afternoon there discussing the political issues that had come from London where John Owen spent most of his time. He learnt that 10 Downing Street, Westminster, was completed as a residence for the Prime Minister, who had recently moved in. Thomas also wanted to question John Owen about policies he hoped to put forward in the next election and repeatedly exclaimed that times were hard, and consideration of peoples' plight should be remembered. Returning to Caerau late that evening, Thomas found Mrs Roberts still up, worried about Frances, who was poorly, having had another coughing attack which the doctor diagnosed as the onset of consumption, though he was not unduly worried. Plenty of rest and fresh air without too much running about should help. Thomas and Mrs Roberts both retired hoping that Frances would show signs of improvement soon.

The year 1732, which then began in March under the old-style calendar, came in very noisily with such high winds that it was difficult for the workmen to do their work. Mary, the kitchen maid, when she went out to feed the hens, was buffeted so violently that Ned the bailiff had to come to her aid, helping her up to make sure that she was not thrown about by the winds before she managed to collect the eggs. He returned her to the house where she was only too glad to give the others an account of what had happened to her, gaining so much sympathy that the cook gave her a bowl of hot soup from the huge pot on the stove to warm her up. It was three days before the winds abated.

Thomas completed plans for the stables, which were built with accommodation for the servants above. The animals' body heat would keep their rooms warm. Planning various open slots in the walls was considered a good idea as it would allow the heat to circulate in the building.

Frances became increasingly weak, causing much anxiety to the family. Emma was too young to understand how serious her illness was, but William was very upset. He had always had Frances near him and any secrets he wished to share were always with her. They were true playmates. Since her illness had started, he did his best to try and cheer her up each day with his funny stories about his adventures around the estate, about his favourite animals and how Emma was always getting the kitchen maids to take her to see newly born chicks. She would sit in the hay for hours watching them and tried on many occasions to catch one to take inside with her for company, but the maids restrained her. Unfortunately, with each day, Frances grew weaker still. Mother Roberts spoke to both William and Emma and told them that Frances would not be with them for long, God needed her to help Him in His garden. This, the children seemed to accept and two days later Frances died.

Once more, Thomas drowned his sorrows through drink, especially when visitors called to see him with their customary sympathy. This annoyed Mother Roberts, though she could understand his despair. She concentrated on making sure that the workmen hired to work on the building of Caerau called on him as often as possible to try and keep him interested in finishing his plans and assure him that they were able to carry out the work needed to finish the stables. She felt that he needed to be occupied rather than sit indoors drinking. She kept reminding him that there were William and Emma to be considered and how important it was that arrangements were made for their education. William would be seven on September 19th, which should encourage Thomas to hire a schoolteacher for him, if only for a few hours three or four days a week.

Thomas heard from his cousin William Owen of Brogyntyn, in Shropshire, who had written to say that he would be calling to see him, as he was travelling to Anglesey for a meeting with the Baron Hill family to discuss a political matter concerning the continued unrest after the last election. He looked forward to this and it helped to quell his grief for a while. On the first night after dinner, they had a most interesting conversation, with William Owen giving accounts of the political situation in London. The news was given also of the stress caused to many travelling long distances, with highwaymen being more prevalent than ever and people becoming frightened of travelling. Thomas heard also that the Convent Garden Opera House was now open in London, and that the Serpentine, Hyde Park, had been laid out, which he found most interesting. He noted this as another place to visit and something to pass on to his many friends on the island, as a place to see when they visited London which most did at least once a year. Having seen his cousin off the following morning, Thomas checked his notes and made sure that the building work was carried out to his specifications, which he hoped would be to the children's benefit, and having listened to Mrs Roberts's worldly wisdom, he interviewed several people for the job of teaching William in readiness for going to school when he was older.

Life resumed to normality again and Caerau was finished in between his visits to Beaumaris where he attended the courts as a member of the grand jury, his visits to Baron Hill, where he was always welcome, being a staunch supporter and many visits to Caernarvonshire. On his return home, Emma would pester Thomas for stories about what went on and he would entertain her with the events of the day at the law court. During the evening, he would discuss the children with Mrs Roberts and ask whether they behaved as expected of young children and whether they were courteous and obedient. This particular evening, he was glad to inform her that life for the poor would soon be made simpler through the courts, as the use of the Latin language had been abolished, making it easier for people to understand what was going on.

A teacher named Mr Tom Jones of Llanfechell was engaged to teach William. He would spend three days a week at Caerau teaching and dining with Thomas so that he could give an account of William's progress. Mr Jones the schoolteacher always complimented Emma, even though she was the youngest. He felt that she was extremely intelligent, always managing to answer mathematical questions before William had a chance to work them out, as she stood gazing through the window watching what was going on around the estate. Without upsetting Thomas, he suggested that perhaps she should be kept out of the room whilst he was teaching William so that he could help William concentrate on what he regarded as the most important subjects, English, mathematics, and some geography so that William would get used to living in the world, not just Caerau. Thomas agreed at once and put it forward to Mrs Roberts. When Emma was told that she was not to disturb Mr Jones when he was teaching William, she decided to play outside and was naughty enough to try and distract him by standing and peeping in through the window. This was soon stopped, and she was taken with Mother Roberts for a walk. They strolled along as far as the church. Mrs Roberts wanted to visit her husband's monument and her daughter's grave. She tried to read out the wonderful memorial to William Roberts, her husband, telling Emma about her grandfather, which Emma did not quite understand never having met her grandfather, but Mrs Roberts felt that one day she would read it for herself and understand. Emma, who did not understand death, would often ask when Frances was coming home. Surely, she had finished planting the flowers by now, and God could send her back. Mother Roberts told her a story as they slowly returned to Caerau and Emma's thoughts were to find William. He was her brother and she looked up to him, though William found her trying at times, being younger than him, and he was still missing Frances with whom he had far more in common.

It had been a busy year and the building work at Caerau was completed, the trees had arrived to be placed along the driveway and in about two years the drive would look just as Thomas hoped. Not only was it going to look good, but it would also give a drive where the wind could not reach easily, and it sheltered the house. Fortunately for him, the ground was lower in that part of the land, which fitted in well. Thomas had been to seek the advice of Mr William Bulkeley of Brynddu, Llanfechell, on trees. Which were the best, not only for growth but from an aesthetic point of view. Mr William Bulkeley was renowned for his knowledge of trees, which he bought in Ireland, both for creating a beautiful corner in his garden or as fruit trees. Thomas admired him and the beautiful garden at Brynddu. It was a relief to have Caerau finished, so that he would be able to invite his friends knowing that he had a welcoming home for them to enjoy. The year came to an end.

Chapter Two

On April 6th, 1734, Thomas Rowlands was visited by the bailiff of the court with a letter which read as follows:

> 'The Great Sessions for the County of Anglesey, being appointed to be held at Beaumaris upon Thursday the 18th Day of April next, your appearance and service there on the grand jury upon Friday 19th will be an honour to your Country and an obligation laid upon your most humble servant. Robert Bulkeley – Sherriff. Gronant.'

This Thomas looked forward to, but before then he wanted to take William, Emma, and Mrs Roberts to watch the football match which was taking place at Maes-y-Cleifion in Tyddyn Rono, between 12 men from Llanbadrig, 12 from Llanfairynghornwy and 12 from Llanrhwydrys. This took place every Easter Day and about 400-500 people would attend. This year it was on April 16th. Much to everyone's enjoyment, the teams played so well that although a tie breaker was expected they decided to declare themselves all winners. After three hours of play it was time for some ale to quench their thirst, which their many supporters paid for them to enjoy. They then all went home feeling merry after having had a wonderful Easter Day.

Thomas busied himself as he prepared for the grand jury at Beaumaris, which meant that he would be away for several days. He set out on April 18th, so that he could settle in at the Red Lion, Beaumaris, where he would meet with other members of the grand jury. He was met by John Owen of Presaddfed, and they dined at the Red Lion when Mr William Bulkeley of Brynddu came forward and addressed John Owen concerning Richard Hughes, of Cefn, whom he described as nothing more than an upstart. He felt that both John Owen and Thomas should not encourage someone who was not considered to be a gentleman. Richard Hughes was a drover employed by many people around Anglesey. He was Thomas's tenant at the time, living at Castellior. Thomas did not approve of Bulkeley raising issues that were nothing to do with him. He felt that he knew how to conduct himself with gentlemen as well as with ordinary people like Richard Hughes, who worked extremely hard, and that he could not ignore the man as he was his tenant.

On April 25th, the grand jury dined at Miles Bull's House. Miles Bull was just 60 years old and had fathered 28 children, 21 by his first wife and seven by his present wife, Lumley, who was the daughter of William Bulkeley's uncle. This is recorded by Bulkeley in his diaries. During dinner, which continued for the rest of the evening, there was much talk of the forthcoming election in the borough of Beaumaris. As they drank, Thomas was glad that he was not standing in the election. The past few months had been tedious, with Mr Owen Meyrick of Bodorgan, whom he liked and who often called at Caerau, hoping to persuade Thomas to give him his vote, always managing to create a dull atmosphere between people. Thomas, liking his drink, enjoyed himself but still went out for a walk in the cool air to clear his head for the next day at court. He would be at Beaumaris until the end of April and would dine at Baron Hill before riding home.

Emma would be waiting and expecting some wonderful stories when her father got back. Thomas could not wait to see William and learn how well he was getting on with Mr Tom Jones, his teacher. He arrived home to find Mrs Roberts dozing in the chair closest to the fire with the embers still bright. He didn't want to disturb her and turned to go upstairs when she woke and told him that Emma had wanted to stay up to wait for his return, but William had told her that their father might not be back until tomorrow. Mrs Roberts went into the kitchen and asked the maid for a bowl of hot broth for Thomas after his journey back through the cold wind at night. He settled to chat with Mrs Roberts for about an hour when both decided it was time to retire. He went upstairs and peeped at William and Emma. How beautiful and innocent they were, he felt. He left quietly, knowing that tomorrow was going to be quite a day with Emma continuously asking questions and William telling him about what had been going on during his absence.

The following morning, Emma was so excited that she couldn't keep still, running and hugging her father each time he moved. William was given time off from attending his classes with Mr Jones so that he could spend time with his father. Mr Jones also had a day off and decided to return to Llanfechell to see family and friends. Emma wanted to know what had happened to the people in court and whether they had been hanged. What had they done to be in Court? Thomas would tell her stories that he had put together whilst riding home the previous evening. He could make some of them sound quite gruesome; this seemed to enrapture Emma, something which Thomas had never understood. Perhaps it was his fault for making them too vivid. William wanted to know about punishment. He was curious to learn what the punishments were and what they were for. Thomas would answer and make the stories sound as real as possible. The children were too young to know the reality of the punishments and Thomas did not wish to emphasise the reality until they were old enough to understand the rules and laws of the land. Now, it was more important that they learnt etiquette and good manners which would enable them to mix in society.

Before lunch, Emma wanted her father to go with her to see her corner of the garden. This was something that had been given to her to do to dissuade her from being an annoyance during William's classes with Mr Jones. She had persuaded the gardener to dig out a pond so that the ducks her father had bought her from Jane Owen of Llanfechell would have a good bath to paddle in. She had designed it all very nicely with some small trees at the front so that the mess created by the ducks went unnoticed. At the back she had an edge of stones to the pond which the ducks used as a stand to dive into the water; between these stones, she had a tower set, which made it look like a fairyland. Her father was most impressed. He could walk around the rest of the garden and the ducks still preferred to stay where they were, near the pond. The trees on either side of the pond sheltered them when the sun was hot. A few flowers in between and a couple of long grasses finished it off. In a few years, no one would notice that there were ducks there. Emma had made them a walk from the pond along the side of the garden, which had been edged with short trees giving the garden a better look which could be enjoyed with no bother from the ducks.

William appeared riding Mother Roberts' horse. He wanted his father to see that he was able to ride and enjoyed it. Thomas thought perhaps he ought to be away more so that he could see what benefits there were to be seen as both William and Emma grew up. William trotted around, then dismounted and made the horse lift each front leg to a whistle he had developed on an old Welsh tune. He then made him trot alongside, and the horse enjoyed this as he kept tossing his head in tune with William. Thomas was astounded. He was so proud of both of them.

The next day he took William out on Mother Roberts' horse and rode his own as they cantered down to the beach where they had a little chase, returning in time for lunch, both very hungry. After lunch, Emma was ready for games. As they chatted together while playing, Thomas explained that the following day he would be riding out to Beaumaris and around certain parts of Anglesey to make sure that people turned up to vote in the election. He had promised that he would help Lord Bulkeley who was supporting Mr Nicholas Bayly of Plas Newydd. When he returned, he would love to ride with William and play games with Emma, besides telling her fairy stories before she went to sleep. Thomas was quite a dab hand at drawing and would draw pictures around her bedroom and then paint them and tell her story after story all relating to the pictures.

Thomas left and rode out to Beaumaris. He would be staying at Baron Hill as a guest of Lord Bulkeley and would be busy riding around visiting the gentry in the hope of a good result. There were just two more days before the election and Lord Bulkeley visited many of his own supporters encouraging them to place their votes in Mr Bayly's favour. He stood for the county, but this was the main election. The morning Thomas was off, Mother Roberts was rather worried. She knew that there would be a lot of drinking and that Thomas never refused until he was quite ill. She wished that he could remember his asthma and the attacks he frequently suffered from.

In Anglesey there were two parties: the Whigs and the Tories. The terms 'Whig' and 'Tory' were freely used between the gentry families. It was considered a family or clan affair rather than party politics. On

May 9th, 1734, the day of the election, the gentry were busy gathering at Mr David Williams the attorney's house in Beaumaris. Around 10.30, Lord Bulkeley arrived with other gentlemen including Thomas and they all ventured forth to the county hall. After listening to the king's writ, Lord Bulkeley polled for Mr Bayly. Mr Owen Meyrick and Mr Bodvel followed and gave their vote to Mr Bayly. Then all the other gentlemen followed and after two hours the sheriff announced the result which went to Mr Bayly. The cheers and shouting could be heard some distance away, along with his name being chanted: 'Bayly! Bayly!'

The elected member and all the electors met and dined at the Bull's Head Inn. It was a grand occasion, and a great entertainment was had. Those who were at the cross were delivered three barrels of ale to celebrate. Everyone, it appeared, was pleased with the result. The following day, most of the gentlemen who had travelled to support Lord Bulkeley and Mr Bayly dined at Baron Hill. There were three tables in the dining room, each sitting about a dozen people. There was entertainment during the evening which was enjoyed by all. After dinner the guests moved to various rooms. Those who sat with Lord Bulkeley were non-smokers. Thomas had followed Mr Morgan of Henblas and several others to a room where they were able to enjoy their pipes. They were joined by Mr William Bulkeley of Brynddu. Here it was expected that the whole company drank a horn, which held something above a quart, and afterwards full glasses. This drinking session went on until seven o'clock when the company broke up, some staying in various inns around the town of Beaumaris and others staying at Baron Hill. Thomas, like several of the other guests, walked along a path towards Friars for a breath of fresh air, later retiring so that he could face the journey home the next day. He breakfasted early and started on his way back to Caerau. Emma would be waiting to greet him, and he wondered what the children had been up to this time while he was away.

The morning after he had arrived home, Emma was shouting with delight and William was chanting some Latin. As they were having breakfast, Emma seemed to be sitting on the edge of her chair, Thomas asked what was wrong, only to hear Emma chuckling away. 'It's the kitten, Papa,' said William. Mother Roberts directly lifted the kitten and took it to the kitchen, and they continued their breakfast with no more disruptions.

When Thomas went out to see the groundsman and gardener to ask what was planted and whether the fruit trees were coming along, Emma clutched his hand, pulling him towards the hay barn where there was a cat and six kittens. 'Look, Papa!', she said, lifting the kittens to her and kissing them.

'Yes, I know,' said Thomas, 'but leave them there.'

'Please Papa, can I have one and take it in? I've had this one in with me since you've been away, and I like its company.'

Thomas hesitated; he felt that Mother Roberts ought to be the one to make the decision. He turned around and saw Emma disappear into the house with a bundle of fluff in her hands and guessed that it was the little kitten. He could not scold her; he wanted her to be happy.

Thomas was glad to be home again, there was much to do and a visit to Caernarvon was much needed, to collect the rents from the many properties around Betws Garmon, Caernarvon, Llanllyfni, Clynnog, Llandwrog. This would take around two weeks. Times were hard and the crops, due to the very wet weather, were not at their best. Prices were extremely low. This meant at times that the tenants could not always meet the demands of their rents. They would pay what they could afford and add the rest to the following year's dues in the hope that the crops would fare better. Thomas felt that to understand their worries did in the end help them out; many would work hard in the hope of a good crop. He was never hard on his people; he understood their hardship and knew that the rent money was safe. He knew that many other landowners would have taken their tenants to court, which helped no one when times were hard. Thomas believed that accepting less one year would help his people to survive. He also knew what it was like to have bad times at home.

On her father's return home, Emma was full of stories about various people living around the area. She had probably been listening when Mother Roberts had her usual visitors, full of gossip from different corners of Anglesey. William was reading extremely well and was able to inform Thomas of the various wonders of the world. It was nice for Thomas to have conversations with his son, and you would often hear them laughing together.

In June, Mother Roberts took a trip to Llannerchymedd market and bought what she needed. The following day she paid Mr Pugh, the exciseman, for the following year, three heads of malt at the rate of 5s a head, and three heads of candles at 5s a head. She was making sure that they had enough stock.

On Sundays, Thomas and Mother Roberts spent time at church and during the evening he would read books on religious subjects. Many he borrowed from friends, especially from Dr Edward Wynne, when he was at home in Bodewryd. The parson, Mr William Morgan, was old and sometimes it was very difficult to understand him. Most felt that he needed a curate, at least to help him through the service. Mrs Roberts said that she would have to speak with Mr William Bulkeley of Brynddu, who took a great interest in matters of the church and its clergy.

During August the weather was very wet, and a hurricane of wind came across and lasted from early morning until about five in the evening for several days. Towards the middle of August, news arrived about Mr William Bulkeley's dog, Ranter, who had been bitten by a viper. Emma was very upset when she heard the news and plagued her father to take her to see the dog. Thomas was not sure what to do, he didn't really know whether the dog was alive or dead. After some debate it was decided that they all should go, including Mother Roberts, pleased to be able to visit as she wanted a word about the parson of Llanfairynghornwy. When they arrived at Brynddu, they found that Ranter had survived his ordeal, and was running around as usual. Emma and William were most impressed when Mr Bulkeley told them the story of how he had saved the dog. He had gone with Ranter to the fields where his workers were reaping the corn. Ranter always enjoyed sniffing around here and there. But this day he was bitten by a viper, which caused him to squeal. Mr Bulkeley realising what had happened killed the viper, opened it and took out its fat which weighed nearly an ounce. He carried Ranter home and found the part where the poor dog had been bitten. By this time, it was quite swollen. Mr Bulkeley put a spatula in the fire until it was red hot and holding it over the swelling anointed the whole area with the melted fat from the viper. By night the swelling was much reduced, and in the morning Ranter was still alive. This pleased Mr Bulkeley very much and of course he had stayed with his dog all night. Emma thought Mr Bulkeley was wonderful to save his dog. She and William went out into Brynddu's lovely garden, William wandering off to where the horses were keeping the groom busy brushing them. Emma sat in a stone-built chair dreaming about Ranter.

On August 19th, the Llanfechell parson and his brother, another Mr William Bulkeley, called, along with Mrs Roberts' nephew, Mr John Owen of Presaddfed. They had been to call on Mr William Bulkeley of Brynddu, to ask permission for the young Mr Bulkeley's marriage to Miss Ann Warmingham. Since her father Mr Thomas Warmingham's death, she was under Bulkeley of Brynddu's guardianship. Having been satisfied that the young William Bulkeley had enough money coming in and knowing that her grandfather had left Ann 100 pounds, the elder Mr Bulkeley consented to the marriage. The next day they were married at Pentraeth. Miss Ann Warmingham was the heiress of Plas-yn-Llan, and young William Bulkeley was John Owen's steward. Emma loved to hear about people getting married, and chatted for hours about what she would do when she married.

During November, a timber boat arrived at Cemaes with a load of things suitable for many of the farmers. There were plough bearers at 4d each, six shingle trees (or *cebystrau*) for 2d each, a master for 8d and an ash plant that possibly would make two plough beams for 2/6d, some shovels for 6d and about 13 joists roughly about six-foot long for 7d each. Thomas had gone with one of his farmhands, but they were both aware that Mr William Bulkeley was determined to get what he wanted first and that they would have to wait and rummage through what was left. Whether those in charge of the boat were smugglers or not, seemed not to matter to the gentry of Anglesey when they needed to stock up with timbers for repairs.

When Christmas arrived Mother Roberts and Thomas attended the early morning service between 5 and 6 a.m. The church looked lovely with extra candles lit all the way. People had placed flowers which gave off a lovely scent. After the sermon they returned to a wonderful breakfast, which the staff presented especially for Christmas morning. Emma and William were running around enjoying themselves. The fire seemed extra bright giving everyone a glow; it was much needed during the very cold winter with its frosty winds.

On January 14th, 1734, Thomas was a bearer at Mrs Lloyd of Rhosbeirio's funeral. He was given, as were the other six bearers, a scarf, *almonde* silk hatbands and gloves. An 'offering' was held over the coffin, something which Mr William Bulkeley of Brynddu could not understand, and which he regarded as more of a superstition than anything else. Over the coffin of the poor, people would offer a bowl of ale or milk and a loaf of bread with cheese. It had become a custom despite what Mr Bulkeley thought. Mr Griffith of Llanddyfnan, Mr Williams the parson of Llanfaethlu, Mr Richard Hughes of Tre'r Dryw, Mr Lewis of Trysglwyn were also bearers. An amount of 2s.6d was given to the parson and 1s to the sexton. Mrs Ann Vaughan, the heiress and daughter of Richard Vaughan of Rhosbeirio, had married Richard Lloyd of Hirdre-faig and had six children by him. It was a very sad day.

In late January, William Williams, the gardener at Caerau, started to sow peas and beans for an early crop. He was very good at getting seeds for vegetables and Mr Bulkeley called and bought some seeds from him. In return he would make suggestions to Williams where to plant some of the vegetables, as the garden at Caerau was new. He was introduced to Mr Bulkeley's fox that had made his home there. He was a fine example, and until that day Mr Bulkeley had not heard him bark, which he did now for the first time.

Emma went off on most days with some of the farm workers who were checking the sheep and counting how many new lambs had been born. She loved helping by holding and cuddling the smallest of the lambs. She had grown a little by now and found other matters around the estate more interesting than trying to distract William from his lessons.

Mother Roberts went over to Llanfechell market the following week to buy some mutton from Richard Owen. She bought a whole side for 1s 8d and carried it back for the cook to prepare into several dishes. If anyone called to visit or to see Thomas, they would have a tasty bite to eat.

In the middle of February, a German Jew called Simon Ballin visited Mother Roberts who was always interested in his selection of bits and pieces for sale. She always tried to buy some small token from him, and now that she had Emma to think about, she would buy special pieces of jewellery to keep for when she was of age. They would sit and chat and she would hear news about members of her own family whom she rarely saw on account of the long distances between them. She bought a tortoiseshell case with ivory leaves to keep for Emma, believing that she would be pleased when she was old enough to attend balls around the island. For William, she bought some buckles for his shoes, again for when he was old enough to collect a young lady and take her to balls.

Towards the end of February, Mother Roberts visited Llanfechell market which she had heard was going to be excellent. Plenty of young horses for harrowing were on sale. There was also a good collection of pewter, brass, shoes, hats, woollen items, and linen cloth. She felt sorry for those selling as money was scarce; not many came and there was not much buying. She spoke to many of the sellers and empathised, realising that they depended on the little that they sold to try and keep their families. She could not stop thinking about them on the way home and prayed that some good luck would come their way in what were very difficult times. How lucky William and Emma are, she thought, deciding that she would make them understand how courageous some people were in trying to earn a living and, the difficulties they faced when nothing had been sold and they had families to keep.

A sudden excitement was spreading around Llanfairynghornwy, people were full of joy. The rumour was that Dr Edward Wynne, the Chancellor of Hereford, whose home on the island was Bodewryd, had sent for his wife to come back after a separation of 17 years. They were married 20 years earlier, lived together for three years and had three children, Susanna, Ann, and John, all of whom died in infancy. They then parted. It was said that this was a reconciliation. Losing her children had caused Mrs Wynne to develop depression which affected her badly; she had left Bodewryd and gone home to be with her family at Plas Einion in Denbigh. The reconciliation came on March 14th, 1734.

Thomas was delighted when he heard the good news and could hardly wait to pay Dr Wynne a visit so that he could acquire the loan of books which he read avidly. It was a great comfort to him that

Dr Wynne always collected books of a very high standard which meant that he could learn many subjects without having to pay out money. They spent hours together discussing serious issues. Thomas read many religious books from his days at Oxford, believing that he might enter the Church if his elder brother was to inherit the Plas-y-Nant estate.

Dr Edward Wynne commuted between Hereford and Anglesey for 45 years. He had a fine collection of books on ecclesiastical matters and on farming. He was always looking for something new and carried it back to Anglesey to help farmers keep up with new trends. He had great faith in sand and encouraged his many tenants to use it; he planned for the Red Wharf sloop to carry sand to the most convenient places along the shoreline so that the men could carry it to various properties. He had learnt from farmers in Hereford that sand was extremely good to encourage the healthy growth of vegetables. He probably rode, as Thomas Pennant recorded, thickly wrapped in cloaks, with jackboots up to his hips, splashing through mud and mire, making light of occasional falls. He was the first person in Anglesey who successfully grew turnips, following instructions in one of his many books.

In accordance with the old calendar the new year started on March 25th. At the beginning of 1735 the great news around the island was that at long last the executors of William Trench, who built the lighthouse in the Skerries in 1716, had succeeded in obtaining an Act of Parliament to oblige all ships coming within sight of the lighthouse to pay tonnage. A clause was included confirming that the title to the same belonged to Mr Robinson of Mynachdy, Llanfairynghornwy and of Gwersyllt, Denbigh.

It was April 20th and duty called Thomas to set out for Beaumaris at 11am. Before attending court, he travelled to Thomas Williams' house at Porthaethwy Ferry and caught a boat costing 6d to Caernarvon. While he was there, he bought himself a new wig for ten shillings and spent eleven and sixpence for two pairs of black stockings. He stayed the night before catching a boat back to Porthaethwy and from there he rode to Beaumaris.

The grand jury were in court on April 24th, all the gentlemen attending dropping a shilling in the glove upon being sworn in and ten shillings and sixpence in the grand jury room towards the expenses of the court. Bills of indictment were made against John Pritchard for burglary and felony, against John Davies, the miller of Frogwy, for killing his maid, and against an old woman from Llangaffo for stealing 40 shillings. The last, having committed no burglary and the offence being her first, was burnt in the hand. The miller, found guilty of manslaughter, was also burnt in the hand. John Pritchard was condemned to be hanged which was executed upon him on May 10th at Beaumaris. After a long court, most of the grand jury and councillors dined with the judge at the Bull's Head, Llannerchymedd.

The following day, Thomas called upon Thomas Lewis of Trefeibion Meurig with a request to deliver something to London. Thomas Lewis was a drover, well-known to many of the gentry families around Anglesey as a trustworthy fellow. Many trusted him to deliver money from Anglesey to London on their behalf. He became wealthy through the payments he received and established himself by buying a large house and mixing in the company of many wealthy estate owners.

Several people travelled to Holyhead in the hope of seeing Jonathan Swift on his way to Dublin where the first four volumes of his collected works were being printed. News had spread that he was staying at Holyhead as the boat had not been able to set sail.

During May, many people flocked to Cemaes as Rogers, a famous smuggler, had arrived. He usually brought materials that were useful to the many farming people such as timber or trees. Should you cross his hand with a piece of gold, then he would produce a barrel of rum, brandy, or whisky. Smuggler or not, he was always given a welcome and many well-known squires bought from him knowing that they managed to do well on price. Gabriel Jones and Lewis Hughes of Cemaes had bought 10 gallons of brandy at 3s a gallon. The boat had been to the Isle of Man with cheese from Chester and came to Cemaes with a cargo of brandy.

Mother Roberts visited Llanfechell market where there was a great asking for potatoes, which sold for 9d and 10d a bushel. She also bought 2d worth of spinach and some radishes. From Richard Owen, the butcher, she bought a quarter of veal for sixpence. Much of the gossip was about the hanging the following day. There was quite a gathering at Beaumaris on May 10th, as this was the day that John

Pritchard was to be hanged. Punishing people in accordance with the law was one thing, thought Thomas, but to want to watch someone being hanged was something that he never understood, or had any inclination to do.

Back at Caerau, the gardener spoke of Mr Bulkeley's fox once more. The one thing he found hard to believe was that the fox, on arriving back at Brynddu, had passed the hens and chicks, and had never touched them. Emma was enthralled with the story and the gardener knew that she too had been making friends with a fox around the Caerau yard. The bailiff had tried to warn her against encouraging it, but Emma loved animals and once she had made up her mind, no one could dissuade her. She fed the dogs every night and left food for the fox which was getting used to the idea and moving nearer to the barn each time, with Emma praying that he would make himself a home there. The dogs ignored it apart from Rŵan, who would sit alongside the fox ('rŵan' is Welsh for 'now', which Emma had heard called out when the men were training the dogs. She thought it was a name, and when pups arrived, she had chosen one as her favourite pet and called it 'Rŵan'). Her other enjoyment was to go with the farm men to the sheep shearing. Once they had finished, they collected the wool ready to be sold for the export market. Emma would help herself and carry some to make beds for the dogs and the fox.

The month of June was very depressing and affected everyone. Many wished that the heavy winds and continual rain would disappear. Emma was restless because she could not go out and would occasionally throw a tantrum which disrupted the whole household. Mother Roberts blamed Thomas for spoiling her and Thomas blamed Mother Roberts for always giving in to her.

Hugh Williams, the joiner of Llannerchymedd, and his apprentice, Richard Davies, came to Caerau. The kitchen had a suitable corner that needed filling, and Mrs Roberts needed a cheese press which would be most useful for the cook and maids. It was so cold that they had fires burning, which for this time of year was most unusual apart from the kitchen fire, used for cooking.

Thomas, travelling from Chester to home, had called at Bangor fair and learnt that there were very good rates for sheep and horses. Cattle and horses had been making good rates at Chester, but not sheep until now. He had a very rough ride home due to the extraordinary weather they had experienced throughout June.

The gardener, who had been over to Brynddu, came back with the news that Mr William Bulkeley had recorded three inches of rain on June 25th, a record never before known. July also was a cold, blustery month with winds stopping work on many of the farms. Shortage of food was not something to look forward to. Many lost their crops, and market prices would be high for the little that could be saved.

The beginning of July saw many landlords organizing for the purpose of repairing the highways. They would send their men to the local quarries to collect stones and rubble to repair the most important parts of the highway. This helped greatly as Anglesey was notorious for having extremely bad roads, which caused many derogatory remarks by those travelling to the island. It was a place according to some where the carriage wheels refused to turn. An Act of Parliament from 1555 placed the maintenance of all existing public highways on the parish, which was to appoint one or two surveyors for the ensuing year from among the inhabitants. All labour, tools, horses, carts and other gear needed for the repairing of roads had to be furnished by the parish. Every occupant of a holding of £50 or over annual value had to provide a cart and a team of draught horses for every £50. All other men in the parish able to labour had to give, at first four, and by a later Act, six, consecutive days annually to work on the roads. This was known as statute labour and was the law of the land regarding road maintenance until 1835. It was, however, mainly the men with holdings who contributed the most. Able-bodied men in the various parishes would have disappeared. Who was going to work repairing roads when they could sit and enjoy themselves or visit the various fairs? The weather continued to be rather wet which did not help the farmers trying to collect rather thin shocks of hay or barley, and the road repairs took much longer than usual.

News came concerning the death of Elizabeth Lloyd, a very well-known character of Llannerchymedd, always to be seen on market days. The gentry chatted with her, and her knowledge was much appreciated by many who invested in sheep and cattle. Mother Roberts had pointed her out to Emma when visiting the market.

She was as straight as a pin and walked well, was 105 when she died and had perfect senses to the end.

Many Anglesey folks were found to be searching for horses from every corner of the island as a rumour had spread that good prices were to be had at Mold fair. A huge crowd gathered to walk the horses all the way to Mold. However, as so many arrived from a wide area, the prices fell considerably.

It was nearly the end of July when many gathered to shoot plovers, always a favourite at that time of year. An extremely good fair at Llanfechell took place on July 25th with woollen and linen cloth, shoes, hats, leather, some cattle, carpenters' tools, and some of their work such as drays and ladders. And filling one corner were the hop merchants. It was some time since Mother Roberts had seen as many goods as possible for sale. She loved rummaging through things, and, having Emma to look after, she was always looking for materials to improve her collection of dresses.

People were also hoping that August would show them a little more sun than had the two previous months. It was a shame to have to watch farmers trying their best to salvage what they could of their hay and rye with far less shocks saved than previously. It was estimated that what was saved was less than half of what they normally had and would inevitably affect food on the island for some time into the future. August was always a busy month when jobs like opening ditches took place before the winter weather which affected the roads and often ruined the wheels of the carriages.

Emma, because her ducks had long since flown away, had been pestering her father for new ducks. One of the farmhands had promised that he would cut their wings this time to stop them flying. That would keep them at Caerau! Thomas, always giving in to her, visited the wife of Thomas Jones, the shoemaker of Llanfechell, and bought seven young ducklings for 1s 9d. This delighted Emma who had been busy making sure that one of the hands around Caerau helped her clean out the pond and make sure that everything was ready for them. They had a way to go before their wings could be cut, but as there was far more in the garden now than when the house was first built, she hoped this would dissuade the ducks from flying away. She accompanied Mother

Roberts to Llannerchymedd fair where there was a glut of herrings. Mother Roberts bought quite an amount to keep everyone fed. These had probably come straight from the port of Amlwch. Various coves around Anglesey produced different fish, so the islanders benefitted greatly from having a variety.

September was busy. First, Thomas had to ride off to Beaumaris to attend court. He was there for three or four days and stayed with Lord Bulkeley at Baron Hill. Once he was back at Caerau, they all busied themselves getting ready for the christening of Ann Warmingham's son. The christening took place on September 16th, 1735, at Glan-Alaw. As we have seen, Ann had married William Bulkeley, the third son of Robert and Catherine Bulkeley of Dronwy. William was agent to John Owen of Presaddfed and was pleased to have acquired this position after the death of his brother, Hugh. They lived at Glan-Alaw after it had been secured for them on a long lease by John Owen through his aunt, Mrs Emma Roberts of Caerau. The godfathers were John Owen and his brother-in-law, John Fowles of Dublin; the godmothers, Mrs Emma Roberts and her niece, Ann Owen, John Fowles' wife. Mr William Bulkeley of Brynddu, who attended the christening, was devastated by the choice of godparents. He believed that he should have been chosen, having been a guardian to Ann Warmingham after the death of her father. He was quite put out, but managed not to cause any disruption and eventually made a gift of one guinea to the baby; he also gave the nurse and midwife five shillings, for having attended to Ann during the birth.

The next excitement was September 19th. This was William's tenth birthday and Thomas, who had been very impressed when William had ridden Mother Roberts' horse earlier in the year, had been busy planning his surprise without anyone knowing. He was aware of the good breeders of horses and ponies around Chester and Mold and had become well acquainted with one Mr John Downing, a well-known breeder who lived at Mold. He had mentioned that he would very much like to acquire a good and stable pony for his son. Mr Downing who had several children himself had been looking after this pony and training it a little so that when William started to ride it, he would feel very comfortable. Thomas had succeeded in purchasing this pony and during the three weeks before William's birthday he had met Mr Downing who had kindly brought the pony as far as Llangefni. From here, Thomas had organised with Mr Robinson of Mynachdy that he could leave the pony with him until September 19th. Thomas himself was quite excited, he couldn't wait to see William's face, wishing also that his wife could see what a polite, intelligent, young man her son had become, and the courage he had mustered to be able to ride Mother Roberts' horse, which could be difficult to handle other than by Mother Roberts herself.

At breakfast, Mother Roberts, Thomas and Emma all wished William a happy birthday and after finishing their breakfast they sat as they gave him his presents. A new pair of trousers from Mother Roberts, and a cravat from Emma. William thanked them and thought his father was rather silent and not taking much notice. He walked towards him to show him what he had been given. Thomas stood still, looking through the window, when suddenly William looked and there, standing outside, was Mr Robinson of Mynachdy holding a lovely pony and waving. William looked at his father and said, 'Why is Mr Robinson standing there with a pony?'

Thomas put his hand on William's shoulder and said, 'I think we ought to go out and see, don't you?'. Both went out and Thomas thanked Mr Robinson for looking after the pony, then turned to William and said, 'This is my birthday present to you, William.'

Disbelief was written all over William's face. He called out to Emma, who came running. 'Look what Papa has given me!'

They both stood there rubbing the pony's head and one of the farm helpers came along and said, 'That's a fine-looking pony there, young William.'

Emma may have acted at times like a spoilt child, which indeed she was, but undoubtedly, she had an affinity with animals. As she kept rubbing the pony's head, she spoke to it and rubbed her face along its head. The pony responded by nuzzling against her neck and up around her head and hair until Emma was shrieking with delight. William made her mount the pony with him and off they went down to the beach about a mile away. As they sat on the stones whilst the pony had a rest, they watched a flock of wild geese flying over on their way to Ireland. Emma thought it was a lovely sight and wondered how they knew the way. The pony kept nuzzling her arm all the way to her neck and again Emma squealed with laughter. William had been quiet all the way to the beach and as they sat there. He was still in shock at having had the pony, something he did not think would be possible until he was older. He admired his father for being kind and the way that he had planned such a surprise with none of them suspecting anything. He would try harder and learn all he could to please his father by becoming a decent fellow with an interest in things that would help others.

During the afternoon, Mr Jones, the schoolteacher, called with a gift for William. It was a book on the anatomy of a horse, which he thought would help William to understand his pony. William was overjoyed and promised to read it until he knew it well. What puzzled William was how the teacher knew that he had just been given a pony for his birthday. What he had not seen was Mr Jones standing there in the morning, but as there was so much excitement he had disappeared quickly and returned in the afternoon with this book which he had been given as a young boy when starting to ride his horse.

The rest of the day was spent in a jolly mood with everyone chatting and laughing until it was time for William and Emma to be taken upstairs and to bed. Mr Jones, the schoolteacher, was invited to stay for supper and he and Thomas indulged in drinking. During the evening, William and Emma could hear a lot of laughter and a rather loud conversation. They crept to the stairs to listen and realised that the schoolteacher and Thomas were rather inebriated. The two laughed as William dropped a coin to make a noise and they fled back to their rooms, hearing the two men walking along the hall wondering what the noise was.

Emma couldn't wait for her birthday to come along and wondered if she too was going to get a pony: but then, she was younger so perhaps she would have to wait. She fell asleep quite quickly.

The rest of the month was wet. The farmers were extremely busy, each day that was dry and windy they collected what was left of their rye, oats, and corn and whatever they could save from various crops. It was a pitiful sight as the workers struggled and much of what they collected just rotted away.

Thomas decided to visit his sister, Margaret, at Caernarvon. He had promised to meet with some of his tenants before visiting some of the shops which were always much improved as the season moved towards Christmas. He knew of a good saddler's shop and where he could buy a new pair of trousers for William, suitable for riding a pony. He asked his sister, Margaret, to look at bonnets and dresses and to choose one for Emma who was busy outgrowing her clothes. Mother Roberts had been quite lucky with having so many nieces who, when they replaced their dresses, had given her what they were discarding. She had Betty Lloyd, the dressmaker, to alter these into dresses for Emma.

Dress worn by Margaret Griffith and designed by Anna Maria Garthwaite, a well-known silk flower designer who had a shop in London. This dress is at the National Museum of Wales, Cardiff.

Shoes worn by Margaret Griffith of Llanfairisgaer.
National Museum of Wales, Cardiff.

Mr William Bulkeley of Brynddu was in Ireland and one of his interests was to browse around bookshops. One day he found four volumes of *The Arabian Nights*, which he purchased for nine shillings, and a copy of Pullman's *Chronological History* for six shillings. He was aware that Thomas amongst others was an avid reader, and Bulkeley thought that once he had read them, he could lend them to various acquaintances as a way of proving to them that he was kind and thoughtful. He had been at Dr Edward Wynne's house more than once and found Thomas going home with a collection of books. This was one way Mr Bulkeley believed would win him good favour amongst those with whom he wished to be included. Unfortunately for him, most people knew of his odd character and that he could be most formidable. His rather sour point of view on many subjects and people, along with his continual bickering amongst good-standing people, could only be thought of as jealousy. His main complaint was that Lord Bulkeley visited Mr Meyrick of Bodorgan, John Owen of Presaddfed and then Thomas at Caerau, which seemed to upset him greatly.

Thomas, however, always saw the good side of him, his knowledge as a lawyer and as a musician. And the garden that he had laid out at Brynddu was a total wonderment. Thomas wondered where all his ideas came from and envied him his interest in growing trees which produced apples, pears, plums, and many other fruits besides all the vegetables that he continued to try out. If they took where he planted them, all well and good; if they failed, he moved on to more exotic ones. Thomas had gained enough confidence in William Bulkeley to allow him to send his own gardener over for advice on many aspects of growing vegetables.

Christmas arrived, which this year was special as William, now ten, would be accompanying Mother Roberts and Thomas to church. Mother Roberts had on days when Mr Jones, the teacher, was not in attendance, instructed William about the church: that when he went in, he would see the altar and the chalice his mother had presented to the church when she was 16 years old and had been confirmed. Inscribed were three lines:

*'The Gift of Ellen Roberts
of Cayrey to LLanfair Church.
1713.'*

St Mary's Church looked a picture with flowers placed around it, and candles lit everywhere. When William saw the chalice thought it looked beautiful; he was so proud that he could hardly contain himself. After the service he was introduced to the parson whom he would soon get to know; it was expected that he, like his mother before him, would be taking instruction in order that he too would be confirmed.

Emma was busy singing and enjoying herself when Mother Roberts, Thomas and William returned from church. There was a glorious fire and plenty to eat. Many nieces and cousins called to wish everyone a Happy Christmas, which was good for Emma. It could be quite lonely at times living at Caerau, so far from the village. She was very good at inventing imaginary people and animals who always talked to her, so she said, but some of her cousins felt it was a sign of being lonely.

During January, the weather was again quite wet, which curtailed Emma's wanderings around to see all the animals. One of the locals called round selling wild fowl which Mother Roberts bought for 6d; they would make a scrumptious meal. By January 21st, snow was falling. Mother Roberts was very protective of both William and Emma when the weather was bad. She did not want them to catch colds or consumption. It was, by the looks of things, going to be a hard winter. It started to freeze, then snow again. William was pleased to have extra time off as Mr Jones had been unable to come to teach his pupil. He played with Emma, who now made him crouch on his knees and she would sit across his back, pretending he was a horse. William had also invented this trick of hiding himself and make Emma find him. This could take hours, which Mother Roberts was very glad of and gave her time for other matters around the house.

On January 13th, Emma's birthday, Thomas greeted her with a smile and a song as he presented her with another new dress and bonnet. Emma was over the moon and kept hugging her father. Mother Roberts gave her a pair of gloves. William suddenly rushed in with a cloth in his hand and gave it to Emma. When she opened it, inside were two snails, which caused Emma to scream. William then told her that he had caught them so that she could give them to her ducks and tell them that it was her birthday. After a while Emma calmed down and thanked William for such an unusual thought. The ducks, when presented with the snails, gobbled them so quickly that they could hardly have tasted them. The rest of the day was enjoyed with members of the family from around Anglesey calling to wish Emma a happy birthday.

William George of Llanfwrog called to make sure that the baskets which the men on the farm had ordered the previous year were still intact. One of them needed a little repair. But Thomas wanted a lobster basket, living close to what he believed would be an ideal place for lobsters, which would be welcome when guests came for dinner. William George left on his way to Brynddu in the hope of another order.

By the beginning of February, the effects of the bad weather and melting snow had many meadows under water with some bridges totally impassable. More snow, followed with many showers of sleet, causing many lambs to die of hunger and cold. This dreadful weather continued throughout most of February. March had cold winds but much dryer weather, with everyone busy once more preparing beds to plant vegetables. On March 15th the moon was totally eclipsed at precisely ten o'clock. From William Bulkeley's diary we can hear the amazement of it all. He had read all the accounts in almanacs which proclaimed that the event would happen 12 minutes before it did. He believed that the 12 minutes were the difference of latitude between Anglesey and London. He was well known to take a keen interest in such matters. Many others were out late to see this once in a lifetime experience.

Chapter Three

Everyone was hoping for a better year in 1736. With the dry weather the people were busy planting. Though it was cold with quite blustery winds they planted vegetables, some making a corner in the garden to fill with seeds – melons, cucumber, kidney beans, carrots, spinach, radish, lettuce. The farm workers were already sowing oats. Visiting Llannerchymedd market, the gentry bought seeds for garden peas at 5d a quarter ounce, leeks at 3d a half ounce, lettuce at 2d, the same charged for cabbage, asparagus, and cauliflower. Henblas, Llangristiolus was known to have one of the best vegetable gardens on the island, with William Bulkeley of Brynddu catching up and becoming well-known for his interest and knowledge. Lewis Morris also was a keen vegetable man and Caerau was becoming more adventurous each year. The gardener there had become quite friendly with William Bulkeley's gardener and often chatted with Mr Bulkeley, as his advice was considered worthwhile.

April came in with extremely high winds causing many trees to sway so heavily that the workers were running to collect the biggest stones they could find to place around the trunks of the trees to keep them from falling. Thomas was worried about the trees he had laid along the entrance into Caerau, but the workers had seen to all the trees. The winds near Carmel Point were sometimes enough to frighten anyone.

Mother Roberts had decided that it was time Emma also, now nine, had lessons from Mr Jones. Another matter that Mother Roberts introduced was the family history. She would choose one day a week to inform them of who they were and where they came from. Emma pulled cheeky faces at the thought that she was to behave herself and be taught by Mr Jones.

The wind also made it difficult for those who had to travel. Thomas had to visit Llannerchymedd post office to collect a letter which he hoped had arrived from John Owen MP who was in London. There was no letter from London, but a letter had arrived from Beaumaris inviting him to attend a special meeting before the grand jury gathered for court on April 19th. Mystified at the intrigue of the letter, Thomas travelled home bemused. Arriving back, he chatted with William and Emma and gave them the rest of the day knowing that he had to travel to Beaumaris the next morning. He instructed them to behave decently to Mother Roberts, William to Mr Jones, the teacher, and Emma to everyone. Mother Roberts had suggested that it was time for Emma to be taught by Mr Jones, which might help to control her. Thomas promised to think about it, but as always, he was never in a hurry over decisions where Emma was concerned.

When Thomas arrived at Beaumaris and met with the rest of the grand jurors at this special meeting, he found that he had been put forward as the foreman of the grand jury. But he declined most profusely. It was then put to the rest of the gentlemen; they all refused thereby causing the court much difficulty. There was only one thing to do and that was to call for a ballot, the result of which fell to Mr William Bulkeley. The jurors then went to Griffith Pritchard's house and appointed Mr Thomas Evans of Tre'r-Gof as treasurer. When he had accepted the position all the squires paid Mr Thomas half a guinea, the rest of the gentlemen paid seven shillings and sixpence and dropped sixpence in the glove. The whole of the grand jury dined with the sheriff which finished with many being drunk. The following day, very little business took place as the sheriff was too drunk to conduct the court business.

Thomas returned home glad to have refused being elected as foreman of the grand jury. He was aware that far too much time was wasted, especially by the sheriff, and that many were too afraid of voicing an opinion. They seemed to treat a day at court as a day out, only important enough to get drunk.

Emma was pleased to see her father and was looking forward to accompanying him on his journey around his properties in Caernarvonshire. Thomas accepted what Mother Roberts had said about her being taught by Mr Jones like William, but he felt that a trip with him would be a nice treat for her before settling down to learning. Mother Roberts strongly disapproved of taking her on this forthcoming trip; giving in to Emma's whims, as she called it, and not accepting that she was growing up! Emma was so excited that she tended to show off, pulling faces at William and members of the household, with Mother Roberts shaking her head and blaming Thomas for having spoilt her.

William took little heed of these peculiar stunts, as he called them, being quite content that he would be accompanying his father to London when the weather was warmer. Emma was looking forward to seeing her aunt and uncle. Margaret, Thomas's favourite sister, had married John Griffith of Caernarvon, related to the Llanfair and Brynodol family. He was the son of John Griffith of Dyffryn and Margaret Whyte of Neigwl Ucha, and grandson of Captain William Griffith of Cefnamlwch, Llŷn, and had inherited Brynodol from his uncle, Hugh Griffith, who bought the estate.

Busily, Emma was planning what she was taking with her and much to both Mother Robert and Thomas' shock, she had filled a trunk until it would not close with all her dresses, smocks and shoes. After much deliberation and a threat that she would have to stay home, it was agreed that she would reduce the amount to what was needed for a week and not a whole year. Resentfully, Emma carried this out with the help of Ella, the maid, who was laughing when she saw the trunk full.

The one pleasure that she looked forward to besides seeing her aunt and uncle was to meet up with her cousins, Hugh and William, and of course the new baby, Frances. She had met Hugh before; he was three years older than her, and they got on very well together even though people referred to her as spoilt. It would be like having her brother around. Her cousin William was younger, and she could help to look after baby Frances. Emma enquired often how they were going to get to her aunt and uncle. Thomas had been busy every night telling her stories about various places that were on the way, which of course included Caernarvon and its castle. He told her all about the high-quality shops that were there and that she would have plenty to see.

Two days later their journey began, Emma beside herself with excitement. She noted as they went through small villages, children hovering around in corners looking dirty and badly dressed; some looked so thin and sickly that even Emma, thoroughly spoilt, felt sorry for them. At times, seeing Thomas and Emma passing through in the coach, the children would run eagerly hoping for some comfort. Thomas, brought up to remember those less fortunate, carried small money as he called it, and would hand it out here and there, much to

Emma's surprise. He explained to her that just because she was brought up in a comfortable house with maids and plenty to eat there were many, many far less fortunate, and that she should understand their plight. Emma just shook her head in disgust. Thomas started to think that much work was needed in educating her.

When they arrived at Beaumaris and got onto the boat, Emma was delighted that the horses also came on board, but she became very nervous when they were made to swim part of the way as they arrived at the Lavan Sands on the other side. Thomas had quite a time trying to calm her down, and she only stopped fretting when she saw that all the horses were safe and standing ready. Thomas hurried her into the awaiting coach which would bring them to Caernarvon, showing her various houses and explaining whose properties they were, thinking of her future, believing that she might marry into one of the prestigious families.

Always tidy about his own business, Thomas had prepared an itinerary for them during their stay with his sister, Margaret, so that Emma would gradually know that she had quite a large family and where she came from. When they arrived at Margaret's house the excitement on both sides was tremendous. A lovely fire glowed in the fireplace and the children surrounded Emma as soon as they walked in. Margaret had arranged with the maids and governess that the children were to eat first so that they could be put to bed when the time came, giving the parents time to dress for dinner and enjoy the evening chatting about various events and political agendas.

John Griffith, Margaret's husband, always enjoyed it when Thomas called, and they chatted for hours. John had recently returned from London, which meant that Thomas could catch up on the latest news. John had heard the latest information on some material found in Brazil called rubber. This was a latex material gathered after cutting into the Para tree. Charles Marie de la Condamine was credited with introducing samples of it to the Académie Royale des Sciences of France in 1736. He went on to write papers on it and rubber became very important to many industries throughout the world. John Griffith was convinced that this was going to make many people rich and felt that a small investment was necessary. Thomas, on the other hand, felt that he had enough to contend with. He was not good with money, and due to his occasional gambling bouts, he suffered losses that he could ill afford. Thomas was far more interested in hearing about Claudius Amyand, a French-born Englishman who became a surgeon. On December 6th, 1735, at St George's Hospital, London, he had performed an operation on an 11-year-old boy for an inguinal hernia with an appendix involved. The appendix had been perforated by a pin which the young boy had swallowed. The boy, called Hanvil Anderson, made a spectacular recovery and was discharged from the hospital after a month's stay. This was what gave Thomas and John hope for their children's future. So content did Thomas feel at such extraordinary news that he encouraged John to join him in another glass of brandy, much to Margaret's displeasure. She knew that her brother at times drank far too much. She was always lecturing him about it, not that for one moment it had any effect.

The following day was an easy day. The men walked and talked as they strolled around the garden, admiring the wonderful view across the Menai Straits. Llanfairisgaer was a pleasant house and the garden to Thomas was completely wonderful. It was a charming place for young children to play. Emma had been kept amused watching the nurse give little Frances a bath. She was fascinated with her tiny hands and feet, then as the nurse wanted to feed the baby, Emma joined the boys playing outside. During the afternoon, many people called to meet Thomas and have cordial conversations, some who had not seen him since his departure from Caernarvon to live in Anglesey. Some of the guests were invited to stay for dinner by Margaret and John.

The next day, Thomas had arranged to visit Plas-y-Nant, Betws Garmon, and he wanted to take Emma to Llanbeblig Church on the way. After breakfast, he gathered Emma, who insisted that Hugh should be allowed to come too. They stopped at Llanbeblig and the lady in charge of the church let them in. Thomas explained about the age of the church as they walked slowly examining everything, until he pointed to a plaque on the wall and said that it had been put there by his sister, Margaret. It commemorated his mother, the children's grandmother. He read it out to them.

> *'Here lyeth that pious and most*
> *Charitable sincere good Christian*
> *Mrs Frances Rowlands*
> *Daughter of William Owen of Clenneny Esq.,*
> *And relict John Rowlands of Nant Esq.,*
> *Who departed this life on the 12th January*
> *1718 in the 63rd year of her age to the great*
> *grief of her children, loss of the poor and justly lamented.*
> *by all who knew her.'*

Thomas then walked them towards the altar where Mrs Frances Rowlands's tomb was and told them that she would be very proud to know that they were there. Hugh had certainly taken in what Thomas had said but Emma didn't seem to have the same grasp. Further along, Thomas pointed to another plaque, which was for his brother, Richard, whom he still missed and for whom had felt a great sadness when he died.

> *'Here lieth the body of Richard Rowlands, Esq., son of John Rowlands of Nant, Esq., and Frances his wife, daughter of William Owen of Porkington in the county of Salop, Esq., who died 3rd December 1719 aged 23. Omnes Lodem Cogimur.'*

They were soon on their way to Plas-y-Nant, which Emma's grandfather, John Rowlands had built in 1671. Emma was quite exciting to see where her father had lived. Mrs Williams from Waunfawr greeted them, she had been a maid there for many, many years, and was delighted to meet Emma. A Mr Lloyd from Beddgelert called as he had heard that Thomas would be there, and they had a long discussion regarding the slate found along some of the mountains at the back of Plas-y-Nant. Mr Lloyd also acted as a part-time bailiff collecting rents when Thomas was unable to attend himself. Both men joined the children for tea which Mrs Williams had been busy preparing. Emma giggled as Mrs Williams kept sending different girls in with various plates of food, but this was a rare occasion and Mrs Williams wanted the girls to see Thomas and Emma as they were the Rowlands of Plas-y-Nant. After tea, Hugh decided to have a look outside and Emma soon chased after him as they ran all the way as far as the lodge near the entrance. Thomas appeared looking for them. It was time to go. He didn't want his sister to fret, and they wanted to call at St Garmon's Church, where again Margaret had placed a plaque to the memory of her own and Thomas' father John Rowlands. It read:

> 'Near this place layeth the remains of John Rowlands of Nant in the county of Caernarvon, Esq. He was married to Frances Owen, daughter of Wm Owen and granddaughter of Sir John Owen of Clenneny in the said county, Knight Baronet. He had by her ten children.'

Hugh approved of the plaque from what he had heard his mother say about her father and understood what a very kind person Margaret herself was.

John Rowlands, Emma's grandfather, who was head of the Post Office Bank in Lombard Street, London.

List of Thomas Rowland's children in the church register, held at Llangefni Archives.

During dinner you could hear the shouting, giggling and laughter as Hugh and Emma were teasing William and telling him about their day out. William was a studious type, always polite and was most interested to hear that Emma had at long last seen her grandmother's plaque at Llanbeblig and her grandfather's brass plaque at Betws Garmon.

The following day, Margaret decided that she would oversee Emma and would take her down to Caernarvon, and have a look at some of the shops, leaving Thomas in charge of Hugh and William. Her husband John was away for the day on business. Emma loved looking at the shops; back home in Anglesey she was more used to markets. Her aunt asked many questions and felt that Emma had a mind of her own. She heard about William and Mr Jones, the teacher, besides many things about Mother Roberts. Margaret was quick to tell her just how lucky she was to have Mother Roberts. On the way back they called on one of Margaret's many friends and had tea. Margaret was proud to show off Emma, she complimented her brother for having put his children first rather than look for another wife. She knew his faults but also knew how affected he had been when he lost his wife and then his eldest daughter, Frances. He had carried on for the sake of William and Emma. That, Margaret felt, showed what a good man he was.

When they arrived back at Llanfairisgaer, Emma showed her cousins a wooden doll which her aunt had bought for her during their visit to Caernarvon. She played with it until she went to bed. Another visit to Caernarvon was to be made the following day as they were starting their journey back to Llanfairynghornwy, this time to see the castle that her father had told her many stories about.

Once Emma and Thomas were ready to leave, John, Margaret and the children stood to see them off. Hugh looked upset. He had rather enjoyed having Emma around and she seemed to understand him. He could not say goodbye and turned to look at the sea. There was a promise from Emma that she would come again and of course Hugh could always visit her at Caerau.

Emma thought that they must be going back to Plas-y-Nant, but Thomas drove a little further than that. He wanted Emma to see the lake that he had been telling her about in the fairy stories before she fell asleep. He had of course to tell her that she would not see any fairies in daytime as they were all asleep. As they walked along the edge of the lake, with Thomas pointing to places where the fairies lived, Emma watched intently, hoping her father was wrong. But she was content, believing that all the stories must be true and that she would have to come back and stay up all night to see the fairies.

By noon they were in Caernarvon where they strolled down towards the castle and Thomas showed the moat which once surrounded it. There were still rooms inside the castle, some beginning to look rather dilapidated. Thomas imagined that probably thieves had broken in and helped themselves to all the wealth that had been left behind. Emma wanted to climb the turrets and Thomas followed and showed her the wonderful view towards Anglesey from the Eagle Tower. This caused him to be a little fatigued by the time they came down, but Emma was full of energy and wanted to climb other turrets. Thomas made the point that they had a long journey and did not want to miss the boat back.

Once they had crossed over to Beaumaris, Emma fell asleep in the carriage. It had been a long journey for her, and Thomas was glad of some peace during the ride back. He was keen to get home before it was too dark and hoped that William would still be up; he just wanted to make sure that he was safe.

Mother Roberts, William, the maids, the cook and the workers around Caerau were all delighted to see them and gave them a good welcome home. Emma was so excited, she couldn't wait to see William and tell him all about Hugh, the other William and baby Frances. Thomas ushered them in so that he could sit down and have a glass of brandy. William came to talk with him and soon they would sit down for dinner. Mr Jones, the teacher, came through and William was sent to look for Emma and accompany her to the dining room. This gave Mr Jones enough time to give a report on William's behaviour and advancement in learning. Mr Jones was very pleased with William and said that if he carried on learning as much as he had, he would indeed be a very good pupil for the Free Grammar School at Beaumaris, where Thomas was hoping to enter him. They walked through and joined Mother Roberts and the children. Emma kept interrupting everyone and telling them all about Plas-y-Nant, Llanbeblig Church and Caernarvon Castle. Mr Jones was most interested and admired her extraordinary ability to remember. Mother Roberts called one of the maids and had Emma taken up to bed. Suddenly silence fell which gave William an opportunity to tell his father what had been happening in his absence.

It was the middle of May and people around Llanfairynghornwy, Llanfechell and other small villages were down at Cemaes, busy carrying sand from boats that had brought it from Red Wharf Bay. Never had sand been so popular and even poor people were carrying some away in the hope of being able to grow vegetables which would help them keep alive. Mr William Bulkeley of Brynddu paid Mr Pugh of Moelfre 16d for two boatloads of sand containing 250 bags.

Mr Lloyd of Rhosbeirio called to see Thomas with Mr David Williams, the attorney. They had been to visit Mr William Bulkeley on private business but were glad to be able to leave and call at Caerau.

Emma had started classes with Mr Jones which meant that he stayed at Caerau for four days, teaching her and William. With Emma, he felt that knowledge seemed to be within her. In mathematics, she was quicker than anyone he had ever taught. The only problem was that Emma disappeared to suit herself. If she felt like going to see the ducks or to visit one of the farm workers, she just went. Mr Jones would have to talk to Thomas and Mother Roberts about this, otherwise his time would be wasted. He had worked out a rota between Emma and William which William dutifully kept, but he was getting to the end of his tether with Emma. Later that day, when the children had gone to bed, Mr Jones sat and talked with both Mother Roberts and Thomas. He explained the situation. Mother Roberts was quick to blame Thomas, saying that if he did not correct her now, in a few years' time he would regret it. Thomas sat silently, though he accepted what was said and understood that most of it was his fault. In the end he relented and gave Mr Jones permission to punish Emma if she disobeyed or decided to disappear whenever she felt like it. They departed amicably on a decision that it was all for Emma's good.

The excitement of her trip was still with Emma. When she entered the room where Mr Jones was already waiting, she started off about the different things she had seen. Mr Jones asked her to sit down and told her that he had spoken with both Mother Roberts and her father, who had given him full permission to lock the door, so that she could not leave. Emma sat in total disbelief. Suddenly she got up and walked to the door, which at the time was still unlocked. She opened the door and screamed loud enough to bring Mother Roberts scurrying from the breakfast room, only to see Emma run out shouting and screaming. This was another tantrum. She fled to one of the outbuildings and ran upstairs to where one of the farm workers was usually found. There she shouted and screamed for all she was worth. All the workers tried to protect Emma. Thomas came along to see what the commotion was all about. Mother Roberts was furious and said that it was due to him. Mr Jones, the schoolteacher, was standing there; he spoke with Thomas, then disappeared. He had realised that there would be no class that day and that it would take some time to calm Emma. He decided to go home for the rest of the day and come back in two days' time to see how the situation was. Thomas was quite unable to do anything, he just hated being cross with Emma. He tried saying that Mr Jones thought she was quite clever, but Emma started to shout again, and Thomas walked off. Mother Roberts couldn't be bothered with a spoilt child: Emma had to learn that she could not and would not always have her own way.

It took William to talk to her. He just quietly said, 'That was a big one, Emm, and it upset Papa very much. We all know that he loves you and always gives in to you, but really, Emm, I've never heard you as bad.' His true pal had been Frances, but he had got used to Emma and did not want to hurt her. Emma turned and looked at William. He said, 'Come along, Emm, no one is going to hurt you, but you will have to apologise to Papa and Mother Roberts.' Emma wasn't sure about that. She just stood and looked around until she saw some of her ducks and went off again to play with them. William followed slowly. Again, he said that she should make an effort now that she was eight and not a little girl anymore. He told her that there would be punishment, that she would have to accept it, otherwise they might get rid of her. Emma looked at him. They could not mean that! But William said, 'They might'. That seemed to quell her.

Emma crept back indoors very quietly, hoping to hide from her grandmother and father. But she was unlucky. Thomas came through from his study and captured her as she walked along the hallway. He ordered her into the study and called Mother Roberts in with William joining too. Her brother felt that it was his duty to be there to protect her if things got out of hand. Thomas looked at her and said in a quiet tone that he would not be telling her fairy stories for over a week. And should she not behave for Mr Jones, she would not visit her Aunt Margaret again. William would come instead. She was to sit for an hour each day reading and in no way disturb Mother Roberts when she was in a temper. He made her promise to apologise to Mother Roberts, the workmen and the kitchen staff. This Emma did, though she did not enjoy the thought of it. Suddenly the thought of being sent away hit home and she disappeared to look for the workers and the staff. Silence ensued for the rest of the day. Mother Roberts had gone off to one of the markets looking for good meat. Thomas went off to Penrhos, Holyhead, to visit one of the boys who was home before going to London.

Emma enjoyed the rest of the day doing exactly as she wanted but William reminded her that she would have to be very careful with her behaviour if she was not to be sent away. That evening she decided to eat in the kitchen with the cook and maids, knowing that they would never fault her even in her temper. One of the maids went with her when she was ready for bed. She did not wish to meet with either her grandmother or her father. Later that evening William called in her room, Emma was still awake, missing her father and his stories. William sat and told her a story until Emma shrieked with laughter.

Next day, everyone sat around the breakfast table. Mother Roberts said good morning to everyone. The silence was penetrating. William was the one to break it by announcing that as Mr Jones was away for a couple of days with no lesson he was going to ride down to the beach. He turned to Emma and said that she could go with him if she felt like it. Emma agreed and soon the atmosphere improved with Thomas announcing that he was going to the post office at Llannerchymedd that day. The children left. Thomas told Mother Roberts what a charming young man William was growing up to be, how he had handled Emma in her tantrum, and then this morning to include her in his outing. He was indeed very proud of him.

Three days later, Mr Jones came back, and it happened to be a day when Emma was to have lessons. He did not rebuke her. In fact, he had brought her a small gift, a pretty little pin to wear on her dress. Emma was delighted. Then Mr Jones, rather than start the lesson immediately, to get her into a good mood started asking her questions about various matters. When he thought she was getting bored, he would ask her what subject she would like to hear about.

It was nice that life was back to normal. Mother Roberts had been going around checking that there was enough of the ingredients needed for cooking. She checked the cupboard in the chimney wall, making sure that there was enough sugar and that it was dry. Due to the rather wet weather, salt from the hanging bacon in the back pantry was dropping over the floor making it quite slippery. This was usually taken as a sign of an improvement in the weather.

On June 23rd a crowd gathered at Llyn Cromlech with dogs to hunt young wild ducks or 'floppers'. None were taken by the dogs, but Mr Bulkeley of Brynddu was able to shoot one. He had always considered himself good at shooting.

Having made her list of things to collect, Mrs Roberts set out for Llannerchymedd and its June fair, commonly known as 'Ffair Dydd Iau Duw' (God's Thursday Fair). Two days later a Mr Lewis called: he was an artist from Shrewsbury with samples of 12 aspects of North Wales. He said that he had already collected quite a few orders on the island and that he would be able to deliver them in a year's time. Thomas was rather wary, but Mother Roberts gave an order saying that she was thinking of William and Emma. Thomas nodded his agreement and wished Mr Lewis well.

July turned out to be another wet month. The cold rain killed turkeys that were about three months old, and news came to Caerau that Mr Bulkeley of Brynddu had lost all his turkeys. The highways were full of water and the farm workers had to open ditches to disperse the water as quickly as possible. The rain abated towards the middle of July and the farm workers started to gather hay into stacks. News came from Caernarvon and Mold fairs that there was no buying of cattle though there was quite a demand for horses. William Bevan of Croes Fechan sold 14 horses out of 17 at Mold.

August 3rd was the day Ann Warmingham's second son was christened, occasioning another family gathering. Emma loved stories about marriage and babies, and she would play with babies for hours. The women chatted while the men celebrated by drinking wine and smoking tobacco bought from Bryan's of Llannerchymedd. Bryan was very well-known throughout the whole country, and people from London continually sent him large orders. This often made the locals wait for their tobacco, as he was always busy seeing to the larger orders from away. News came later that Mr William Bulkeley was most upset because he had not even been asked to attend the christening. He believed that being the mother's guardian he had a right to be there. Everyone attending had a very good day and were glad that no gloom from Mr Bulkeley cast a shadow over them.

On 25th August, an overcast day, an eclipse of the sun took place. Tomorrow would be another day to be off to the sessions at Beaumaris. They would go on until September 5th, when Thomas could return home and see what his children had been up to. He was very glad that Emma was showing signs of being more settled and getting on well with Mr Jones, who thought she was an excellent pupil. Thomas found everyone in a good mood. There appeared to be no tantrums and no ill feeling. Emma chatted at such speed that Thomas had to ask her to slow down, he had time to listen to her. William informed his father that he had ridden several times as far as Llanrhwydrys one way and Llanfaethlu the other, teaching himself routes to travel upon. He suggested that the two of them should ride out one day so that Thomas could show him how to get to Holyhead, which Thomas agreed to do.

Many people had been told about the eclipse of the moon which was to take place that night. Many, however, had forgotten. And some – knowing of William Bulkeley's keen interest in astronomy – decided that they would leave it all to him. He recorded it in his diaries as a total eclipse of the moon which happened at three o'clock in the morning.

September 14th brought news of Thomas Roberts of Bodior's death. Married to Margaret Owen, daughter and sole heiress of John Owen of Bodior, he was a brother-in-law to Mother Roberts, her husband's brother. Thomas and Margaret Roberts's son, William, had married Emma Owen, heiress of Presaddfed. Emma Rowlands, despite her indifference towards many members of her family, was related to many, many families through various interlocking marriages around Anglesey.

Later in the month, Thomas visited his sister Margaret and took both William and Emma with him. This would be a break before the long winter months which often caused Emma to lose her temper through being bored and unable to go out. Llanfairisgaer looked wonderful, the garden beautifully kept. The children loved it, and Thomas spent many hours with his nephews, Hugh and William. Little Frances had passed away leaving Margaret bereft of the only daughter she would have.

When they returned, Mother Roberts had been busy sorting out many things. She had the maids put up thicker and warmer curtains in William and Emma's bedrooms. She had woven beautiful rugs for them and had placed them by their beds. Always very resourceful, she knew that it would please the children to have something new, though it might not be as grand as Emma would have liked. All the coal buckets were filled by the maids with coal recently delivered to Cemaes in boats. Anglesey had its own coalfields which belonged to the Holland family at Berw in the township of Ysgeifiog.

October went by with people still busy on the farms collecting what they could of what was left of the grain, and many cutting gorse to dry ready for the winter fires. All the men around Caerau had been busy making sure that everyone was going to be warm, and they would often tell stories about what they had found when cutting the gorse. Emma loved listening to their stories because they were of animals and birds. They would tell her the colours of the birds and their eggs; totally fascinated, she listened intently. Thomas asked the men to make sure that the ditches either side of the drive were open and clean. Now was the time to do it. Some of the men were still building a wall which should finish off the walled garden, a mammoth job. Thomas managed to occupy himself with all that had to be overseen. It certainly was a busy month between visits to Dr Wynne, Lord Bulkeley and sometimes to Mr William Bulkeley.

During November the weather was cold, dark, and cloudy and on November 12th Thomas Lewis, the drover of Tre Feibion Meurig, was buried. Drovers were rather like lawyers, not popular men, but Thomas Lewis was one who had learnt to better himself by being honest. William Bulkeley's diary states case follows:

> *'This day was buried Thomas Lewis of Tre Feibion-Meyrick, a very great dealer in sheep and hogs, and of late in oxen and cows, and had acquired thereby considerable fortune considering the time he had begun (about twenty years ago) brought up seven children, one at university and purchased a £20 a year estate and died worth £1,400 or £1,500 in money and stock in the 51st year of his age. Nov 12th, 1736. Thomas Lewis was formerly of Brwynog.'*

This was a huge compliment from William Bulkeley, who had changed his mind about drovers when Thomas Lewis proved his honesty to him, carrying money to London for his son. Later in the month Thomas Rowlands joined Mr Meyrick and others to walk five miles hoping for a woodcock, partridge, or hare. None were found, being a good shot Mr William Bulkeley managed to shoot a plover and teal.

There was an epidemic of cholera, which made many to be despondent. On December 26th Llanfechell Church had over 90 in attendance, with people from other parishes attending from lack of a service in their own. The parson continued to read his sermon which he had started a week before, then went on to read an Act of Parliament against profane cursing and swearing, which made it very late. William Bulkeley was furious that the parson had wasted so much time over this Act of Parliament when so many people were dying.

The following day, December 27th, one of the men came running with news that the post boy of Llannerchymedd had died of cholera. Mother Roberts, anxious about the children, called them in and started telling them a story about various members of her family, anything to distract from this depressing news.

There was worse, as news arrived on the 29th about the death of young William Bulkeley, leaving his wife, Ann Warmingham, with two little boys, one just over four months old. Many were concerned about her circumstances as it was known that her husband, who was John Owens's agent, had spent a lot of money on Presaddfed, believing that he was making it fit for John Owen whom he hoped would become a member of parliament. The truth was that John Owen had never thought of this and considered much of the expense unnecessary. Bulkeley had died after just 24 hours of sickness. He was buried on December 30th at Llysdulas. The shock to Ann Warmingham caused many to gossip, as she seemed not to care how she looked on the day of the funeral.

The month of January brought with it an epidemic of distemper which fell mostly on labouring people. At Presaddfed it was reported that 17 servants were sick all at the same time. Caerau had three ill, with Mother Roberts giving out homemade medicine from her mother's recipes.

Emma's birthday was a warm occasion, with William teasing her. It was nice that he now played with Emma and gave her more attention. Thomas had refrained from buying her bonnets and dresses, giving her instead some quills and ink so that she would understand the importance of continued learning. Emma accepted them as though they were just what she wanted, which pleased Thomas immensely.

Towards the 24th January, it began to snow and people everywhere were praying that this would wash away the distemper. It did not. Pleurisy were still very common in many parishes all the way to Holyhead, where they were busy burying almost every day.

On the 8th February, having been out to Llanfechell market, Mother Roberts heard the news that her brother-in-law, Simon Langford, had died of the epidemic. He was buried the following day, leaving his wife, Sina, sister to Mother Roberts, with two or three daughters. Simon Langford was rector of Rhoscolyn and lecturer or reader of Holyhead, and had struggled a long time with so little money coming in to keep him, his wife and his daughters. Many a time Mother Roberts had felt sorry for her sister, Sina, feeling that her children always looked a little drab and poor. Emma was always scathing towards the girls and how they dressed, never remembering how lucky she was to have all she wanted. Little did she know that Mother Roberts used to make sure that anything she did not like and would not wear went to those in need. After the funeral, Thomas and the children went for a ride as far as Cemaes where they saw two 14-ton boats taking barley from Cemaes to Warrington.

Many young men from around the district were disillusioned, with work and on February 29th people watched as several local youths gathered together to walk to London in the hope of getting work. Their families and friends worried that they might not see them again, even though many promises were made by some that they would be back within a year. It was March and the weather was not encouraging, but life went on.

Chapter Four

The year 1737 again started cold, blustery, and wet. Each dry day found most farm workers busily harrowing in readiness to sow hay seeds mixed with clover in the hope of a good crop. Holes were prepared to plant fir trees. They would grow tall and wide providing a firm screen or wind break.

The sessions were held as usual at Beaumaris between April 14th and 19th. There was an interesting case when Joseph Davies of Cheshire, master of a cruiser held now at Beaumaris, was accused of killing one of his comrades in Holyhead Bay by a blow to the head with a hand spike. Custom officers from several counties attended the court on his behalf, but the jury brought in a verdict of guilty to murder. Several of the crew members who had given evidence against their master were dismissed by the custom commissioners who claimed that they were ashore the night when the death took place. The commissioners also petitioned the judge for a delay of execution and prepared another very long petition to the king and council in the hope of a pardon.

The jury were at the Bull that evening, Thomas, Mr John Owen of Presaddfed, Mr Owen of Penrhos, and Mr Jones of Plas Gwyn with several others, when Mr William Bulkeley arrived along with his cousin, Mr Henry Morgan. They all drank together until most of them were rather drunk.

The excitement during May for Emma and William was seeing a 60-ton sloop arrive at Cemaes from London. It had come to pick up barley and oats which had been bought for the London merchants. The sloop brought with it 1400 deal boards and some oak, to be left at Cemaes until sold. The children loved to hear the chatter of the crew and the laughter of the crowds standing watching.

Emma was in the garden at Caerau when a flight of fieldfares arrived, 20 or more in number. When she asked Mr Jones about them, he told her that they were known as birds of passage, as they never stayed here in breeding time. That was it, he had to answer one question after another, and the afternoon soon disappeared.

On May 22nd the news arrived of Mr John Holland of Berw's death. He was married to Jane White, the only child and heiress of Mr William White of Friars, Beaumaris. Mrs Roberts took the message as Thomas was out. She ordered the maid to make sure that his coat and gloves were clean and ready as he would be attending the funeral.

Emma and William had decided to visit Mynachdy, where they knew the housekeeper, Mrs Jane Hughes. Mr and Mrs Robison were not in residence, but Mrs Hughes always gave them a warm welcome and made them tea. She loved to hear their chitter-chatter and what they had learnt from Mr Jones.

The end of May saw most farmers busy shearing. It was also the time when corn was exported to England and Ireland. There was always something being exported from Anglesey, 'Môn Mam Cymru'.

In June, Emma and William looked forward to their holidays when Mr Jones would be away for three months. He had taken a post with a family from abroad who wanted their children taught during their visit to Britain. Emma and William were pleased but Mr Jones had left plenty for them to study while he was away. When June 27th came along, many people grumbled because it was the day when the parson set out the tithe tax. Disagreements could be heard everywhere; even Mother Roberts and Thomas complained.

July proved to be a better month. At least everyone had sun. Thomas was off again to the quarter sessions where they levied 20 shillings on the county to repair the bridge over the moat for the gaoler of Beaumaris Gaol. The jury condemned a woman of Holyhead to be whipped the following Saturday for petty larceny. When Thomas was back home, telling Emma the story as she always insisted that he should, she was shocked to hear that this woman was to be whipped. Thomas explained that he thought it was better she was whipped otherwise she might be burnt on the hand which could maim her for life.

It had been so hot that many had to water their gardens to stop the fruit from falling too soon and vegetables and plants from withering. It was a time when plenty of crabs were found and some young lobsters which were always welcome for a tasty meal. Many of the people passed their time busily weeding so that the vegetables had a good chance of growing well. Those who took their oxen to

Aberffraw fair found that prices there were good, though many wondered how long this hot weather was to last. Emma made herself busy, making sure that there was enough water for her ducks and helping William Williams, the gardener, water some of the vegetables.

On August 7th many from Caerau called at the parson's house at Llanfechell. John Griffith of Plas-y-Bais, Llanddyfnan had come to introduce Mr James Bulkeley, Lord Bulkeley's brother, to the country. He was shown around the Llannerchymedd market, then they went to Presaddfed, then on to Caerau before ending up at the parsonage. A few more gathered, including John Owen and his brother, the doctor. Mr Lloyd of Rhosbeirio was sent to meet them at Llanfechell. There they drank hard, everywhere they went little did Emma realise that this James Bulkeley would eventually be her husband.

At the August sessions, a judge by the name of Mr Roger Holland attended – his first visit to Beaumaris. Holland of Gray's Inn had been made Justice of Caernarvon, Merioneth and Anglesey. On August 29th the grand jury were sworn in, putting their shillings in the glove, and amongst them was Richard Hughes of Castellior, Thomas' tenant, about whom William Bulkeley had been so scathing. This time, Mr Bulkeley was seen talking to him, which caused many of the jurors to smile.

On September 8th a great many people from all over Anglesey gathered at Gallt Ben Ddu outside Llannerchymedd where the foundations of a windmill were laid. Many cheered and sang, regarding this as a historical event, and the men of course walked down to the Bull where they had plenty to eat and drink.

Thomas was pleased to hear from the bailiff that merchants from Liverpool and Warrington had bought what Caerau had to sell of barley, rye and pilcorn. Cemaes was full of farmers wanting to sell their goods to the merchants. Drays were to be seen everywhere carrying barley and oats when it was dry. Making some money was important as the markets over the year had been quite poor. Suddenly a lot of fishermen went to Wylfa to fish for herrings and a great many were caught. It had been more than 20 years since any herrings had been found there and many had believed that they would never come back. Everyone was overjoyed and had herrings twice a week for over two months.

Mr John Lewis, the artist from Shrewsbury, came around delivering paintings and prints he had made of views of North Wales. It was an exciting day, waiting to see what he had brought. Thomas and Mrs Roberts were very pleased, and they would get John Roberts, one of the farm workers, to put the pictures up. Thomas felt that now he could tell Emma stories to do with each picture and that she would soon recognise the various places around North Wales.

Newborough market was not very good, with only a few old cows and some oxen. Drovers had been collecting the best cattle to take to Chester and London. There was still much buying of wheat and corn in October by those who were commissioned by the Liverpool and Warrington merchants.

The following week, Thomas, William and Emma travelled to Llannerchymedd to witness the christening of Dr Evans' baby on October 14th. They met many friends, had tea and chatted, and soon it was time to ride back to Caerau for dinner. William and Emma were enjoying themselves as Mr Jones only came twice a week now as he had other pupils. They were hoping that either their cousin, Hugh, would come over to stay or that they would go over to Llanfairisgaer to stay with their aunt and uncle. Thomas teased them, saying that they could only go if they had done all the work expected by Mr Jones.

A week later a letter arrived from their Aunt Margaret inviting William and Emma to stay for a week. There was such excitement as Emma enjoyed Hugh's company, and she behaved herself so that she could go. She would tell William all that she remembered from her previous visit and ask her aunt to take them to Llanbeblig Church where they would see the plaques in memory of their grandmother and their father's brother, Richard. Hugh took them, telling William that it was good for him to learn about his family. Their Uncle John was pleased to have them around and William, their cousin, always the quiet one, spoke of his interest in the church and that he felt it was his calling. His knowledge of churches, going back many centuries, astonished William and Emma, though they both felt that he was rather young to be saying that he was going to be a priest. They played games, laughed, and ate well, which rendered them quite exhausted each night as they went to bed.

Thomas called on them a week later, visiting his people and collecting some rents. Caernarvon had done well with the sale of barley, oats and corn, and the farmers were able to pay their rents, many of which were overdue. Thomas stayed the night at Llanfairisgaer and the following day they set off on their long journey back to Caerau, where all the staff were glad to see them, Mother Roberts sitting with a lovely fire to greet them.

Many people were sad for King George II, whose wife, Queen Caroline, died on November 20th at St James' Palace, aged 54. William Bulkeley, who regarded the Prime Minister, Robert Walpole, as a ruthless rascal, believed that things within the country might improve now that there would be no more support for him from the late queen. Caroline was the first Princess of Wales to be invested with her husband and was later crowned at his side. She was politically active, a firm supporter of Walpole, and proved that her intellect far outweighed her husband's. An avid reader, she established an extensive library at St James's Palace. She supported vaccination against smallpox by having her three youngest children inoculated. She had gained the trust of the people, who mourned her much.

December was a dreary month, but Caerau had good fires, Thomas had instructed the men to make sure that they collected plenty of gorse to make the fire crackle. Dry gorse ignited in seconds, with the sound of it crackling accompanying breakfast. Thomas had been given a load of coal from a man living at Cemaes because he had helped him over an issue that he did not understand, being unable to read. He insisted on paying, but Thomas, knowing of the man's circumstances, did not want to accept anything. However, one day when Thomas was at court, the man had come with a load of coal and insisted that the workers unloaded it into the shed where coal was kept along with the gorse which was drying.

As Emma's birthday got closer Mother Roberts told William that there was only a week to find her a suitable present. She had saved to buy a lovely rug for Emma's bedroom, giving money to one of her nieces who lived not far from Chester to purchase it. When Emma was away at her aunt's in Caernarvon, the niece had brought it to Caerau, where it was hidden until the birthday. The week before, Mother Roberts had been busy arranging that various members of her large family would visit on the birthday. She was extremely thoughtful, realising that without a mother, Emma would be lonely.

Thomas had been away in London. On his way he had called on his friend, Mr Downing, who lived near Mold, a man famous around the district for knowing everything there was to know about horses. Thomas had asked him to find a pony for Emma. When he called on his return journey, indeed his friend had found a beautiful pony. Thomas fell in love with it and was convinced that Emma would love it too. He had already decided to leave it with Henry Morgan at Henblas, to be collected on the morning of Emma's birthday. There was great jollity when Thomas arrived back; the children adored their father and he in turn adored them. Mother Roberts gave a good report of their behaviour while he was away. She had overseen the work that Mr Jones had left and made sure they spent some time each day on their lessons. Thomas felt he was lucky to be able to depend on Mother Roberts who was so astute and intelligent and kept an eagle eye on the running of the estate.

On January 13th, her birthday, Emma woke wondering what she was going to get. The maid came into her bedroom and gave her a bath, so that she would look special for the day. When she arrived downstairs and walked into the dining room for breakfast, she was greeted by Mother Roberts, William, and her father. After breakfast, Mother Roberts took her upstairs and told her to go into her room where she would follow in a minute. She went to a cupboard, took the rug and brought it to Emma in her room. Emma was delighted, she hugged Mother Roberts and at the same time wondered how she had managed to hide it. Downstairs again, William gave her a red bow for her hair. Thomas was outside, and with him stood this lovely little pony. Emma could not believe it. She went over to her father who kissed her and wished her a happy birthday. The pony was soon making friends with her, nuzzling its head on her shoulders. William suggested that they should ride together down to the beach. All three went off for a canter. Emma had always dreamt of having her own pony but never thought that she would get one as lovely. She would have to think of a name and ride down to the beach each day, so that they would become good friends. Emma was in such a good mood for the rest of the day, enjoying every minute of it, and William showed her the book that Mr Jones had given him which gave the names of various parts of the horse's anatomy. Hours passed, both in deep conversation about how they would ride together to various places.

During February, Mr William Bulkeley called at Caerau to buy seeds from William Williams, the gardener. He bought onion, carrot, and parsnip seeds, admiring the way Williams had everything in order. Emma insisted that Mr Bulkeley saw her new pony. He walked with her to the stable, where she had been busy brushing and combing the pony ready to be put outside in the field. When he asked the pony's name, Emma said, 'Fancy. She fancies herself and I fancy her.' Mr Bulkeley said that the pony was indeed a very fine example and gave her some advice how to get the best out of her.

The following week, Mother Roberts went to Llanfechell market and was surprised to see such an abundance of corn of all sorts, veal, salt, bacon, and eggs. It was such a long time since she had seen anything like it. She stocked up on several things and as she rode back to Caerau it was beginning to snow. She was glad to be back as the snow fell very quickly and was soon a foot deep.

Nicholas Oughton, who taught people to sing at Llannerchymedd, was at Llanfechell Church on February 26th to teach people how to sing psalms. Mother Roberts and Thomas were looking forward to the time he would be at Llanfairynghornwy Church.

On February 28th there was such thunder and lightning that some of the staff at Caerau were afraid. William became anxious but Emma delighted in the storm. She stood in one of the windows so that she could see the flashes as they struck and then seemed to be swallowed up by the sea. She found it extremely exciting and shouted each time another flash came. Mother Roberts took no notice, having been used to lightning over many years. As her part of Caerau was much darker than the big house, it did not affect her much.

March brought in more bad news as many children had caught smallpox, many of them dying. Alongside this ran another distemper which was called the hen pox. As many as eight coffins could be seen near the cemetery in nearly all the villages of Anglesey. At times like this, Mother Roberts made sure that William and Emma had malt and plenty of good food and did not make contact with anyone outside Caerau. At church the following Sunday. A sad end to the year.

The year 1738 started much as any other. People running the many estates of Anglesey were busy making notes to cover the year, which fields would bear crops, and which were to be used for the animals. It was a custom that each field had a change of use each year. The field where the pigs had been would now be ploughed, sown, and prepared for growing hay. Other fields were prepared for barley, oats and pilcorn. The gardener would be clearing out the garden, ready to be sown with a variety of the most popular vegetables, hoping for the adventure of a good selection for the kitchen. There was a keen interest in vegetables around Anglesey. William Morris, the customs officer at Holyhead, was well-known for his vegetable garden, as were Henry Morgan of Henblas, Mr Bulkeley of Brynddu, and Thomas Rowlands of Caerau, to name but a few. Often stories arrived about the wonderful garden at Plas Newydd and other estates around the island.

Most people were hard at work ploughing and harrowing. Those who had several properties would visit to see what their tenants were hoping to grow. In many ways it was an audit of all that they had and to what purpose it was being used. Then there was the land tax to consider, whereby owners of estates had to declare their interests. Thomas had to account not only for the Caerau estate but for all his lands in Caernarvonshire – Betws Garmon, Beddgelert, Llanwnda, Llandwrog, and Clynnog besides houses owned in Caernarvon itself.

So far, the weather had been extremely cold and wet. By April 22nd there was snow on Garn, Llanfairynghornwy, with Mr William Bulkeley recording that it was there by five in the morning. All the planting had to be stopped and the workers put to other tasks such as making sure that all the ditches were cleaned out and open for the melting snow and the heavy rains that usually followed. Emma loved to see the snow and would walk in it watching her footprints, which could be seen from nearly every window. William declared that his sister should live in the wilds. Mother Roberts' warning that she would suffer from chilblains fell on deaf ears. Emma was in a world of her own, watching the snow on the trees creating patterns, the most beautiful lace she had ever seen.

She became bored again and had a very bad bout of temper, setting Mother Roberts, William, and Thomas all on tenterhooks. She threw such a tantrum that even Ella, her favourite maid, could not handle her. She hated where she lived with so few neighbours and wanted to go and live with her Aunt Margaret in Caernarvon. Thomas suggested that it might be a good idea for her to go for a month, then see how she felt. His sister could arrange for her to attend a school in Caernarvon to learn about life. It would be good for her to have sewing lessons to make dresses for herself. Letters were exchanged which pleased both Thomas and Emma. He gave a day when he would travel with her, making sure that she was safe. Then he would take William on a trip to London and show him some of the things that Mr Jones had been telling him about.

On their journey to Caernarvon, Thomas spoke with Emma, trying to tell her that it was time she behaved like a young woman which she would soon be. He did not want to hear his sister making any complaints about her. Emma promised that she would make every effort to behave. When they arrived at Llanfairisgaer, Emma flew out of the carriage and ran into her aunt and cousins. She was in her element and never stopped talking. This her cousin Hugh loved and off both went. Thomas explained to his sister what had been happening, how every few months they would suffer Emma's bad behaviour when she would yell, scream, and kick out at everyone. Margaret said that she would watch and agreed that to engage her at the school in Caernarvon might be an excellent idea. Thomas stayed the night and left the following morning. The journey back was wet and difficult. After the snow in late April, May brought in rain and many bouts of thunder and lightning. Mother Roberts and William were pleased to see him and after a few days' rest he planned for the trip to London. Mother Roberts informed him that Mr Lloyd of Llwydiarth was not in good health, suffering from dropsy. Thomas called to see him on May 8th before going on the journey.

Everything seemed to fit in well, Thomas and William off to London and Emma with her aunt. All this helped, as the bailiff had suggested bleeding some of the working horses, which would probably upset Emma. First the farrier would cover the horse's head with a sheet, then place a fleam near the jugular and quickly knock it in with a fleam stick so that the horse would not know what had hit it. This bleeding was done in order to keep the horse's blood balanced, which helped to keep it in good health. The workers went around collecting all the sheep to be washed before they were sheared. Ned, the bailiff, felt that it would be a strange event this year as Emma was missing. She loved to watch as the men washed and sheared the sheep, they would laugh with her as they often struggled to catch a sheep.

At the end of two weeks, Thomas and William returned, William full of stories which he was looking forward to sharing with Mother Roberts. She thought that he had grown at least a foot since she last saw him, which made William laugh at the impossibility.

On May 29th, a boat arrived at Cemaes from Liverpool with coal. Everyone arranged that their workmen collected between five and six tons to last over the summer and into the winter.

Excitement came with the news from Baron Hill that the wife of Frederick, the Prince of Wales, had given birth to a son on June 4th at Norfolk House, St James's Square, London. The Whigs and the Tories celebrated. This son would eventually become George III.

On June 10th, a boat belonging to John Edwards of Llanfechell was cast away near Corwyn y Cawr in the bay of Cemaes. It broke up in pieces and the load of 115 pegets of oats was lost. All the people on board were saved and then went to Llanfechell to made a protest against John Edwards.

News came on June 30th of Mr Lloyd of Llwydiarth's death. He left two daughters, bringing an end to the 500 years of male heirs. Thomas was invited to be one of the bearers. The funeral had to be held the next day, July 1st, because the body could not be kept any longer due to the dropsy. Mr Lloyd's body was taken from Llwydiarth, Llannerchymedd to Amlwch to be buried.

On July 12th, the small son of Mr Richard Lewis, the vicar of Llanidan, had a terrible accident, killed on the spot when the horse that his nurse was riding fell.

It was time again to collect sods and peat which would be piled up and dried to make long-lasting winter fuel. Farmers had begun making hay into stacks, and the wind helped to dry them. The gardener was busy clearing the remains of used vegetables, making room to plant spinach for winter use and saffron roots. The harvest saw most workers busy reaping rye and barley.

Soon thoughts turned to Emma. Thomas decided that he should visit to see what the situation was. Would his sister and brother-in-law want to be rid of Emma? In all reality he would very much like to have her back home at Caerau. What he found when he arrived was a great welcome from Margaret and John, with Emma shouting and running around her father and hugging him. When he asked Emma if she was ready to return home, he received no reply but rather a sullen face. He told her that William missed her and that her pony wanted her back. Margaret suggested that Emma needed time to say goodbye to her cousins and that they would love to have her again. Once she understood that, she would have something to look forward to. Nothing more was said until the following morning. Her behaviour according to Margaret had been impeccable, with no signs of moods or temper.

An early riser, Thomas was ready for a brisk walk before breakfast. He loved the view overlooking the Menai Straits towards Mr Bayley's house, Plas Newydd. There was a little wind, nothing compared to the howls he had become used to around Caerau. During breakfast he told John Griffith that that it would be late afternoon before he was back from several visits to discuss rent issues with the new tenants of various properties. John told him that he was more than welcome to stay another night which made it much easier for Thomas. Emma could not believe that there was no Thomas when she came down for breakfast with Hugh and William. Her aunt and uncle explained to her that he had a very busy day and would be staying again that evening, which took away her anxiety immediately.

All was well and Thomas and Emma returned to Caerau, where she entertained everyone with all her tales. The kitchen staff were delighted to hear about her adventures. Thomas asked her into his study as he wanted to explain to her that William was now a boarder at the Beaumaris Free Grammar School. Emma was shocked. What was she going to do? She would not have William to ride with or play, and he would not be able to tell her all he had learnt through Mr Jones. She stormed out of the study and went outside. Beside himself in fear that Emma would throw another tantrum, Thomas tried to follow when he was met by Mr Jones. Thomas explained to him that he has just told Emma about William at the school. Mr Jones asked where she had gone, then went and strolled around Caerau until he found Emma busy talking to her horse. Mr Jones joined in and asked many questions about the horse. Her answers revealed that she must have read the book he had given William. He told her that she was indeed very good and that he was pleased that the book had been helpful. Emma then turned and said that she would not like living at Caerau anymore because William was not there. Mr Jones listened and interested her in the idea that perhaps one day she would be going to a school. He told her a lot of stories about what some of the pupils did if they did not like a teacher, which had Emma laughing for all she was worth. By the time they returned to the house everything was normal. Mr Jones had managed to stop another tantrum.

On August 19th Thomas was off to the Beaumaris Quarter Sessions. He was also to meet with the Tory faction as Mr Bayley wished to stand again at the next election. The grand jury were sworn in on August 21st, with many more jurors than usual, all dropping their 6d in the glove and 10s 6d at the grand jury room. All the jurors dined with the sheriff and there were many balls and feastings during the session. On August 23rd they were discharged, and Thomas most certainly would be riding home that evening.

During September, the weather was fresh and cold, with a shower of hail followed by heavy rain. Mr Owen who looked after the horses at Caerau took Mother Roberts' horse to John Hughes of Gwredog so that they could have the service of his stallion. By the end of what had been a very wet month there was hoar frost in the mornings and evenings. All the workers were busy collecting gorse to give the fire a sparkle during the winter season. October came in, too wet to allow the workers to collect the rest of the barley.

There was a meeting at Llannerchymedd where many had travelled to receive information exhibited by the officers of excise regarding tea and coffee. There had been much grumbling the previous year when the Prime Minister, Sir Robert Walpole, had introduced the excise scheme. The dissatisfaction caused him to withdraw it.

On October 24th the Llwydiarth mill began to grind its first corn. Many people had travelled to see it, regarding the day as an important historical event.

During this late October time, the weather had been better than in many summer months. Thomas joined Mr William Bulkeley of Brynddu and Mr Fortunatus Wright, his son-in-law. They then met up with Mr Hugh Owen of Penrhos, the counsellor, the parson, and Mr Thomas Morris of Rhyd-y-Groes along with some others to go hunting. A crowd of young men beat the bushes, but the day proved rather fruitless. They found one hare, but it escaped and those with guns only managed to shoot two woodcocks. Thomas felt it a complete waste of time as they had walked around nine miles with very little gain.

Mother Roberts visited Betty Parry at Llanfechell to have her winter cloak repaired, something she would need very soon, as living near the sea they suffered horrendous bouts of extremely cold winds. On her way back she was met by the head worker and presented with handfuls of thick rushes which were used as watch lights. These were much appreciated and helpful when anyone needed to be out in the dark. The rushes would be set to light the way, so that visitors would be able to see the house when riding along the driveway. Many were still busy carrying gorse to dry. They scoured the hedgerows to find whatever little was to be found. Rumours had spread that it might be a very cold winter. Throughout December there was hail, thunder, and lightning. Emma as usual was excited watching the lightning bolts as they appeared to drop into the sea.

This was the time of year when the workers checked the outhouses, making sure that the roofs were safe. If not, they would make lists of what repairs were needed. Those in charge would carry out the repairs and attend to any thatching that might be needed to keep the house dry. This was done before the harsh winds of winter arrived.

When the post boy of Llannerchymedd arrived William and Emma went forward to give him 6d as a Christmas present. He told them that he liked this time of the year as he did well in tips.

At the end of December, a boat called the Cloxan, jointly owned by Mr William Griffith and Mr Gabriel Jones of Cytt arrived at Cemaes, where it found many arriving to collect the coal it was about to deliver.

It took some time as the people pushed forward wanting to be the first to be served.

January came in with more bad weather. It had become darker and the winds at times were ferocious; there had been so much rain that the water just stood on the ground everywhere. Much grumbling went on, especially by landowners who knew that if the fields were not ploughed it would be a difficult year.

Emma was thoroughly fed up at not being able to go out. Mr Jones knew by now how to keep her from throwing a tantrum, he would play games with her, hiding something which could take hours for her to find. Emma was in her element and quite determined to work hard at finding all the items hidden, not that she was always successful. It did, however, help to pass a day when nothing else could be done, all due to the weather.

When Iris, one of the kitchen maids, arrived back having been home to visit her sick mother, she was full of news. Her brother had called home just before she left for Caerau and had given them the news that Mr William Bulkeley's daughter had just given birth to a little girl. Mother Roberts was very pleased to hear the news and immediately arranged for one of the maids to visit Brynddu with a gift for the new baby. Emma wanted to send something too and found a shawl suitable to carry the little baby in. The baby was born on February 5th at 4:15pm and on the 10th she was christened. The godparents were Mr Bulkeley, his mother, and Mrs Wynne of Bodewryd. After the christening many accompanied them back to Brynddu, including Thomas who stayed there until well past midnight and was rather the worse for all the drinking that had taken place.

On January 16th it was the election for an usher at the Beaumaris school. This caused a slight uproar as Lord Bulkeley had chosen Hughes of Denbighshire as a candidate. He was the curate of Beaumaris. However, there was opposition. Some had chosen a young man of nineteen, Vincent of Llanfachraeth. His myrmidons were Mr Thomas Rowlands of Caerau, Mr John Griffith of Garreg Lwyd, Mr John Owen of Presaddfed, Mr Edward Owen of Penrhos, Mr Hugh Hughes of Plas Coch, and Mr Lloyd of Rhosbeirio. Lord Bulkeley was very upset at this unexpected opposition. He did not appear but sent his brother, James, down to challenge these rebels who had dared to dispute his authority. The rebels huffed the ambassador away and carried on in their own way. Thomas had an interest in the school especially now that William was a boarder there.

February 14th saw a great fair at Llanfechell, and people had gathered from a wide area to enjoy it. It was also known that an old fair which had been neglected for well over 100 years was revived at Caernarvon. Mother Roberts and Thomas thought that Llanfechell Fair was great fun and Emma had a wonderful day. Mother Roberts paid 4s and 6d for 13 pounds weight of ordinary Irish candles so that she could save what they had at Caerau for common use.

March brought some improvement to the weather, and this helped to ease the worries of many who had had not been able to carry out any ploughing because of the excessive rains. This had also affected the markets as difficulties had arisen in collecting meats for sale, causing prices to rise, and upsetting the regular customers. On March 15th it snowed heavily with a very cold, raw wind. This held up the workers in their efforts to plough and harrow the fields. They were led to other jobs such as repairing hedges and helping the gardener with dunging to make hot beds.

It was still snowing when a messenger arrived with news that upset many, that Lord Bulkeley had died. Both Thomas and Mr William Bulkeley received an invitation which read as follows:

'March 22nd: Letter from John Bulkeley of Bwchanan Lord Bulkeley's agent.
Sr. Baron Hill March 21st, 1738.
My Lord desires the favour of your company here at nine o'clock next Saturday morning to be one of the bearers to attend my late Lord to his grave.
I am Sir, your obedient Servant and Kinsman.
John Bulkeley'

Richard, Lord Bulkeley, died without issue. He was the 5th Lord Viscount Bulkeley, born in 1708 and only 30 when he died on March 15th, 1738. He was the Chamberlain of North Wales, Constable of Beaumaris Castle, and Member of Parliament for Beaumaris, 1734-38. He was married to Jane, daughter and heiress of Lewis Owen of Peniarth in the County of Merioneth. She was to have a jointure out of the estate of £800 per annum, made up to £1,400 per annum after the death of the Dowager Lady Bulkeley, the late lord's mother, who had £1,400 jointure. The lord's brother, who succeeded to the title and estate under the encumbrances, had likewise (they said) a debt of £40,000 to pay. Lord Bulkeley was buried on March 24th, and the funeral was recorded in detail by Mr William Bulkeley of Bryndddu.

'March 24th, 1738:

The wind E blowing very cold and a great hoar frost this morning as thick as moderate snow, was a horseback this morning half after 5 to go to Lord Bulkeley's burying, came to Town by 10 and having cleaned my boots, and put on my best wig; I mounted my horse again to go up to Barnhill (understanding after I came to Town that the Bearers were to accompany the Hearse on horseback) being come there and conducted to the mourning room to console with the present Lord, (who were present with him as mourners his 2 Uncles Dr Thomas Price of Rhiwlas and Mr Lewis Atkinson and his servant John Bulkeley of Bwchanan) which being done, I was conducted to the room where the bearers were, who were Mr Rowlands of Caerau, Mr Richard Lloyd of Rhosbeirio, Mr Morgan of Henblas, Mr Lewis Llysdulas, Mr Griffith of Llanddyfan, Mr Hughes of Plâs Coch, Mr Jones of Pentraeth, Mr Williams of Ty Fry, Mr Wynne of Llanwnda, Mr Roberts Bryn-y-Neuadd, Mr Edmund Meyrick of Trefry, Mr John Rowland of Porth Llongdy, son to Mr Harry Rowlands author of Mona Antiqua, Lewis Tryslwyn and myself; and 4 clergymen (3 of whom were Bachelors, the care was to have all the lay gentlemen married men) the clergy were: Lloyd, a younger son of Grwych and Parson of Llanuwchlyn in Meirionethshire in the neighbourhood of Rhiwlas, Robert Lloyd Parson of Aber, Owen Lloyd Parson of Llansadwrn and Thomas Owen Parson of Rhoscolyn and Schoolmaster of Beaumaris, who had married, John Bulkeley's sister: there were the Bearers, 18 in number, who having had scarves, hatbands and gloves and dimensions taken of each finger to fit them with rings at a proper time and being all served with Cakes and Wine, the corps was brought out to the green Court before the front, where it was fastened on the carriage of a Coach drawn by 6 Horses which were covered with black Cloth, with Escutcheons fastened on the Cloth on both sides of the Horses – as also on the Velvet Pall that covered the Coffin; The coffin was very large and contained I presume the Leaden Coffin where the Corps was laid in; it was covered with black Velvet having on it several Gilt Plates in the following order; over the face was a carved gilt plate representing Time having in his right hand a branch of Palm, and a Trumpet on his left, over the breast was a coronet, below that was a large plate representing an Erected Monument, with Pillars, Bases, Frieze and Cornish and an Oval smooth place in the middle of it with these words engraved on it: 'The Rt Hon Richard Lord Viscount Bulkeley dyed March 15th 1738'. Below that at the lower part of the coffin was another plate representing a Flowerpot with Flowers: and in the intermediate spaces and about the coffin were small Gilt plates representing Angles. When the coffin was made fast on the Carriage the Mourners and Bearers mounted; The present Lord as chief mourner rode next the corps, then his 2 Uncles after him side by side, and John Bulkeley singly after them, then the Bearers followed by 2x2. The Bearers' Servants had hatbands and gloves, as had abundance of other people, in this order they marched silently till they came to the Church yard without any prefatory Prayer at seeking out, nor singing Psalms on the way; The corps being taken down, the Corps was carried from thence to the Church on the Arms of 8 persons, the bearers in 2 rows taking hold of the tassels of the Pall, and the mourners following after till it was placed on the Brier; then the service being performed he was put in the Tomb in this manner; a very wide deep pit being opened at the West End of the Tomb discovered a hole of about 32 inches square, the upper part of which hole might (I believe) by level to the surface of the Church floor, and having place planks over and across the pit, the Coffin was shoved thereon to its proper place in the Tomb thro that hole: Then was used on this occasion that Popish Superstition of this Country of giving Meat and Drink and Money over the Corps with black wooden Bowls to receive the drink with the above mentioned inscription upon them, only his age added which was 31. I gave the Minister 5s & 2s to the Clark, as all the bearers I presume likewise did, when the Burying was over all the company went to Baron Hill, where we dined and having sat about an hour after Dinner my brother Lewis and I took our leave of his Lordship came to Town and having paid 6s at my lodgings we set out about 5and came to Llysdulas by 8.'

Thus ended the year 1738.

Chapter Five

The usual blustering winds continued at the beginning of 1739. It was cold and dark in the mornings and the evenings darkened early. Thomas arrived home after the funeral of Lord Bulkeley wondering how long it would be before his brother would take over the late lord's lead. It would probably take some time and now everyone was missing the 5th lord viscount who was much admired. He had always been very pleasant and allowed the most ordinary person his view on various matters. He was interested in Anglesey as a whole and its people. There were not many who had a bad word of him.

Back at Caerau it was soon time once again to sort out the various taxes needed including the land tax. Thomas spent much time in his study sorting everything out and was pleased to hear a very good report from Mr Jones regarding Emma.

Stormy weather arrived which caused substantial devastation. Many lost their corn and hay as the wind damaged the stacks and several houses suffered the worst of the storm. The wind was blowing so high that it singed the March blossoms and new shoots on trees. The workers at Caerau feared that if they were unable to plough and reseed the fields by May, they would lose most of their stock of food.

Thomas was pleased that Emma seemed calmer, and more interested in her lessons. Mr Jones always gave her some work to do when he was not attending at Caerau. Emma delighted in finishing within a day of him leaving, so that she could be out riding and visiting friends. Now that she was 12, the teacher had reduced his time at Caerau, believing that Emma like William would soon be attending school.

Thomas received a letter from his cousin, William Owen of Brogyntyn, who would be calling as he was travelling to Anglesey to speak with the new Lord Bulkeley. There were many issues concerning politics to discuss. Thomas looked forward to this and asked Mother Roberts to make sure that they had enough meat to make a good feast when he arrived.

Emma chatted with Thomas as he told her stories each night which she loved, though some were now used as a direct lesson in many aspects of life. He had been telling her stories about horsemen, ghosts, burglars, and of course highwaymen, the most famous being Dick Turpin. Many of the Anglesey drovers had claimed to have either met or seen him and their gruesome and hair-raising tales would frighten people. This sort of excitement filled Emma with wonderful dreams, and she looked forward to the stories each night. She was more grown up and Thomas hoped that would continue until she was of age to mix in society and perhaps find a suitable husband.

When William Owen visited on his way back from their London house in Conduit Street, he was full of Dick Turpin's execution, which had taken place on April 7th. Richard Turpin started life in Hempstead, Essex. Born at the Blue Bell Inn (which later became the Rose and Crown), he was the fifth son of John Turpin and Mary Elizabeth Parmenter. His baptism took place on September 21st, 1705, in the same parish as his parents had been married ten years earlier. John Turpin was a butcher and innkeeper. It was believed that Dick followed in his father's profession and became a butcher, though some said that he was apprenticed elsewhere. Unfortunately, he joined a group of youths who wandered around the countryside pillaging whatever they could find and causing much disruption when they stole horses and deer. It could be that they encouraged Dick as he would know how to cut up a carcass. He became a notorious horse thief and later went as far as killing people to escape, probably to Epping Forest which was one of his haunts. After many exploits and having continuously to hide from the authorities, Dick Turpin, now calling himself John Palmer, travelled across the River Humber from the East Riding of Yorkshire to Lincolnshire where he settled with his wife, Elizabeth Millington, whom he had married in 1725. He went around declaring himself a horse trader and mixed quite often with the gentry. John Palmer not only bought a house but spent lavishly. His wife had her own maid, and this caused suspicion. Many questions were asked as to who John Palmer was. His mistake was to shoot a man's cockerel and threaten to kill its owner, causing much speculation that things were not quite as they should be.

Three local justices of the peace made enquiries as to who John Palmer was and how he had made his money. Enquiries went to many counties, eventually leading to the arrest of John Palmer, who was handcuffed and transferred to York Castle. Found guilty, Dick Turpin was executed on the Knavesmire (now York Racecourse) on April 7th, 1739. When the news arrived in Anglesey, mostly through the *Gentleman's Magazine* (which William Owen had also brought for Thomas), with details of his cruel world, his arrest and execution, it was as though everyone had lost a friend. His barbaric life seemed to matter little. Most people had come to accept him as a notorious character, but had learnt to travel without valuables, leaving the highwaymen empty handed.

Thomas was looking forward to reading all about Turpin, wondering how he could think of a story to kill off one of Emma's favourite characters. Everywhere Thomas went, people were full of Dick Turpin and in some quarters, there was consternation that he had been executed. Stories had built up about him, most likely fictional: that he was a character brave and strong who had ridden 200 miles overnight on 'Black Bess' from London to York. It was said that he stood at 5ft 9ins, with dark hair and was quite good looking, except for the scars left after the pox on his face. Thomas would have to work hard at making a story that Emma would believe. Emma now had her story before going upstairs to bed. Thomas brought in Dick Turpin and when he had finished, he told her that they would hear no more about him. Emma accepted it though it would mean that she had one hero less to dream about.

Walking around the Caerau yard with the bailiff, Thomas and Emma noticed the first swallows. It was April 18th, and they were busy flying around their old haunts looking for a safe place to build a new nest. The odd thing was that the martins had also arrived which was unusual as they normally arrived after the swallows.

There was quite an excited noise coming from one of the fields on April 20th, all the farm men were shouting that they had heard the first call of the cuckoo. They were turning money in their pockets for luck.

Mother Roberts had taken Emma out with her to visit one or two people at Cemaes. During their time there, Mother Roberts found some young lads walking around selling oysters. She bought 20 for a shilling.

It was a pleasant day on May 22nd when Lord Bulkeley's servant arrived with a mourning ring which all the bearers had been measured for at the funeral; Thomas was in his study when the maid came to inform him, and he gladly entertained the messenger and ordered him a drink after his long and tedious journey.

George, the new farm lad, went with a horse and dray to Cemaes to collect sand from a vessel which had just arrived from Red Wharf Bay. It was always first come, first served. George knew one or two of the men who made sure that his dray was full.

Young lads were often seen walking around the countryside selling fish and, on this day, they were selling crab-fish for 6d. Anyone visiting the Isle of Man was always asked to bring back tea, which usually cost 14 shillings. The young lads selling various foods were bright enough to watch which fields were busy and where they could sell their goods quickly. In some fields the workers were winnowing corn and others preparing to sow more hay seeds.

A report was heard that there had been a very good fair at Bangor, that Lord Bulkeley's servant had sold two of his lordship's oxen for £16, and that four others went for £12 a pair.

Mr William Bulkeley of Brynddu was very pleased when his camelias arrived. The last time he was in Dublin he had ordered some, the first in Europe from the Far East. Mr Bulkeley, always keen to try to do something different, prayed that the wet weather would soon stop so as not to rot his new acquisitions. Many of the workers were busy cutting sods and peat to dry out in readiness for the winter. The Llanfairynghornwy parson was busy collecting his tithe lambs which he received once a year. This year they were plentiful. William Williams, Caerau's gardener, was at the Llanfechell market when he met with Mr William Bulkeley. They chatted and discussed vegetables. When Williams told him that he had seeds for late carrots and beetroot, Bulkeley pounced, declaring that he would very much like to try some. He was surprised to find that Williams had some in his pockets, which he kindly gave to Mr Bulkeley.

On June 21st everyone was running around. The parish constable came to inform people to be vigilant and keep an eye along the coast in case bodies were found. On enquiring why, they were informed of the tragedy of the previous night. Mr William Robinson of Mynachdy, Llanfairynghornwy and Gwersyllt Uchaf, Denbigh, had drowned along with 12 other wealthy young men who had been with him for the day on the Skerries. On their way back the weather took for the worst, the storm was horrific and all of them were drowned. It is claimed by some that the son and heir of Garreg Lwyd hid himself under a manger so that he was not with them when they left, probably because he knew of the dangers associated with the island. Again, it is difficult to ascertain whether it was, as some claim, an after-dinner frolic or whether they had spent a night on the Skerries and tried to return the following day. Whatever happened it was a tragedy.

William Robinson had married his cousin, Elizabeth, daughter of William Robinson-Lytton of Knebworth. They had two daughters but only one was alive when the accident occurred. His estate was in financial trouble and was sold by an Act of Parliament in 1737 for the benefit of his creditors. Mynachdy was sold to Mr Lloyd of Rhosbeirio, except for the Island of Skerries, which had been on a 99-year lease at a very low rent from William Robinson to a wealthy Irish merchant called William Trench. He had been given a patent by Queen Anne with the help of a petition from the Irish traders to build a lighthouse. This he proceeded to do, paying a crown rent of £5 per annum with the right to charge a levy of one penny per ship and two pence per ton of cargo. The first light was seen on November 4th, 1716. In a round tower of 35 feet, the light was created by coal-burning. William Trench's failure to make it pay was due to the mean tricks of traders, mariners and merchants who refused to pay the levy. He fell heavily into debt and died a broken man in 1729. He left the lighthouse to his daughter who married a Morgan Jones from Cardigan. They rebuilt the lighthouse, which never really paid; eventually it was bought by Trinity House.

People around a wide area knew of the many shipwrecks that occurred around the Skerries, but to lose 12 young men was a shock. Thomas and Emma were devastated. Mother Roberts visited Mrs Robinson and Emma accompanied her. Thomas would wait to see how the situation was before visiting to pay his condolences. He remembered how kind William Robinson had been when he joined in to hide William's tenth birthday present, looking after the pony until the day. He knew also that both William and Emma visited the housekeeper and that Emma called to see the little girl when she went out riding on her own. Having adjusted to what had happened Thomas instructed the farm workers that should a body appear along the coast, they were to send for the constable as soon as possible. He paid a visit to Mrs Robinson who was travelling back to Gwersyllt the following day to be with her family and friends.

On June 29th, the Custom House cruiser was seen leaving Cemaes Bay, a large boat coming from the Isle of Man with brandy was thought to be a smuggler. Amongst the men were three locals who were taken by the customs cruiser to Beaumaris. They were Owen Edwards of Llanfechell parish, Rowland Morgan, the Llanfairynghornwy parson's son, and John Pritchard Samuel, a shoemaker of Llanfairynghornwy. The three were home the following day but no one knew whether that was by consent or not. They were known locally for going off and trying to smuggle brandy and other liquors, and though some people supported them, they also knew the danger of carrying out such actions now that the customs had their own boat. On July 2nd, the collector of customs at Holyhead went to Hugh Price's house to hear information about the smugglers. The goods were seized, but the men discharged without penalties.

Many young girls were excited having heard that some soldiers were going to be around Llanfechell. William Bulkeley of Brynddu had staying with him on July 17th two recruiting officers who had come over from Dublin – Captain Tonge belonging to Lieutenant General Patrick's regiment and Lieutenant Captain Roberts belonging to Colonel Philip Bragg's regiment. They had 17 or 18 recruits with them to be sworn and certified. They came by boat from Holyhead to Trefadog and walked from there to Brynddu. Around 12 noon they returned after they had refreshed their men with meat and drink at Llanfechell. There were girls running around the young men who were about to become soldiers, shouting and waving them goodbye as they walked away from Llanfechell. William and Emma had ridden to Llanfechell so they could see the soldiers. Emma thought how smart the lieutenants looked in their uniforms. The venture had lifted their spirits after the tragedy of Mr Robinson.

Workers around many estates were still busy winnowing and cleaning oats ready for the mill. Some of the oats would be taken to the boats at Cemaes for delivery further along the island. Ships came in and out of Cemaes to carry produce to Warrington, Liverpool and sometimes Chester.

Emma was walking around Caerau when she found William Williams busily sowing lettuce, cress, radishes, onions, carrots, and turnips which had been introduced to the island by Dr Wynne of Bodewryd, as well as cabbage and cauliflower. Williams was making sure that they would have plenty of food in a wide variety. Emma chatted with him for some time before returning to the house to learn that Mrs Wynne of Bodewryd had died and that Thomas was invited to be a bearer. On August 3rd Thomas and Mother Roberts prepared themselves to go to the funeral. Mrs Wynne was buried at two in the afternoon and after the service they all dined with Dr Wynne. The bearers were Thomas, Mr Jones of Pentraeth, Mr Williams of Tŷ Fry, Mr Griffith of Llanddyfnan, Mr John Lewis of Llanfihangel, Mr Lewis of Trysglwyn, Mr Lloyd of Denbighshire and Mr William Bulkeley. Thomas was glad to be home again after the funeral. These events tended to make him rather melancholy, and he would drink too much. His spirits were soon lifted when a letter arrived from his cousin who was back in London. William Owen was very good at letter writing and kept his friends up to date with all the news, of politics as well as more mundane matters. This letter contained information about the 'Foundling Hospital' which had just opened in London by Royal Charter after 17 years of campaigning by the shipbuilder and philanthropist, Thomas Coram. He was fortunate in having good support from many leading figures, including William Hogarth, well-known for depicting the poverty around London through his art, and another faithful supporter, George Frederick Handel. Thomas read part of the letter to Mother Roberts and Emma, knowing that Mrs Roberts would be most pleased at the generosity shown by Thomas Coram, and hoping that his charity would show Emma how important it was to help those less fortunate.

Emma had made friends with one young girl whose parents were not wealthy but regarded as very respectable and intelligent and keen to be part of the church. Mother Roberts was very pleased to hear this and suggested that Emma ought to ask her parents to allow her to come to Caerau for tea. Elizabeth Hughes came, and it was such a relief for Mother Roberts when she heard the two girls laughing together and playing tricks on William.

The farm workers were busy checking the outbuildings in case any thatching was needed before the high winds around Caerau lifted the roofs off. Other workers were busy collecting hay, returning next day to rake all they could from the ground. Nothing was to be wasted.

Mother Roberts took Emma to a market at Llanfechell where she bought a side of lamb for 8d. As they returned home, they were met by the young lads selling fresh herrings which Mother Roberts enjoyed for her tea. William appeared. He had been out meeting with some of his school friends. He was enjoying his summer holiday apart from the tragedy of Mynachdy, which cast a shadow over his and Emma's visit to the housekeeper. It was lunch time and they all met in the dining room where Thomas announced that Mr William Bulkeley would be calling during the afternoon to discuss something to do with the tragedy of Mr Robinson. Thomas asked Emma and William to find some useful exercise to do and not disturb him.

Mr Bulkeley arrived, and Thomas escorted him to his study where there was a welcoming fire. After chatting about the weather, with Thomas asking him various questions about the sun and the moon, Mr Bulkeley arrived at the account he wanted to give, as written in his diary:

'Having now some certainty of a melancholy accident that happened two months ago, I am now to give an account of it. Mr William Robinson of Gwersyllt in the County of Denbigh having come to Mynachdy an estate of his this Country about the 11th or 12th of June last went into the Island of Skerris on Wednesday the 20th of June accompanied by one Mr Edwards of Shansty in Denbighshire and a gardener that came along with him to this country from Holywell to lay out ground for gardens and plantations of trees (he designing as it was said to live in this country) his own servant, Wm Thomas tenant at Monachdy, and his son, leaving behind him at home three other children, John Humphrey ap Richard Owen, Wm Thomas's servant, Hugh Jones, a freeholder in Rhoscolyn, the father of three small children, John Lewis of Llanrhwydrys, the father of one child, Owen Pritchard of Cemlyn the father of a child born less than a week after he went off, these are all that went from Henborth, being

there they found another boat came from Wylfa, Wm Watkins, son of the Watkins as son Wm Watkins Wylfa, in it were Richard ap Sion ap William Probert of Gwyddolyn, the father of four children and his wife with child, Richard Owen ap Wm Bedward of Tyddyn Ronwy, the father of four children; about six in the evening the wind rose very high, Mr Robinson and these people being heated with liquor (as people that kept the light in the tower reported) resolved to go home through the storm; it blew so high and rained so fast with all, that the people in the Island soon lost sight of them; it was at first hoped that they had gone to the Isle of Man, accordingly a boat was dispatched there to have tidings of them; but to no purpose; afterwards various reports of their being come to this place and that place, all proving false; advertisements likewise having been published in public papers of this accident, the Collector of White Haven sent to Chester an account of a boat come to a creek near that place, empty and miserably broke with the lid of a butter box with Wm Thomas's name on it; this being sent to this country by Mrs Robinson to know if anyone knew the butter box. Upon it being produced all the family of Wm Thomas knew it, where upon John Thomas of Wylfa the nephew and heir of Wm Hughes of Wylfa who had built the boat was engaged to go to the place where it was to see if was the same, who going there upon his return reported it to be the same boat these unfortunate people went into the oars and rudder were lost and all the sails and shrouds of the foremost broke in the middle, carried off the main mast, nothing in the boat when found (which was the 24th of June in the morning) but broken pieces of bottles, and a large wooden basket found floating by the boat, in which they had carried their meat. So that of 13 persons most of them masters of family and fathers of small children, not one is to be found alive or dead; Mr Robinson was a young man not long married and had living only one girl; William Watkins the son of Watkin ab William Watkin of Pandy Budr in this Parish was the only stay of an aged father all the rest, but Mr Robinson's servant and Wm Thomas's servant were married people and lost in following the caprice of a hot headed young gentleman.'

Thomas ordered tea and thanked Mr Bulkeley for the trouble of coming and discussing it with him. He was indeed shocked at the account and the added difficulty of knowing many of those who were lost. He felt for all the families left bereft and suggested that perhaps a collection should be made for those most needy. Mr Bulkeley promised to speak with the bishop at Bangor to ask permission that the collection from all Anglesey churches be given to the various families.

In two days, Thomas visited Llannerchymedd market which from all appearances was very busy, traders saying that business had been brisk from eight in the morning until about four in the afternoon. Thomas was meeting with a Mr Host who had come quite a long way with potatoes. William Williams would appreciate them, and the field was ready for planting. It had been a good month for the Caerau estate, which was growing hay, corn, barley and oats, but as the year came to its close the heavy rains began to slow the work.

Between clearing old hay out of the barns, some of the workers were reaping peas which were not fully ripe, keeping them for the horses over winter. Coal would be ordered, malt and candles would be bought, usually enough to last until June the following year.

Mr Jones came twice a week 'to keep Emma out of mischief' according to Mother Roberts. On other days Mother Roberts would interest Emma in many matters such as deportment, good manners, and etiquette and how to address people. She also started telling her about her rather large family, so that she would understand how many relatives she had. Emma was a little distraught; William had gone back to school at Beaumaris, and she felt lonely. Yes, she had a friend in Elizabeth, but William was interesting and made her laugh, and she enjoyed riding out with him.

Life carried on and after the 7th of September, Thomas heard the results of the sessions held at Beaumaris, when owing to very little business only one case took place, that of a man accused of stealing the goods of another man who had unfortunately become shipwrecked at Llanfaelog.

During October, Thomas received a letter from Mr Bayley who was busy preparing for the next election, asking for his vote. This meant that Thomas would be expected to visit several people encouraging them to vote for Mr Bayley.

The weather was getting colder. It was freezing every night and every morning saw the hoar frost as far as the eye could see. Later in the month there was heavy thunder and lightning which continued for four hours much to the delight of Emma. Excessive rains caused the land to be underwater. As there was little point in venturing out, Mother Roberts and Thomas stayed safely indoors, spending the evenings beside a glorious fire playing cards. By November everywhere was covered in snow causing many problems.

Thomas was pleased when news arrived concerning the Spanish War which had started on October 22nd with an attack on La Guairá and the capture of Porto Bello during November. He decided to visit Mr Meyrick at Bodorgan, but on his arrival there he learnt that Mr Meyrick had that day left for London.

During December the weather was worse than ever. It was very raw and cold, and a great storm blew up that continued for days. The farm workers had to take pickaxes to cut up the ice so that the cattle had water. Many of the corn stacks were damaged.

January, which was extremely cold, saw only a few attending churches where prayers were said by order of the king to implore God's mercy against our enemies in the Spanish War. The highways were frozen to the extent that carts could not travel. A result of all the bad weather was the number of burials, mostly of the poor who, due to their diet, could not survive the severity of the hard freezing weather. By the end of January people were afraid that a terrible sickness would arrive on the island. At Peniarth in Merionethshire, where Lady Bulkeley lived, there were six dead at the same time in the house. The illness first seized people with terrible pains in the head, then a hard swelling of the head and face along with a fever, which later moved down to the stomach. People feared any visitors to the island.

On March 1st, Mr Jones, the teacher, called at Caerau giving news that Mr John Bulkeley who kept a school at Llanfechell had been found dead in bed after a night of heavy drinking with the company he kept. He lodged with William Mathews's widow. John Bulkeley was the third son of Robert Bulkeley and Elin, his wife, who was the daughter of John Owen Wynn of Ucheldre. He was christened on April 7th, 1703, and buried during the evening service on March 2nd, 1739, aged 36 years.

Chapter Six

The new year of 1740 brought with it the usual yearly humdrum of planning and organising the work on the estate. Thomas and Mrs Roberts would sit and discuss matters, and Thomas in turn would discuss the best use of fields with the bailiff, William Edwards. There was also the organising of Plas-y-Nant to sort out, which would take two to three weeks. There were taxes to check and light taxes to pay. All this Thomas would settle.

The workers were anxious to plough and sow seeds but were having to hold the work back due to the very cold weather. The farm men would walk the fields looking for signs of spring. The seeds sown were not showing any signs of growth and the grass was wanting. The poor cows were beginning to look thin, and it was getting rather late to turn them out. Most of the standing water everywhere was frozen solid, and the men had the extra work of carrying water to the animals. This extraordinary weather was extremely hard for the workers around many of the Anglesey estates. Coping with such conditions proved how tough the men were as they carried on doing what they could, knowing that if the weather showed no improvement soon, many would be out of work, causing more havoc than ever. It was April and time to venture forth to collect sand from the Red Wharf boat which had arrived at Cemaes.

A pleasing occasion was to see the swallows who had just arrived searching out their old haunts ready to build nests. As it was April 16th, the men believed that the swallows were three days earlier than usual. On April the 19th, there was excitement and cheers when the men heard the first cuckoo. They all claimed to be the first to turn money over in their pockets, believing that luck would be with them for the rest of the year.

One or two sunny days did not put things right and meat was getting scarce in the markets. This long winter could only be attributed to what modern climatologists call the 'Little Ice Age', which covered the period from 1300 to 1500 and then after a short break continued from the 1700s to 1850, when everything changed. During the 'Little Ice Age' Scotland still had glaciers. The River Thames became totally frozen in 1607, and this happened for the last time in 1814.

There was a slight improvement in the weather during May, but it was still very cold and wet. The wind scorched plants trying to grow, and by the end of May the trees had lost their blossoms. It was time to spread the fields with lime, which no one looked forward to in these hurricane winds.

Everyone looked forward to visiting the markets at Llanfechell, Llannerchymedd and Newborough, but feared the prices might be too high for replacing their stock. Mother Roberts was surprised to see white bread from Ireland at Llanfechell which she bought to try. She also bought some cod fish. By June corn prices were high at Llannerchymedd market, which many noted, hoping to recoup what they lost by late sowing.

June brought many hot days. Emma was able to ride her horse along the water's edge in the sun, which made her feel better after the frustrations of the long winter. She was aware that some of her tantrums had caused much disappointment in the house, and she wished that she had better control of her temper. When she returned to Caerau it felt desolate. Most of the men had gone over to Cemaes where a timber fair was taking place. Most people found something useful to buy even if it was only for repairing rotten or broken wood.

William, the gardener, arrived back, very pleased with himself as he had bought half a pegget of potatoes to plant so that cook would have enough to feed them all.

Thomas wanted to visit Caernarvon and Emma accompanied him. Mother Roberts gave her a list of spices that the cook needed, usually found at the Caernarvon fair. She gave her enough money to pay for them; what was left over, Emma was to have for a little treat. Thomas visited the quay where he met with Robert Foulkes who was to bring his boat from Caernarvon to Cemaes carrying 4,000 slates which cost £1-16-00 for William Bulkeley. And as Owen Warmingham was bringing corn from Cemaes to Caernarvon, Thomas waited for him to arrive so that he could take what Robert Foulkes could not.

Thomas travelled to attend the funeral of Owen Jones of Bryn Hir, Criccieth, who was buried on July 31st, 1740. He was the widowed husband of Thomas's Aunt Margaret; a sister of John Rowlands of Plas-y-Nant. She had died in 1708. Thomas looked forward to meeting his cousins: the Reverend Rowland Jones who was rector of Edern; the Reverend John Jones, rector of Boduan and later of Llanymstumdwy; Ann, who was married to Owen Lloyd of Tyddyn Annes, Llanllyfni; and Grace, married to Ellis Annwyl of Parkia, Criccieth. It was a long time since he had met up with them. He stayed the night at Llanfairisgaer before his return to Caerau.

On August 21st, William Roberts, the saddler of Llannerchymedd, called with a new saddle for Mother Roberts, some saddle cloth and two bridles. One was for Emma's horse. William Bulkeley records in his diary:

> 'On August 27*th* news was heard that Lord Bulkeley's second sister Ellen was married to Bertie a clergyman and her first cousin. It was presumed that it was a match courted by the mother to fix the estate in her own family in case her son died without issue. The Lord's eldest sister always pretending an aversion to marriage, though if what is publicly reported of the eldest sister being contracted with John Bulkeley of Bwchanan, if not actually married should prove true, her Ladyship's scheme would be quite spoiled. This same John Bulkeley in 1715 wore my Livery; the year following he kept a little school at Llanfechell which was worth to him perhaps 40 shillings a year. From there he went to Coytmore where he lived in service a year or two longer from where he went to Baron Hill, at first as an under trapper, but he being a forward, impudent fellow and a great party man which was the most valuable recommendation in a servant, to that grand tyrant and Jacobite, this Lord's father, he in a short time made him a gentleman to this Lord's brother upon Mr Edmund's decease (who was both prime minister and manager) made him his steward, where he has so improved himself that in 12 years' time he is said to have made a fortune of 1600 pounds at the same time that his Lord's debts increased that sum or more every year. His interest with the family was so great that he not only procured himself a long lease upon Porthamel for good at half the rent, but he got them to lay out 300 pounds at least in building him a fine house there, while the Lord's family were sinking under a load of debts.'

The lord mentioned in the story eventually became Emma's husband. Another visitor called on September 15th. He was the collector of the king's chief rents who came once a year to collect the land tax. Thomas would always give time to people collecting taxes so that he could put forward what he felt was unwarranted by their demands.

It was also an important time for William who would be 16 on September 19th. He had been, when he was home on his holidays, under the tuition of the vicar towards being confirmed as his mother had been before him. He knew that his father and grandmother would appreciate his efforts in carrying on the family tradition. His gift in memory of his mother was a new Bible presented to the church. This time he had enjoyed his holidays, notably by the occasional presence of Elizabeth, Emma's friend. He found her most interesting and her knowledge well advanced.

October the first brought a shower of snow which did not last long. Owen Williams, the Llannerchymedd glazier, died and was buried on October 13th. Thomas attended and Mother Roberts took Emma with her to Llanfechell market, where she bought a side of beef from Shadrach Evans for 15 shillings. Workers around Caerau were busy starting to cut and collect gorse for the home fire, though one of the kitchen maids kept complaining that it sparked and made holes in her apron.

William, the gardener, called in the kitchen to tell Emma's maid a story which she could tell Emma. He had just returned from Brynddu, and the story was about a cuckoo that William Bulkeley had been feeding since July. It died. But someone had told Mr Bulkeley that often cuckoos could revive, so he placed it in a basket of feathers and hung it up in the kitchen near the chimney. The maids and the cook laughed, as did all the workers who were in for their food. They thought that Mr Bulkeley must be the cuckoo to believe such a story.

The gardener had been busy planting trees, shrubs, and vegetables. The excitement this year was that he was growing asparagus and had been busy for some time collecting fresh pigeons' dung to cover them. This was the best sort of natural fertilizer and would also keep slugs away. This effort should produce excellent strong, healthy asparagus.

The horses were put in a field further down for grazing. They had been working hard during the week and the workers believed that they deserved two days off, if only to keep their spirits up. Nothing was worse, according to one of the workers, than to break the horse's spirit.

Caerau's bailiff had acquired much knowledge around the island and knew who were the most efficient farmers and the best breeders of sheep, cattle, oxen, and pigs. He visited Hugh Charles of Foel who had ewes for sale and ventured to buy four at 13 shillings and sixpence. The following year should show good, strong, healthy sheep. The weather was warm and the sun shining, but people feared increasing their stocks after the long, tiresome, cold winter, which had carried away many animals. The losses were great, leaving many to depend on the drovers to buy for some money to cover their losses.

Mother Roberts was concerned that Emma was no longer asking Elizabeth over as she had done for some time. Since William had shown an interest in Elizabeth, Emma had behaved with a little jealousy which had not passed unnoticed by her astute grandmother. For several months, all Emma chatted about was Elizabeth and now she never mentioned her. Mother Roberts was hoping that because she had chosen to shut her out, there would not be another tantrum. As she was contemplating what to do, there was a knock on the door. It was Thomas Williams, the tailor, who had made a winter coat for Thomas. He was welcomed in and given a glass of wine. Thomas was more than pleased with the new coat and felt that he would be much warmer this coming winter.

This time of year had the collector of land tax calling. Many might not have enough money to pay their dues because of the dreadful time everyone had suffered. They would beg leave of full payment in the hope that somehow, they would, through being thrifty, pay up next year. Thomas understood their difficulties and knew how his own tenants often had to delay their payments but always paid up when they could.

Emma had ridden to Cemaes with Mother Roberts where they saw the boat called Cloxan, sailed by its owner and master, William Griffith, returning from Liverpool where he had taken wheat, barley, and oats to one of the merchants. Emptying his boat, he was able to bring provisions back for the Anglesey people. He brought in salt, New England wheat, raw hemp, tram oil, vinegar, flowers, and a variety of trees such as damson, peach, and codling. When people saw the trees, they thought of only one person, that being Mr William Bulkeley of Brynddu, Llanfechell. Over many years he had shown such interest in growing as many different trees as possible, whether for decoration or use. It was to him that many went for advice, always gladly given.

Emma was amused as she watched a young lad running around the boat and feared that he would fall overboard at any minute. But hearing Mother Roberts call she joined her as they made their way back to the horses and to Caerau. As they approached the road where Elizabeth lived, Mother Roberts stopped and told Emma to come with her to see Elizabeth. Emma looked at her grandmother, gave the horse a gentle spur and sped towards home. Mother Roberts was beside herself but went and knocked on the door of Elizabeth's house. Mrs Hughes, Elizabeth's mother, answered and invited Mother Roberts in. It was a small house, but very neat and tidy. Mother Roberts was informed that Elizabeth was indeed quite poorly; the consumption had set in and she had great difficulty breathing. Mrs Hughes asked after Emma, and Mother Roberts did not hesitate to avenge her shame regarding Emma's distasteful behaviour.

Emma knew that she had behaved badly and had gone riding down to the seashore where she sat thinking about her temper. She was blaming everyone else for her misdeeds and claimed to herself that it was because she missed William. This was partly true, but she had to accept that he had a right to an education and to have a girlfriend. She had calmed down enough to see her own faults and decided that she would return to Elizabeth's house, hoping that Mother Roberts would still be there. She mounted her horse and rode back only to find that Mother Roberts' horse was not there. She waited a while before finding enough courage to knock on the door. Mrs Hughes opened the door and was surprised to see Emma standing there. She invited her in. Emma apologised profusely for not asking Elizabeth to come over to Caerau and for not having made enquiries about her when she heard that she was poorly. Mrs Hughes explained that Elizabeth was indeed very poorly, with little hope of any improvement. Emma asked to see her, and Mrs Hughes reluctantly allowed Emma to enter Elizabeth's bedroom. Elizabeth looked very pale; her eyes were very dark. Emma moved close, held her hand and talked to her for a long time. Elizabeth just had to listen and not tire herself out trying to speak. After a while she left, telling Elizabeth that she would write to William and tell him of her woes. But Elizabeth said, 'No'. She did not want to upset William, and they had enjoyed themselves the little time they had had. Emma thanked Mrs Hughes for allowing her to see Elizabeth and later that evening, when she found that the cook had made pheasant soup, she insisted that one of the maids or the gardener took some down for Elizabeth. Mother Roberts was stunned by the sudden change of heart on Emma's side. She just couldn't believe it.

Emma hurriedly wrote to William and told him how poorly Elizabeth was. She hoped that he would come home at half term rather than go off with some of his friends. There was a week to go before half term and Emma was waiting impatiently, hoping that he would make the effort. The sad news of Elizabeth's death arrived a few days later. William, once he received Emma's letter, was most concerned and as the half term started the following week, he asked his master if he could go back home the following day so that he could see Elizabeth. He was granted his wish but returned home to learn of Elizabeth's death, which left him beside himself. His father did all he could to try and console him. He visited Mrs Hughes and enquired about being a bearer. Elizabeth's parents agreed.

When William returned to Caerau, Emma greeted him saying how sorry she was. He shouted back at her, 'As if you care, you were so rude when I took her down to the beach or if I was having a conversation with her!' Emma apologised and said that she had not realised he thought so much of Elizabeth. After some time, William calmed down, feeling that perhaps he had not thought things out properly, but whatever excuse he came up with did not stop the hurt he felt at losing Elizabeth.

The morning of Elizabeth's funeral William was up early. He visited his father in his study to consult about a bearer's duty. He felt lost and bewildered as he realised how much he had grown to love Elizabeth. Having spoken with his father, he left and arrived at Elizabeth's house. Elizabeth's parents appreciated him and after the funeral he accompanied them back to their house where they chatted about Elizabeth.

William, on his return to Caerau, hardly took any notice of Emma, and when she complained to her father, Thomas warned her to calm down and not upset William. Mother Roberts also warned her to leave him alone to grieve as he wanted to. It was soon time for William to return to school and this time he had a friend who would travel with him back to Beaumaris. Emma felt lost once more.

Mother Roberts wished to visit the market at Llannerchymedd. Indeed, it was very full, and a few days later, on a Monday which was also a fair day, she visited again taking Emma with her, believing that it might lift Emma's spirits. She realised that it was lonely for her without William and that perhaps Thomas should think of sending her to school or to stay with her Aunt Margaret at Caernarvon. The fair held at Aberffraw proved to be poor. There was such a scarcity of fodder all over the island that people everywhere were cutting down their stock. The drovers however bought around 140 fat bullocks.

During September, when Emma was down on the beach, she noticed a flock of wild geese arriving earlier than usual. October the first saw snow over the Caernarvonshire mountains, and by the 23rd there were showers of hail. November brought in the hurricanes, tearing down slates from the roofs and damaging many hay and corn stacks. This was followed by the thunder and lightning, which Emma loved! William Bulkeley writes:

> 'On November the 25th, Ann Roberts was buried in her father's grave at Llanflewyn. She was the daughter and heiress of Mr Hugh Roberts of Ucheldre. She married sixty years ago to Robert Lewis of Bodwine by whom she had two sons. Richard the eldest married when an old bachelor, Margaret the daughter of Mr David Williams of Glanalaw, and an old maid past bearing, she was also a sister to Mother Roberts. Richard settled his own estate and Bodwine upon her and her heirs forever. Hugh, the other son died a student whilst at Oxford. Mrs Lewis having lost both her sons without issue settled her estate upon Mr Thomas Roberts of Bodior. Having lived to the age of eighty years, she was left impoverished by the selfish servants and having 0 credit, it is said that she died for want. Both Ucheldre and Bodwine were taken from the right heirs.'

The weather once more had become so frozen that the animals could not get to the grass beneath the snow and ice. On December 3rd 1740, people were out watching the coffin of Owen Hughes, Master of Arts, Bachelor of Law, Chancellor of Bangor, Prebendary of Penmynydd and Parson of Aberffraw and Trefdraeth.

News quickly spread that at long last there was plenty of butchers' meat to be had at Llanfechell market, and everyone turned up to buy even the smallest piece as they had gone so long without any. The weather continued to be bad, and a hurricane gathered the snow in such heaps along the roads that they became impassable. Everyone prayed for a thaw.

Mother Roberts, having visited Llannerchymedd, called at Cemaes on her way back, where she bought 200 oysters for two shillings.

When Emma's birthday arrived, she was greeted by her father and Mother Roberts and received her gifts, but William had not returned home to celebrate. Losing Elizabeth was still very much on his mind at that time, so he cared little for Emma. She spent the day indoors with a few visitors calling to wish her well. Mother Roberts felt that she had become subdued and thought of what to do in case depression set in. She had always blamed Thomas for spoiling Emma but now felt that perhaps she too had contributed to allowing her too much of her own way.

All the brooks and rivers were frozen hard, and it threatened snow again. There was a great ring around the moon, which made everything appear colder still. February 4th, 1740 was a day throughout England and Wales when everyone was praying for blessings upon the king's arms. The country was now at war with Spain. Emma thought of the soldiers she had seen staying with Mr William Bulkeley and prayed that no harm came to them.

Emma and Mother Roberts found the fair at Llanfechell extremely good with a great variety of woollen and linen cloth, shoes, stockings and hats, which Emma enjoyed trying on. When they got back to Caerau, the gardener was busy sowing parsnips, lettuce, spinach, cress, and radish. A few days later he sowed onions, leeks, and carrots. At the end of the day, the gardener called at the kitchen to tell the maids to be careful how they told Emma that Mr William Bulkeley's fox had died, two weeks after it had been mangled in the night by a strange dog. It had lived happily as part of the Brynddu household for nine or ten years.

Thomas had to ride out to Penrhos as Mr Edward Owen had died and was being buried on March 21st, 1740. The following day the Llannerchymedd people joined with those of the Llanfechell congregation in singing psalms. A collection was made to pay for their dinner.

Chapter Seven

Freezing weather continued during 1741, with many deaths due to the outbreak of influenza and consumption, and devastation for the farmers, losing most of their animals.

There was a good market at Llanfechell, with plenty of fish and corn, but the butchers' meat was very poor. It was said that a third of the cattle and horses within the county had starved to death due to the dreadful weather. The corn sowed in early February was just beginning to show. With the easterly winds blowing fresh, cold, and scorching, several people had been driven to unroof their barns and stables, making use of the thatch to try and keep their animals alive.

Time had come around again for the Beaumaris sessions and Thomas was soon preparing for the event. On April the 5th he rode out to Beaumaris where he met up with other members. There were three bills to be dealt with, to do with indictment against felons who had stolen sails and rigging of a ship anchored at Llanfaelog. The business took longer than was expected as Martin, the judge, was drunk each day. There were so many complaints that on the last day, and keeping the jury longer than necessary, he muddled through and managed to get the business done. Thomas could not wait to return to Caerau. Having been at home but a few days, he had a visit from Lord Bulkeley who was accompanying Mr Bayley as they travelled around Anglesey hoping to secure votes. Mr Bodvel was also with them. Thomas this time had promised to help John Owen of Presaddfed, who was a Whig, many feeling that a change was needed. Mr Meyrick of Bodorgan, a well-known Whig, supported John Owen, and an agreement was put forward that he would support John Owen if he was willing to promise the seat for Meyrick's son in a future election.

News arrived that Admiral Vernon had taken Cartagena in the West Indies and that the Spaniards had sunk all their men-of-war and galleons for fear of their falling into the hands of the English.

The farm workers were once again collecting sand from Cemaes, where the boats would discharge it. This went on for weeks, many believing that sand mixed with their soil was beneficial to the vegetables. Many were preparing what little stock they had left, hoping that things would improve.

May 27th, election day, arrived with great excitement. John Owen and many voters were in Beaumaris by 6pm. Mr Bayly arrived privately with a few accompanying him. A Mr Herbert of Oakley Park, who had been sent by the ministry, arrived in the hope of dissolving the union between Mr John Owen and Mr Meyrick, but all his attempts failed. Mr William Bulkeley of Brynddu, a great supporter of Mr Meyrick, voted this time for John Owen. There was more voting and discussion the following day and it looked as though Mr Bayly accepted that he would not win. On May 29th, John Owen was declared the winner.

Mrs Roberts felt that Emma was very subdued. If only she had listened and not been so selfish. William still would not speak with her when he was home. Emma wished that she could put things right and that they could ride out together once more. When William came home, the first thing he did was to visit Elizabeth's parents and then visit her grave. Mother Roberts had suggested to Emma that perhaps if she visited the grave with William, it might break the awful atmosphere that hung around. But Emma decided that she would not go this time just in case William thought someone had put her up to it. She would wait until he was next home; knowing that on the first day he would visit Mr and Mrs Hughes, she would wait until the following day and wait for him at the cemetery.

The weather was wet and sultry making it very difficult for everyone. The water corn mills from every corner of the island were standing still and the people feared the droughts.

Mrs Roberts visited Llannerchymedd and bought four pairs of brown thread stockings of three thread, and three pairs of stockings of five thread made of silk and worsted mix for 29 shillings from John Fursise, the Scottish pedlar.

Thomas travelled to Tre'r Ddôl for the funeral of Mrs Ann Meyrick. She was only 40 years old and the wife of Mr William Hughes, the parson of Llantrisant.

A few days later it rained, and people were so overjoyed they danced in the rain. Soon the mills would turn again, people would have flour and the animals would have plenty of food.

William was home again for the summer holidays and Emma was on her best behaviour. She asked questions about some of the boys that William had mentioned from time to time, trying her best for a conversation with him, but William was quiet. Emma couldn't understand how he had changed. The following day, as he had done since Elizabeth died, he visited her parents. This gave Emma time to plan how to be at the cemetery before William arrived. She was up early, had her breakfast and then did some chores, listening to hear the door being shut as William left. She got the gardener to saddle her pony and she was ready. She went through the gate into the cemetery and wandered around having pulled the hood of her coat up over her head until she saw William. She slowly walked towards him and when William heard some rustling along the ground, he turned quickly, and Emma spoke to him. William remarked how busy someone had been in keeping up with the flowers and Emma told him that she had been every two weeks with flowers, to show him that she was truly sorry about the way she had behaved. William accepted her apology and accompanied her home on her pony. Mother Roberts sighed with relief that William and Emma were talking once again. The atmosphere improved and they were able to enjoy their dinner with all the pleasantries. Thomas was in good form and glad that William was friendly with his sister.

William announced the next day that he was going to Caernarvon to stay with his aunt and uncle and to have a little fun with his cousins. This was quite a shock to Thomas and Mother Roberts, so soon after being reconciled with Emma. Emma began to sulk and once more everyone was on tenterhooks. Everyone knew of her temper and even the kitchen maids were waiting for the explosion. William left and Emma stood there in dismay. She just could not believe that William could be so cruel to her. She believed that having apologised, it should have been enough. Thomas called her into the office and asked her if she would like to accompany him to Holyhead, as he wished to call and see Mrs Owen of Penrhos. Emma sulked and Thomas explained to her that she just had to accept what had happened, and let William do what he wanted. He was after all growing up and probably would not find her company as exciting as it used to be. Mother Roberts knocked on the door and Thomas called her in. She asked Emma if she would like to visit Llannerchymedd with her, calling in the bakery for some cakes. But Emma stood there looking rather blank.

When Thomas was ready to leave, he called Emma, but she refused to accompany him, feeling sure that it was going to be some dull affair or other at Penrhos. She did not accompany Mother Roberts to Llannerchymedd either, but stayed at home and later took a ride down to the beach. There was a pleasant breeze blowing through her hair. She smelt the salt of the water and wondered why everyone had to be so cruel to her. She watched some children playing further along the beach and the game was to throw stones into the sea. One was very clever, making a stone ripple over the water.

William arrived home two days before his school started its new term. He was extremely busy getting all his attire ready. Thomas called him into his study and chatted about his aunt and uncle. William said that he had much enjoyed his visit, especially with his cousins. Thomas asked him not to be too hard on Emma and that he should realise how lonely it was for her once he was at school. William apologised to his father and said he would spend his last day with Emma.

William met Emma for breakfast on his last day and asked if she would like a ride down to the beach. Emma was delighted and when she was ready mounted her horse and waited for William. They rode down to the beach and sat where they always did and chatted, watching the birds. Emma loved to see the oyster catchers and the way they kept trotting around. The sea birds were busy making a lot of noise, probably because they were feeding their young along the rocks.

It was time for William to return to school and Emma once more was alone. She was invited by her aunt to visit. Though the boys attended school, she would have her aunt's company and they would be able to visit other people to introduce Emma. She was not keen to go, but reluctantly accepted the invitation. This would help to break up the winter and the boys would be home every weekend. Emma became very interested in the people her aunt knew and would ask questions about them. They received many invitations for tea and Emma enjoyed the chatter they had. When Thomas came to collect her, during dinner he was most interested to hear the news from his brother-in-law, John Griffith, that roads were to be improved under the new Highway Act. The other piece of news was that the Royal Military, Woolwich had opened. Hope for the country yet, he thought.

It was soon time to return to Caerau once more and suffer the cold winds and hard weather, which Emma often complained about, but she enjoyed the fires and her father's company. Mother Roberts had been informing her of her rather large family; not that Emma took much notice of many of them. She thought some of them were very poorly dressed! Mother Roberts took little notice of her sarcastic remarks knowing that Emma was a snob. She continued with stories about many of the family and advised Emma that she should write some of their names down, as she might one day be fortunate enough to benefit from one or two of them. Emma, now bored with all this information, skipped outside, and found the gardener busy planting tulips, anemones, ranunculi, and jonquil roots. She loved the varieties of the ranunculus and the yellow of the jonquil flowers. He had a lot of patience and always spoke to Emma giving her much knowledge of the plants. She went back inside, and Thomas was telling Mother Roberts that news had come informing them that Owen Williams, the glazier of Llannerchymedd, had died and was being buried the next day.

Two days later Emma strolled into the vegetable garden walled in one corner. The gardener was busy planting cabbage and carrots, parsnips, and onions to get seeds to sow after Christmas. Other members of Caerau were carrying the cut gorse to dry out in the sheds ready for the winter fires.

Mother Roberts bought a gallon of butter for 14 shillings to keep them over the winter months and paid Shadrach Evans seven shillings for a quarter of beef. The weather was cold and freezing though it thawed a little during the day, but the ground was so hard that the dogs could not run and stood looking at the hares as they ran away.

One of the Caerau workers who had gone to Henborth to watch the ships sailing, brought back a cask which had come from Liverpool for Mr William Bulkeley of Brynddu. He was given a shilling for his kindness.

It was freezing and the earth entirely covered in snow which the rain was unable to thaw. Thomas was getting prepared for the quarter sessions and Mother Roberts was glad that he had the tailor make a very thick coat, which would at least keep him dry. The wind blew such a hurricane, carrying rain with it and also accompanied with thunder and lightning. Tiles came off roofs and stacks of hay and corn were broken up.

An old vagabond from Caernarvon used to travel to Anglesey and sleep in farmers' barns when asked to catch moles. He was usually paid two shillings for this, and by the time he had visited many Anglesey people who needed his service, he would return to Caernarvon with very heavy pockets.

Emma was delighted that her birthday was, as usual, white. She loved to see the snow. She had been busy over the last few months sewing and showed a great talent. She used to spend some time in the kitchen with the maids and they had been showing her what she could achieve by sewing, at which she became very adept. She never told Mother Roberts what she was up to, knowing that there might be some trouble especially when she had cut two dresses up and had sewn one part of one dress to the other. How smart they looked! Emma felt that she could show them off anywhere.

In the newspapers on 2nd January there was a report that Sir Robert Walpole, finding that the majority in the House were against him, went to the king in the evening and vowed never to return to the Commons. It was said that he would be made a peer.

Many people in Anglesey were extremely poor with no food and a concerted effort was made by many to keep all leftovers and give it to them to keep them alive.

On February 18th the newspapers announced that parliament met after an adjournment of 15 days when Walpole retired to his house in Norfolk. This would of course mean another election.

The fairs at Llannerchymedd and Llanfechell had very poor meat which was expensive. The last two severe winters were showing the effect. The weather continued cold with hoar frost every day, but the workers continued to plant and kept hoping.

On March 15th at about nine at night an aurora borealis appeared in the sky. Mr William Bulkeley of Brynddu, well-known for his interest in such matters, thought it should be called aurora universalis because the whole firmament was filled with beams of light that darted from the horizon to the zenith. Emma enjoyed listening to stories to do with the sky. She thought that Mr Bulkeley was a very knowledgeable man and listened intently when he was discussing matters with her father. She remembered every detail so that she would have something of interest to discuss with William when he was home.

At last, the fair at Llanfechell proved well worth visiting as it had proper butchers' meat, which was a great change from what had been on offer over the last year or so. People were very sickly in most of Anglesey and the news out of Llannerchymedd was that a great many farmers, regarded as being substantial, were dead within the last few days. People became wary when they heard this sort of news. Another very cold day brought an end to 1741.

Chapter Eight

The year 1742 started with the dreariness of dull dark weather which after a week became very cold. Not a good start. People everywhere were making the most of their fires and Emma loved to hear the crackling of the gorse. Thomas had a bout of asthma which lasted a few days with Mother Roberts fussing around him as though he was a little boy. He was soon fit again and busied himself with all the bills that needed sorting out for Caerau and his lands in Caernarvonshire.

William Bulkeley records that on April 4th he went with others to meet the body of Mrs Meyrick of Bodorgan, which arrived at Llangefni having travelled from London, where she had died.

> 'Her body was to be deposited in the family vault at Llangadwaladr Church. Arriving at around 9am, the hearse and Mourning Coach were waiting along with the bearers who were fitted with scarves. About 10 am they proceeded to Llangadwaladr Church in the following order: two men in black cloaks carrying black poles with black scarves tied to them Mr Meyricks's tenants having gloves and hatbands then the bearers six in number, then the hearse covered on the sides with escutchions drawn by six horses and the Mourning Coach followed with the undertakers. The body was enclosed in three coffins one being leaded and weighed 800 weight was taken out of the hearse and a velvet pall placed over it which was then carried by eight men's shoulders to the Church where the ceremony began. Later after the body had been placed in the vault everyone travelled to Bodorgan where they were wined and dined.'

The reason for three coffins is that Mrs Meyrick died of dropsy.

In all the markets around the island, potatoes had been very scarce over the last two years and sold for 8d and 9d. Liverpool potatoes sold for 1s and 14d. Those who had been growing potatoes became more vigilant and kept watch over their fields in case they were plundered by thieves. Fortunately, the gardener at Caerau had planted enough potatoes for use at the hall and for selling to the markets. Thomas thought him very astute.

Through a church collection, enough money was raised to apprentice the son of John Jones of Penhesgyn to a glazier at Denbigh.

Emma had heard the cuckoo and seen the first swallows. Very excited, she ran in to tell William. Later they both took a ride down to the sea. William returned to school. He had enjoyed being home and listening to Emma's unstoppable chatter.

The workers were pleased to hear that Thomas and Emma would be missing for a week or more as it was time to bleed the working horses, a ritual carried out every year. Thomas decided to visit Caernarvon and took Emma with him. While Emma chatted with her aunt, Thomas liked nothing more than to hear what news his brother-in-law, John Griffith had to share. John was full of some cotton factories that were opening around the country. He spoke of Paul and John Wyatt who had opened a factory called Upper Priory Cotton Mill in Birmingham. It had 50 rollers which were turned by two donkeys walking round an axis where the spindles came out. Another was about to be opened in Northampton, which would be the first to be driven by waterpower. This had 250 spindles and, as John said, how lucky they were to be living in a world when many worked at improving things. The cotton fabrics would be welcomed by the females in society. The only sadness was that it would always be the poor producing for the rich. Both had enjoyed their visit. Emma said that she would like to come again, and her aunt said that she wished she would. When they returned Mother Roberts had seen to it that there was a nice meal to greet them and told them many stories of what had been going on during their absence. Mrs Roberts stated that they had to be very careful as there was a fever raging through the country which had killed many, with others taking six weeks to recover having relapses in between. They all understood that the country suffered either from bouts of heavy flu or from raging fever. Mother Roberts instructed Emma to always keep lavender in her handkerchief and hold it to her nose if she thought there was an illness around.

On June 8th a messenger came around with a ring in memory of Mrs Meyrick of Bodorgan. He went around all the bearers and others who were named on his list.

The following day Mr William Morgan, the parson of Llanddeusant, was buried at Llanfairynghornwy. He was regarded as a cheerful person without a care in the world.

Many complaints were heard about the ships that came from Sussex, some to Caernarvon, other to Dulas, Red Wharf Bay, and Beaumaris. Not only did they take all the corn but caused all the markets to have nothing to offer the local farmers. It was soon time to cut and pile the turf and peat ready to dry. To the Anglesey farmers, seeing to the home fires was a ritual every year.

There was hope around the country, as the fair at Aberffraw showed that fat cattle made very good money. This pleased the workers at Caerau who, during the severe winter months, had managed to fatten the cattle indoors. Two could now be sold, keeping the others for breeding.

On June 24th Francis Lloyd and his wife arrived to settle at Rhosbeirio. He was known as 'doctor', having spent six weeks at Guy's Hospital for a cure to some ailment. We must remember that this was Mr William Bulkeley's view. He was known to be quite sarcastic at times.

The weather was getting colder again and very dark until 11 am. When thunder and lightning occurred, Emma was in her element, wanting to go out and dance in the storm. Mother Roberts had to see that she stayed indoors and became quite convinced that there was something wrong with Emma. Never in her life had she seen a young woman behave like her. Nothing like her mother, she thought. Emma couldn't understand why Mother Roberts made such a fuss. She was looking forward to seeing William, who would be home soon for the summer holidays. She decided a few days later to ride down to the shore, where she sat alone for a few hours contemplating what she was going to do with William during his holidays.

William arrived home and there was such a hustle and bustle that he wondered what was going on. Everyone wanted to welcome him, and it took quite a time before he was able to sit and feel at home. Emma was so excited that as usual she could not stop talking, but was careful the first few days, knowing that the first thing he would do was visit Elizabeth's parents, then her grave. It was after the first week that she started pestering him about going out for rides. She had been busy making plans, not that William agreed with many of them. Thomas and Mother Roberts were delighted that they were friends again and both sighed with relief hoping that this year things would improve. Among Emma's plans were one or two things she knew that neither her father nor Mother Roberts would agree with, but in her mind, that was what made her plans exciting. She would wait until they went to bed, then call William in to see her and start telling him what she had in mind. She wanted him to pretend that they were going out for the day down to the beach, but instead they would ride out to different places around the island, then sit and have lunch and ride all the way back. William thought about the idea. He himself had often thought of riding out to other places for practice and learning about different ways back to Caerau. He agreed that the plan was feasible, which pleased Emma. 'As long as you keep quiet about it,' was his warning. They hung around Caerau. Riding down to the beach they would often call to see the housekeeper of Mynachdy, who now lived in a small cottage along the coast. She loved to see them and would make them fresh Welsh cakes over the fire, which they devoured very quickly.

The first week went well and then it was time to put the plan into practice. Emma was very cool, William less so, as he did not want to upset his father. After collecting food from the maids in the kitchen they set off. During lunch, Thomas asked where Emma and William were. Mother Roberts's quick reply was that they had gone down to the beach. But Emma and William were sitting in a field eating their lunch. They had chosen a little lane which took them through Llanddygfael Hir, and they had stopped to look at Arthur's Rock. They then rode as far as Llyn Hafodol where they decided to give the horses a drink.

William had been making notes about how many left and right turns they had taken, to make it easier for when they returned. When he eventually mounted his horse, Emma started without him with William calling her back. But she went on until she disappeared out of sight. William rode as fast as he could in the hope of catching up with her but there was sign of her. He was getting hot and perspiring. This was not what he had expected. He was already regretting his decision to do what Emma wanted. He feared the repercussions when they got back, and he certainly did not want to have to face his father and must explain that it was all Emma's fault. He knew that Mother Roberts would be in a panic if they were not back for their dinner. Things seemed hopeless. He kept riding, not knowing whether he was going the right way.

Then he came to Rhos Goch, where there was an inn. Outside was Emma's horse which was a relief in one way for William, but he was rather cross finding her at an inn. He dismounted and stood for a while just to get his breath back. He asked a maid if she had seen the girl who had left her horse outside, and the maid told him that she had gone round the back to a collect some water. She was very thirsty. William tied up his horse so that it could also have a drink after that chase. As he went to sit, he heard a voice which sounded quite familiar to him. When he turned to look, he found it to be one of the boys who attended school with him. He was there with his father. William explained to Charles what had happened, and Charles called his father and introduced William to him. They sat and spent some time over pleasantries, when William asked if they knew what time it was. He told them that he was very afraid that his father would reprimand him severely, because of Emma. He asked Charles's father if he would be so kind as to speak to her and make her understand how important it was that they made their way back. Charles had disappeared round the back and found Emma busy talking with some chap in the kitchen and telling him all about herself. Charles asked in a firm voice, 'Excuse me, are you Emma?'

Emma, shocked, replied, 'It all depends on who is asking.'

Charles, again in a firm voice, said, 'If I were you, I would find your brother, William, and start for home.'

Emma looked around and then started walking to the front, where she found, William sitting talking to Charles's father. She cheekily asked, 'Were you looking for me? Because someone came to the back and asked if I was Emma.'

William stood up and said, 'This is Charles from our school, and this is his father, Mr Hugh Woodcock.'

Emma looked at him and Mr Woodcock asked her to sit down for a moment, explaining that she should not have ridden away from poor William as he did not know which way she had gone. Again Emma, exasperated at being told off by a stranger, said, 'I'm not going to listen to you, you are not my father.'

Mr Woodcock thought that she was very feisty and told her that her father would not believe what he was going to tell him when he met him. That seemed to calm her down a little and Mr Woodcock told her that he understood that she had enjoyed her ride out with William, but that she should not play stupid games and chase off as she had done. 'William,' said Mr Woodcock, 'already knows that he will be reprimanded by your father, which is not at all fair as it is you who should be punished.' By this time Emma was very quiet, and Mr Woodcock advised them to start riding back home with no more nonsense from Emma.

William mounted his horse and Emma hers and they started out the same way as they had come. Unbeknown to them, Mr Woodcock had already summonsed a messenger from the inn to travel to Caerau and inform Thomas that William and Emma would be home that evening, perhaps a little late. William instructed Emma that they now had to keep turning right rather than left and that they had to pass Arthur's Rock. Then they would know that they were not far from Llanfechell and then on to Llanfairynghornwy and home. When they turned down towards Caerau, the relief was tremendous though Emma had sulked most of the way back with William taking no notice.

When they arrived back in the house, they were met by Thomas who looked quite stern and ordered Emma to bed and William to his study. William stood and said, 'I'm terribly sorry, sir.' But Thomas interrupted him, saying that he already knew that they would be returning a little late and that he also knew that it was all Emma's fault. William could not understand how his father knew. Thomas never let on about the messenger simply because he wanted Emma to understand just how cross he was with her. He explained to William that he expected him to start learning his way around the island, but he did not like that Emma had put William in such a situation. He told William to go up and have a bath as he could see how hot he was after riding. William obeyed immediately.

Emma had already had a bath by the time William went up, having complained to her maid how hungry she was, and couldn't believe that her father had sent her up without even asking if she needed food. Emma was beside herself. Her maid, however, had been down to the kitchen and had brought a tray of food for her. Emma sat and ate it.

Her maid said, 'You know, you are a one to go off like that. You're just like a bunch of monkeys climbing a tree, always in trouble.' Emma laughed as her maid was always using that saying.

The next morning, Emma refused to go downstairs for her breakfast. Thomas was having none of it and ordered her maid to bring her down even if she was not dressed. Emma was shocked and once again her tantrums started. Thomas called her from the bottom of the stairs to stop her nonsense and come down. A very shaky Emma appeared and didn't say good morning to anyone. Mother Roberts was extremely quiet and just left Thomas to deal with the situation.

When breakfast was finished, he told Emma and William to go to his study. He sat down in his chair and told Emma that he knew from earlier in the afternoon that they were going to be late arriving back. Emma looked at him quite astonished. How could he possibly know? He explained that a messenger had been sent at Mr Woodcock's request. Emma started by saying, 'William' but before she could get any further Thomas stopped her by saying, 'That is enough, Emma, we all know whose fault it was, and it certainly was not William's. If you had asked properly, I would have refused an adventure for you, but to do what you did to William and ride ahead with no care in the world was not fair. When William arrived home last night, he was coughing and very hot, which is not good for anyone.'

Thomas turned and asked William how he felt, and William replied, 'I'm well, thank you, sir.'

Thomas stood looking at them. Emma's cheeks somewhat flushed and then he said, 'Both of you can ride out a little and learn your way around, but no more bad behaviour from you, Emma. You can go now.'

As Emma was climbing the stairs, she asked William how her father knew that they would be late, William replied that he did not know and was quite shocked when his father told him after arriving home. Emma asked if he had mentioned to anyone about their secret and William assured her that he had not told anyone. Emma got dressed and William went to his room. As soon as she was dressed, she went knocking on William's door. 'What are we going to do today?' she asked. William said that as the horses would need a rest, and they could either stay around Caerau or walk down to the beach, to which Emma agreed.

They walked into the walled garden and found the gardener busy planting cauliflower in the north bed and English cabbage and sugar loaf cabbage in the south bed. They chatted with him for a while then went to look at the ducks, which were still a great favourite with Emma. They were called in for lunch and decided that later they would walk down to the beach. When they arrived back in the house, they found that Thomas had already left. He had gone to attend the funeral of Dr Richard Evans, the surgeon of Llannerchymedd. Many felt his loss and felt for his wife and six small children.

After lunch, William and Emma prepared themselves for walking down to the beach. They called to feed the horses first then went off. William told Emma stories about some of the boys he kept company with and what they did to new members of the school when they arrived. Emma was in giggles over some of the things. When they arrived at the beach, they paddled and sat on some stones looking out to sea. They could see one or two boats and William told Emma that they were out to catch herrings. He had recognised one boat from Cemaes. Further along there was a very large pool of water surrounded by many wild plants and when they looked, they saw a moorhen with about eight little chicks. They sat quietly just watching. Emma did a little shiver so William said that he thought they should make their way back to Caerau. Emma said, 'Let's watch them just for a few more minutes. Then we'll go home.'

William said again, 'Come along, Emm, it's time to return home.'

When they got back, Thomas was home and they soon got ready for dinner. They chatted about various activities that they had been up to when a knock on the door could be heard. It was William Bulkeley wanting a chat with Thomas, and as they were about to start eating, William Bulkeley was asked to join them. When they had eaten, Mother Roberts beckoned to William and Emma to follow her as she left the room so that Thomas and William Bulkeley could talk. It was about John Owen of Presaddfed having an agreement with Bulkeley's son-in-law, Mr Wright, regarding some payment from a tenant. John Owen had suddenly sent a note to eject the man, and William Bulkeley wondered if Thomas or Mother Roberts knew anything about it.

They didn't. But William Bulkeley said that it would be in court soon as John Owen had presented Mr Wright with a declaration of ejectment. It was decided to leave the matter until it arrived at the court.

The attendance at church had increased a little and on August the 7th, the parson spoke about a collection for propagating the gospel in America. He had received a copy of a letter from the king, which had come from parliament in the hope of persuading the people how zealous the king and his ministers were in the cause of religion. Many agreed, but there were also many who believed that the money would be better spent elsewhere. William had been to church as he was going back to school the following day. He had a slight cough, but Mother Roberts had seen to it that there was a bottle of medicine in his bag. Emma, though she missed him terribly, had accepted that he had to go. She was hoping to visit her favourite aunt in Caernarvon before too long.

Emma loved accompanying Mother Roberts when she went shopping to the Llannerchymedd fair. She was fascinated at seeing people around the countryside reaping the wheat and then bagging the corn, which went to the ships to be transported to other parts of the country.

The Beaumaris sessions that began on August 23rd did not sit until 7pm in the evening. Mr William Bulkeley had delivered what was called 'examinations and recognisances' regarding a murder, to the proper officers at Beaumaris.

The matter concerning John Owen of Presaddfed had been settled. He had received two years' interest, which were in arrears, so he stopped further proceedings regarding the ejectment of his tenant. A group of men which included Thomas Rowlands, John Owen Presaddfed, Lewis of Trysglwyn and Thomas Morris of Rhydgroes were criticised by William Bulkeley for not finding a bill of indictment against the murderer of George Warmingham during the Llanrhuddlad Wakes. He finished his comments with, 'These are the good, honest and fine gentlemen of the country as they are called.' Thomas and the other gentlemen knew better and would not concede just to please William Bulkeley. It was George Warmingham who had started the fight, always thinking himself stronger than anyone else. That he was beaten up was for the asking.

On September 11th, people saw something that they would normally see during December; the Caernarvonshire Mountains covered in thick snow. At 3pm that day, William Rowlands died of smallpox at school. This was devastating news for Thomas, Mother Roberts, and Emma. Thomas, in Beaumaris for the sessions, had received news that William was ill, but never for a moment thought it was as dangerous. Several others at the school also died. A correspondent wrote that, *'Ye smallpox is very rife now. Master Billa Rowlands is now ill of the smallpox in his fifth day... it is now the eleventh day. He died and his sister Emma became the heiress of Caerau and Plas-y-Nant.'*

Thomas was stunned and did not speak. His world had crumbled. Once he was home, he locked himself away in his study, which worried Mother Roberts. She understood he had to cope with his grief, but there were things to do. The parson called and sympathised with Mother Roberts and Emma, and it was decided that William would have to be buried on September 13th as it was not good to keep bodies that had a disease. They would have to put him in two coffins so that the disease could not spread. Mother Roberts made all the arrangements. Emma was practically hysterical. She received plenty of comfort from the kitchen staff. They looked after her as though she were their own. Mother Robert's concern was to deal with Thomas. The parson had tried when he had called, to no response. She sent letters to John Owen and to William Bulkeley, who arranged for Lord Bulkeley also to be called. Mother Roberts spoke outside the study door and told Thomas what arrangements had been made and when William was to be buried. The house was suddenly full of people. Thomas took little notice of all the callers and what they had to say, but just before midnight he opened the study door knowing that everyone would be in bed, and slowly went up to his bedroom. He knew that he had to be prepared for the burial. His heart hurt, thinking that perhaps if he had gone to see William or called a doctor sooner, he might have saved him. He remembered what a kind and thoughtful son William had been, how he had stood up for Emma, had managed to talk her out of one of her tantrums, and had forgiven her when she had shown how jealous she was of his friendship with Elizabeth. This was too much to bear.

Mother Roberts was first up, arranging everything. She sent the maid to see to Emma, who was in a bad way and failed to understand what had happened. She couldn't believe that she would never see William again. She hated everything and everyone all at the same time. The maid had to calm her down, telling her that this day was not the day for tantrums and to think of her father who had lost so much. It was a very dark day for everyone at Caerau and that included the farm workers and all those in the kitchen. Emma and Mother Roberts were not allowed to attend the funeral. Thomas insisted that their duty was to be home waiting for those who had kindly attended.

William Bulkeley, though critical of Thomas and his friends when they refused to be influenced by him in court matters, felt very sad indeed and in his diaries, he left a blank square the day William was buried, as though to say that there was no word to express how he really felt.

Thomas looked dreadful as they walked to the church but carried out his duty and thanked everyone who attended. He now would have to write letters to inform people of what had happened. When he arrived back at Caerau, Mother Roberts and Emma were standing to greet everyone. Thomas and his friends drank quite a lot. When many left rather late in the evening, Thomas went to his study and Mother Roberts knew that it was best to leave him to his grief. Emma too was heartbroken. She felt shocked, betrayed, and utterly lonely. As spoilt as she was, nothing could make up for how she felt now. The servants around Caerau kept calling to ask Mother Roberts if there was anything she wanted doing apart from seeing to their work. The kitchen staff also were concerned. Mother Roberts, always stoical, had been through many deaths, and understood how important it was to carry on.

For weeks after William's death, Thomas was hardly to be seen. Everyone was worried about him. The rest of September seemed to have disappeared until news came that Mr Hugh Owen, Penrhos, had died. He was married to Mother Roberts' niece and had a baby daughter just six weeks old. He had gone down to Bristol for his health, very ill before starting out, and his journey was horrendous. But he believed that he would get better once he reached Bristol. His fever could not be controlled, and he died. It was decided that he was to be buried at Bristol.

A Flintshire smuggler arrived at Cemaes from the Isle of Man. One of Thomas's workers had gone over as it was said that you could buy five gallons of brandy for 25s, which was indeed very cheap. Thomas had already given money for the cause!

The weather had been growing cold for some weeks, but this day, October 3rd, such a storm blew up that it uprooted trees and broke others in half. The devastation was frightening. It lifted slate and thatch roofs, hay, and corn stacks. The winds were so high that two ships were cast away southwest of Holyhead. At Trefadog in Llanfaethlu a large West Indian man from Liverpool was staved to pieces. All men perished except one Welshman who swam to shore. The ship was laden with rum, sugar, and cotton. The sugar melted away in the sea, the casks of rum came ashore, and the story is that the country people, after drinking as much as they could, knocked the heads out of the casks and destroyed the rest.

On October 21st Mr Meyrick arrived back at Bodorgan, having been away for some time after his wife's death. William Bulkeley went to welcome him, before going over to Henblas where he stayed the night. Once Mr Meyrick had time to catch up with all the news, he called at Caerau to commiserate with Thomas over William's death.

In November, Emma's cousin, Emma Owen, who had recently married William Roberts of Bodior on October 12th, called on her way home from London where she had been on honeymoon. She told Mother Roberts and Emma that her brother, Robert, now a doctor, had been pleased to see her. Dr Robert Owen of Presaddfed had qualified at Luton in 1731 and had practised in London with his father-in-law, John Douglas. Emma Roberts became the heiress of Presaddfed after the deaths of her two brothers.

Mother Roberts had been to see a weaver, whom she paid 2s to for weaving four blankets to help keep warm. It had started freezing every night and was as cold as the bitter weather experienced during December 1739.

During this time of tribulation at the loss of William, Thomas's sister, Margaret, wrote to Mrs Owen at Porkington. She thanked Mrs Owen and her cousin, Mr Owen, for the welcome she had received and for Mrs Owen's great servility in taking notice of Margaret's loss when she had lost a son at the tender age of seven years to a dreadful distemper. She then went on about her concerns for her dear brother, Thomas. *'He writes me word that he endeavours to submit to God's will though thinks time cannot efface his memory, he has had a pain in his stomach but finds benefit by something that was ordered. He gives you and Mr Owen his humble thanks for your kind enquiry after him.'*

Margaret then mentions Miss Dolly Wynn who was married to that noted pretty Mr William Thomas. Dorothy Wynn was the daughter of Thomas Wynn, 1st Baronet of Boduan and Glynllifon, and Frances Glynne. She married William Thomas on October 10th, 1742, and came to live with him at Coed Helen, Caernarvon, which was his home. William Thomas was the son of Rhys Thomas and Gaynor Wynn. Margaret also states that she was very proud of the fact that Mrs Owen's five-year-old daughter, Miss Margaret, had not forgotten her. She was exceedingly glad that the cold bathing agreed so well with Miss Nelly, who had obviously started walking.

Margaret's letter confirms just how deeply hurt Thomas was at the death of his only son, William, for whom he had built up so much hope over the years. His pain was probably made worse by his overindulgence in alcohol. Margaret conveys her best wishes to Mrs Godolphin, Mrs Owen's mother, who was staying at Porkington. She finishes off with, *'Pray my services to Mrs Sky'*, whose husband was the Reverend Sky, headmaster of the free grammar school in Oswestry and vicar of Llanfillan, Denbighshire.

William Bulkeley called round to chat with Thomas in the hope that he could lift his spirit. He told him that he had been with Mr William Lewis the younger of Trysglwyn and Mr John Hughes of Glan-yr-Afon to see Mr John Hughes skating on the ice. He had skated from Cae Rhos y Fawnog in the south end of the pool to Nyth yr Alarch in the north end in three minutes.

Mother Roberts visited the market at Llannerchymedd which was much better than the last except for butchers' meat, which was still very scarce. She met some boys on the way back to Caerau who had some rabbits hanging around their necks, so she bought two for a 1s. Mr Bulkeley reported that there was a good market at Llanfechell, full of corn, butter, and cheese, but no butchers' meat.

Emma's birthday was a dull affair. She wasn't interested in anything, and she missed William. In a way she was still in shock and couldn't believe that she would never see him again. His grave was to remind her of his being. Her grandmother gave her a pretty brooch to pin on her dress, but Emma hardly looked at it. She was worried about her father and kept thinking that she might die at any minute. Members of her family called to cheer her up and give gifts, but Emma was sullen most of the time. She even wondered why gifts were necessary. There was nothing she wanted apart from having William back. Her father and Mother Roberts took everything in their stride and kept talking with her, trying to make her understand that she alone was now the heiress of Caerau and Plas-y-Nant.

On January 14th, the day after Emma's birthday, the famous astronomer, Edmund Halley, died. He wrote a synopsis of the *Astronomy of Comet Sightings* from 1456, 1531, 1607 and 1682, all so similar that he concluded that it was the same comet returning each time. He predicted that it would next appear on Christmas day 1758, which Halley did not live to see.

On February 24th a great circle appeared around the moon, which many thought of as a sign of something to come. Coal from Liverpool arrived at Cemaes with everyone rushing to buy tons. The poor who watched as it was loaded ran to pick up the pieces that fell to ground. On the 9th of March the aurora borealis blazed throughout the night. William Bulkeley stayed up to watch it. A letter from William Morris to his brother Richard states: *'Roberts had got Mr Rowlands of Caere to keep his horse whilst in Dublin.'*

By the 12th of March it was snowing hard but then it rained and washed all the snow away by ten in the morning. At Llannerchymedd fair, butcher's meat at an extravagant price and many could not afford to buy it.

At the end of his diaries for 1742, William Bulkeley wrote that, *'A year remarkable for the scarcity of all sorts of Butcher's meat in this part of the Kingdom, and indeed all the Kingdom over London. A year likewise remarkable for plunder and oppressing of the people with excessive taxes by those very people (now at the helm of affairs) who for several years had been the remainder of Walpole's administration and are now making larger strides that ever he did. 700,000 pounds being raised this year and the last to procure satisfaction from Spain for their insults and depredations, while these last eighteen months past everything continued in a state of inaction. 15,000 Hanoverian troops paid by the English for appearing in defence of their own country and paid 10 months before they came to the field.'*

Most people who knew William Bulkeley would understand just how much he disliked Walpole, just as he criticised the parson when he preached on various subjects. This was the end of 1742.

Chapter Nine

The year began with hail and sleet making life dreary. This was also the time of year when the moles had been busy, and Thomas was glad when the head of his workers told him that the mole catcher was due. When he was ready to leave Thomas paid him 9d for having caught a dozen. The weather grew colder still and even the water in the house froze.

Mother Roberts decided to ride out to Holyhead. She needed some soap. It cost her 6s for 12lbs of soap, whereas in 1739 it had cost 4s 6d. On her return she found Thomas busy with piles of paperwork around him, which pleased her as it proved that, at long last, he was beginning to take an interest in life once more.

On April 10th there was great excitement as the cuckoo was heard for the first time and Emma saw the first swallows to arrive at Caerau. Thomas was having to pay window taxes, which he disagreed with, and told Mother Roberts that he intended to take some of the windows out and block them up.

The papers were installing fear in everyone regarding a raging infectious distemper that had been in London for over six weeks. Should it arrive in Anglesey it would cause devastating suffering which every epidemic did each year. In London they were burying as many as 25-30 bodies a day.

At last, there was plenty of butchers' meat at the Llanfechell fair, which was a very good one, with plenty of everything. There was nothing like a fair. Everyone was usually glad to see people they only saw at fairs, and they would chat away, telling each other about their families.

On Monday May 8th, 1743, the Bodorgan Mill was laid near Llanfarian. People from around had gathered despite the winds, which were quite scorching. Then it turned very cold, killing the vegetables that people had struggled to grow. The gardener at Caerau could not believe it when he saw the kidney beans black and withered. The ash and walnut trees were as black as coal.

Emma was away staying with her aunt at Caernarvon. Her aunt wondered after the first day how Emma and William, her son, never tired of talking. She had never heard so much talking but was very kind to Emma, realising that she was still missing her brother, William. Emma was sorry for her aunt too, at losing her young son aged seven years, so they were both able to console each other.

At the beginning of June, Thomas decided that he needed a change. He had worked hard sorting many bills out and visiting his lands in Anglesey and Caernarvonshire. It had taken longer than usual with everyone wanting to console him about William. He spoke with Mother Roberts about his intentions, and she agreed that a break was well and truly overdue. She also told him that it would do Emma good to see different places and people, rather than feeling alone at Caerau. With permission they were allowed to stay at Lord Bulkeley's house not far from Church Street, London, and Emma suddenly felt very important. Having arrived safely in London without being held up by highwaymen, Thomas started making a list of all the suitable places they should visit. He was determined to go and see Hyde Park having followed all the news regarding it and then perhaps to see the Serpentine, the recreational lake which had been built at the wishes of Queen Caroline, wife of King George II. She had planned it with Charles Bridgeman who dammed the Westbourne River to create an artificial lake and, who had dug the 'Round Pond' in the centre of Kensington Gardens to be a focal point for pathways in the park.

Thomas waited for Emma who was taking her time getting ready for the excursion, fussing about how she looked. She had spent weeks choosing what she was taking with her, and her Aunt Margaret had given her a dress to wear for the theatre. He father was shocked at the amount she had brought with her, but his sister had warned him that women had to have enough dresses for various occasions, and as this was Emma's first time, he had to accept it. When Emma eventually arrived, her father had to admit that she looked lovely. He led her to the foyer and hailed a carriage to Hyde Park.

They could not believe the vastness of it and though the Serpentine was not finished they liked the walks around it. Emma was dumbstruck, she had never seen such a place before and she couldn't wait for the time that she could make notes of what she had seen. A copy of *The Gazette* had been left for Thomas to read and he would also arrange what and where they would be going to the next day. He had read about George Frederick Handel's 'Messiah' and had seen the wonderful reviews, so Thomas was hoping that he could arrange a musical evening. They could be lucky enough to hear Handel's oratorio 'Samson'.

So many people called to wish them well and Emma's cousin, William Griffith, called to see her and arrange to take her out. She was also invited by Mrs Mostyn for tea, which lightened Thomas's load of trying to find so something for her to do all the time. He made a note of one or two people he wished to call upon whilst he was in London and he was very pleased when his cousin, Mr William Owen, called and invited him along to a few clubs, knowing that he liked to gamble.

The following week, Thomas wanted to go and see some galleries where they would be showing some of Hogarth's paintings, including his new collection, 'Marriage à la Mode'. William Hogarth was an engraver in his own right and knew exactly what to do to make the colours stand out just as he wanted. This collection was the talk of the town. It was written: 'He delights in the unruly theatre of life afforded by society in London from the slums of St Giles to fashionable St James's.'

One day, Emma asked her father about getting some silk. She had promised Mother Roberts that she would do her best to find something suitable for her. Thomas agreed with her but all he knew about silk was that the Huguenots had a place at Spitalfields. Having made enquiries, he learnt that the most famous shop was in Artillery Lane, run by Nicholas Jourdain, a silk mercer who was also director of the French hospital. They enjoyed their visit and especially examining the silks. Emma loved to see the weavers and all the things that they produced, and she couldn't get over how warm the silk felt on one's skin. She purchased a small piece to give her grandmother, hoping that if she wore it around her neck, she should be very warm. There was so much to do and to arrange that Thomas found that time was flying by.

A visit from Lord Bulkeley surprised them. Thomas offered to move out, but Lord Bulkeley refused, and he said there was plenty of room for them all. That evening, Thomas treated Lord Bulkeley and Emma to dinner and Emma was thrilled, not that she took much notice of Lord Bulkeley. She was too busy talking about other young gentlemen. One had taken her fancy, the handsome Owen Meyrick, a barrister-at-law, the son of Owen Meyrick of Bodorgan. His family were known as the purest and noblest Cambrian blood and had possessed the same ancestral estate and residence at Bodorgan, Anglesey without interruption for over 1000 years. He and Emma got on extremely well. Owen Meyrick was known for building a family vault at Llangadwaladr Church in Anglesey.

Many called to wish them well as they set off for Anglesey, with promises that when they were home or rather visiting the island they would call and see Emma. Thomas realised for the first time that Emma had grown up and that it would soon be her time to enjoy herself, being accompanied by young men to balls and dinners. He wondered where time had gone. He sat thinking about various possibilities whilst Emma was saying her goodbyes and promises of keeping in touch.

The news before they left London was that the king was taking troops from Britain and Brunswick to Bavaria for what came to be called the Battle of Dettingen. He led them to victory over the French, the last time a reigning British monarch participated in battle. During the journey back, Thomas decided to stop overnight at Chester, as he was tired. Emma had not stopped chatting about the people she had met and the places she had visited. All Thomas heard was her excited voice as he fell asleep.

When they eventually arrived back the following day at Caerau, Mother Roberts was delighted to see them. She'd had the maids prepare high tea, which both Thomas and Emma enjoyed. After tea Emma told Mother Roberts about all the things she had seen. Mother Roberts suggested that a hot bath and a good sleep would do her good and that they finish off about London until the following day. Later, Mother Roberts sat and chatted with Thomas, asking about various people and what he thought about some of the places he had visited. Thomas grew rather tired and went into his bedroom for an early night where he hoped that he would be able to sleep.

When Emma was up the following day, she rushed downstairs to find Mother Roberts, who, since Emma had arrived back, thought how much she had grown. In her mind she was busy making plans to get her married off. Emma did nothing but talk about Owen Meyrick and Mrs Roberts assumed that now there was hope. It was difficult to keep up with Emma, there was so much excitement. Mother Roberts decided that she would wait a few days until Emma had calmed down before discussing the matter of having a young man and of marriage.

Thomas was unwell again, coughing and his asthma was bad. He had to stay in, and Emma was instructed to be quiet around the house. She decided to take a ride out down to the beach, there she could dream as much as she wanted. However, plans had been made that she attend a school, or rather a finishing school, so that she would know how to conduct herself should she marry into the aristocracy. Mother Roberts dreaded the day when she and Thomas would have to tell Emma about this school, knowing that it could cause another tantrum. Emma, however, told Mother Roberts that, as she had attended school when she stayed with her aunt in Caernarvon, there was no need to send her to another. And Mother Roberts herself had taught her etiquette and good manners. Mother Roberts could not discuss the issue with Thomas. His asthma was really bad, and she realised that there was no point in upsetting him about Emma. She also knew that what Emma had said was quite true. During the evenings, when they were both together, Mother Roberts would ask what she would like to have, should such a thing as marriage occur and that every young woman would be collecting different things for their wedding. Mother Roberts did not tell her that she had started a collection to make sure that she had plenty of the right things. Thomas, however, felt that a finishing school would certainly prepare her for marriage and improve her behaviour.

Emma was busy, there was a ball to be held at Baron Hill and she was hoping that Owen Meyrick would be home for the occasion and that he would escort her to the ball. Owen Meyrick had hired a coach to take them both to the ball and Emma felt wonderful and very important. From that point, her grandmother heard nothing but this and that about Owen Meyrick.

In September she visited the Owens at Porkington and got on very well with Mrs Owen, who liked her. She taught her many things and Emma became very good with needlework. She also met many ladies and they all played cards together and had interesting conversations. They laughed, they joked, and they criticised. She also heard much about Mr Thomas Pennant with Mrs Owen telling her that he was a most likeable chap. Emma had seen him of course when he attended some of the balls and she quite fancied him.

Emma would walk around the grounds of Porkington and sometimes she took a walk further afield. She enjoyed riding, and another chap now took her fancy, the groom who looked after Mr Owen's horses. She would question him on various aspects of the horse's body just to see if he was as good as her grandmother, who was exceptionally informative about them. She was enjoying herself but there were occasions when she was homesick. She would play with Robert, better known as Bobby, the young son. He loved to tease her by hiding in places and gushing forth giving her a fright. She thought he was very bright because he found a new place each time and still managed to frighten her.

Emma found the three youngsters, Robert, Margaret, and Ellen, great fun. She played for hours with them and taught them games but was always glad when the *gouvernante* came to collect them and take them to bed. During the evening, she played cards with Mr and Mrs Owen and whoever else was staying there. It had been nice and now she would have to prepare to travel back Caerau and see how her father was and Mother Roberts.

Mr Owen travelled with her as far as Wrexham, feeling that she would be safe from there. They had lunch, then Mr Owen went on his way and Emma towards Anglesey. She slept most of the way, and it took some time to cross from the Lavan Sands over towards Beaumaris. A horse was waiting for her, and she rode as fast as she could to be home. One of the kitchen maids saw here riding down the road and ran in exclaiming that Emma was back. Mother Roberts went out to meet her and they hugged, Emma was glad to be home. Tired after her journey, she still insisted on trying to tell Mother Roberts all about the people she had met, until poor Mother Roberts' head was in a spin. Her father asked about Mr Owen, his cousin, and said that the Jacobite threat was a great strain to many. Emma did not know anything about this; but having heard various bits of conversation between Mr and Mrs Owen, and having seen some letters from Mrs Owen's aunts, the Godolphins, she put the matter in order in her head. Later in the year, a notice appeared in the newspapers: *'James of Scotland by Grace of God, King of Scotland, England France and Ireland, Defender of the Faith, to all our loving subjects of what quality so ever, greeting. Given at our court at Rome 23rd December 1743. The 43rd year of our reign.'*

Emma was looking forward to the winter ball to be held at Plas Newydd, hoping that Owen Meyrick would be home to escort her to it. But Owen Meyrick could not be home, he was too busy, so Emma had to go alone, hoping to meet someone who might take her fancy. Another ball was to take place at Bodorgan, Owen Meyrick's home, and Emma couldn't wait. When she arrived at Bodorgan, she was met by Owen himself and had the first dance with him but there were so many good-looking young men that Emma wanted to dance with them all.

Her father was now thinking that she might decide soon that she wanted to get married, and that he would have to provide for her. He thought it best to leave the matter. Her intelligence, he felt, was her strong point and she would certainly not throw herself at anyone. There was talk about Owen Meyrick and Thomas Pennant; she was young, and he could not blame her for having fancies. It was all so natural, and one day she would find the right person. Thomas himself was not well; ever since he lost William he had been suffering with a heavy cough and asthma. He knew that his heavy drinking had not helped. As he sat and thought he remembered when he first met Elin, his wife, how deeply in love he was with her and the sadness of losing her and the baby, then to lose two more of his children. He felt that he had to get well again for Emma's sake. He was glad that Emma was having such a good time with many invitations to various balls or concerts and sometimes just dinner. He would have to make a new will as Emma was now his heiress and that alone should make anyone interested in having her as their wife. He believed that his wife would have approved of how he had brought Emma up with the help, of course, of Mother Roberts.

There were rumours everywhere that Emma and Owen Meyrick were going to get engaged, but Emma herself never mentioned anything about it. Thomas could only believe that there was some sort of stalemate in the relationship. However, Emma ventured out as often as possible if she had a companion. Perhaps she wanted time and felt that everyone was pushing her towards marriage. Being a strong personality, she was determined to choose for herself.

On January 3rd, Thomas' sister, Margaret Griffith, having been over to see Thomas as she was still concerned about his health, wrote to Mrs Owen of Porkington hoping that her cold was better and giving her some news regarding Mrs Dolly Thomas, who according to Margaret was certainly expecting a child as was her sister, Wynne, in London. She then went on to say that Mrs Thomas had a new gown and coat of a rich silk, yellow ground with blue and silver flowers with a pink tabby night gown and a very broad, laced head and a Dublin handkerchief. After giving Mrs Owen some gossip, she went on about historical facts regarding families of estates around North Wales, giving the history of various well-known people,

> 'such as Sir W. Jones, Knight of Castellmarch, whose son had married Margaret Wynne of Gesail Gyfarch, supposedly descended from Wynn of Gwydir. His eldest son married the daughter and heiress of Plas Mawr in Caernarvon. They had two daughters; the eldest married Sir Griffith Williams of Vaynol and the other married his brother Thomas Williams of Dinas; she married for the second time Thomas Bulkeley the younger son of Baron Hill. Sir Griffith Williams had a son, and he married a daughter of Baron Hill and had a son, Sir William, who became the last in the line of Sir William Jones, Knight. He had another son, Charles Robert, and a daughter that married to Wynne from which I think Sir I. Wynne came, Francis to park one married to Lord Keeper Littleton and another to Tokkenbridge, one to Price of Rhiwlas. I will enquire further if you wish. Sir W. Jones's wife was a daughter of Cefnamwlch, her mother Catherine Buckeley of Baron Hill and her mother was a Griffith of Penrhyn.' She finishes by saying, 'If you cannot satisfy yourself, I will write it out in a better manner.'

This shows the interest Mr Owen of Porkington had in collecting people's ancestry, which had for a long time been kept by Mr Wynn of Gwydir. Whether Mr Owen took on this task from Mr Wynn of Gwydir is not known.

Thomas was in his study when a knock on the door woke him up. It was Mother Roberts, who had been out to Llannerchymedd fair and had heard the rumour about Emma and Owen Meyrick. Thomas said that he was aware of the rumour but as Emma had not mentioned anything, and even more importantly anything to do with marriage, they both agreed that it was better to keep quiet about the rumour.

On January 10th Emma wrote to Mrs Owen at Porkington telling her that she was abroad, *'and on my return found a letter directed to me from Mr and Mrs Owen.'* Obviously, Mrs Owen had mentioned Thomas Pennant when she said,

'You were pleased to mention the gentleman in yours so lately whose agreeable chit-chats gained so much of your governante's attention.' She goes on to say, *'his name is Thomas Pennant a gentleman of family and fortune in the county of Flint.'* Then she writes about Mrs Owen's children, hoping that Master Franky is weaned. She wishes them, *'much joy of your safe arrival in your new settlement and I hope it will be as productful of happiness as the old and may your good family be increased and multiply sevenfold into your bosom My Dear Madam Owen.'*

The Owens had moved to Brongyntyn, which became their home and housed a huge library. She mentions that Mrs Owen going to Bath, then refers to Sir Watkin Williams who had broken one of his ribs, which she did not believe until she received Mrs Owen's letter. Emma had sent Mrs Owen patterns for a poplin to choose and approve, *'so that I may send immediately to Dublin for them.'* She then goes on to say that Miss Freeman has had a cold and is in dreadful apprehension that she has lost the use of her fingers. Emma is worried that she may not receive any more letters from Miss Freeman. She finishes off by calling herself, *'obliged humble servant, Emm Rowlands. P.S. Papa and Grand Mama desires their compliments to you Mr Owen and family and please to make mine acceptable to them a thousand services to Miss Freeman just commit this to the farther end of the Gallery.'*

Emma had met the Freemans whilst staying with the Owens, and as Mr Pennant had been mentioned to Mrs Owen, Thomas was thinking that this was more of a match. Thomas knew Mr David Pennant, Thomas Pennant's father. Thomas Pennant had been born in 1726. He became a naturalist, traveller, writer, and antiquarian.

He lived all his life on his family's estate, Downing Hall near Whitford, Flintshire. He attended the Wrexham Grammar School before moving to Thomas Crafts School in Fulham in 1740. Thomas was hoping to hear more about Thomas Pennant. Perhaps now that Emma would soon be 17, she should think about inviting him over to meet them and see Caerau.

Emma was very busy. She had many lady friends who now called on her. They would play cards, which she enjoyed because of the gossip and discussions on fashion, besides their beaux. They were of similar age, everything was exciting, and Mother Roberts was kept informed of all the gossip when they had gone. She was amused to hear the various stories and would at times have to leave the room just in order to have a laugh. Emma was so precise about matters; Mother Roberts thought she had to have her fun and Emma had grown used to the fact that she could tell Mother Roberts anything. When she told her something naughty Mother Roberts took it all in her stride.

It was Emma's birthday and Thomas had arranged for her and some of her friends to have dinner in Beaumaris, something to remember. Thomas and Mother Roberts were there too. The table was beautifully decorated with flowers and the food was very good. Emma looked lovely, thought Thomas; he wished he could send her mother a picture. She would be so proud. They stayed the night at Beaumaris and returned home the following day. Emma was in wonderland. She was now 17.

The month of January was unusually cold. Thomas suffered quite a bit from colds and a fever, and Mother Roberts kept a watchful eye over him. He just could not shake it off. They kept a fire going most of the time and Thomas had to call the men in to see him when it was necessary to discuss farm matters. Mother Roberts did her usual, going to market to make sure that Thomas had the best vegetables and meat.

Emma was away in London at a finishing school, where she chatted and laughed with the other girls and thought that she knew most of what had taught her. However, she had promised her father that she would stay and obey orders. Many people from Anglesey who had houses in London and knew her had often entertained her.

So really this was 'a life' rather than what she called the dull atmosphere of Caerau.

The weather was much as usual. Plenty of snow and hard frost. Most people had become accustomed to this weather and would often have made sure that there was plenty of water near the house with enough coal and wood to see them through the winter months. Many stayed in and kept warm. It worsened and by February the violent storms frustrated the planned French invasion of Britain.

On March 1st a comet was seen, seemingly the brightest ever. Everyone thought this a good omen, but on March 15th France declared war on Great Britain, leaving everyone in rather a gloomy state. Cardinal Fleury of France and Robert Walpole had both felt that peace was a necessary aspect of national prosperity, but Walpole had resigned in 1742 and Cardinal Fleury died in 1743, which left everything open to the troublemakers. The French made plans for an invasion across the Channel in the company of the Jacobite pretender, Charles Edward Stuart. However, all the bad weather which had damaged the fleet caused the plans to be abandoned.

Chapter Ten

1744 was a leap year starting on a Wednesday so, there would be plenty of talk about marriage, which caused a furore amongst all the young ladies. Thomas, whose health problems were still with him, had decided to visit London and Bath. London, because he had been called there due to Emma's illness. He felt frustrated and ill at the thought that if she did not get well, he would have lost all his family. This was a most anxious time for him and on April the 5th he wrote to his cousin Mr William Owen of Porkington from London.

> *'Dear Sir,*
>
> *I acknowledge the favour of yours and am much obliged for your kind concern and enquiry after my health which really hath been very indifferent all the winter and spring hitherto having plagued with the most violent colds and intermitting fever which lasts still it hankers about me with a great cough attending it of its bad consequences I am sufficiently apprehensive and to escape them I am determined to spend a month or five weeks at Bath being well advised under God I shall thereby find relief. My stay in town I do assure you is not very agreeable to me but as I came up purely for the benefit and advantage of my poor girl I could not leave her in a hurry but shall now soon quit it with greater satisfaction than I entered it: if my time and conveniency will permit I shall with the greatest pleasure accept of your invitation and wait for you at Porkington in my return if otherwise happens I hope you will excuse me would you but once vouchsafe to come to Cayrey I should esteem the visit as a most particular favour and believe me dear sir no person more welcome to what you there find than yourself. I hasten the sooner home in hopes of seeing you I delivered your message last night to Mr Pennant his curiosity rendered him somewhat suspicious but do believe that he continues a bluff and firm Patti one of his daughters is just recovered from the smallpox Cousin Lewis, I saw him some*

time ago and was much surprised to find him look so thin. I know where to meet Master Owen, I would make it my business to wait of him. I have not a word of news but what the public papers afford with my best regards and honourable service to Mrs Owen and Miss Owen I am dear sir your most affectionate obedient honourable servant.

T Rowlands'

So, Thomas spent some time in London with Emma until she was better, then went to Bath for the waters which obviously helped because he was able to attend court and other political meetings which was, according to Mother Roberts, a very good thing.

During April, *The Female Spectator* (a monthly) was founded by Elizabeth Haywood in England, the first periodical written for women by a woman. Thomas had purchased a copy whilst in London to give to Mother Roberts on his return. It was an anxious time yet there were so many interesting things happening which helped quell most misgivings.

The 'Cousin Lewis' mentioned by Thomas was William Owen's brother, the Reverend Lewis Owen D.D., rector of Barking in Essex (1725) and Wexham in Buckinghamshire (1742). Thomas must have been aware that he was ill; he died two years later.

The story of the war continued and in Mrs Margaret Griffith's letter we find reference to Prince William who later became the Duke of Cumberland. She is writing this to Mrs Owen at Porkington:

'Hon Madam,

Be so good as to pardon me for giving you this trouble and indulge me in the satisfaction I take in writing to you by which I have a second pleasure in hearing how yourself and Mr Owen and your dear little ones are whose health I am solicitous to know as well as render to you my humble thanks for the favour of your obliging as very entertaining letter which should be acknowledged by me sooner but forbore out of compliment to you Contrary to my inclination least tire you with my stupid stuff having nothing that is agreeable to acquaint you that Prince William of Bristol has taken a French privateer of 50 ton with abundance of small Arms and handcuffs with about 44 men, she is now here on her way to Bristol with only 6 Frenchmen the rest are sent by land and the Arms are taken by Prince William to go in quest of more Welshmen put about of her to bring it to Bristol, they are gone this tide.'

We learn a little of Caernarvon's history. Margaret Griffith then writes with some sadness of a friend:

'I lament the Death of Mrs Thomas, she died of Fever our Doctor tried his utmost skill to save her life by applying 12 blisters but all would not destroy her to her senses which she lost after keeping to her bed 3 days, tho not well a week afore was abroad Thursday and Delirious Wednesday and Died Thursday night the 31st May so that she was 12 days very ill. A good woman soon gone, that her husband to the last for we thought him declining daily before she died but since has picked up his crumbs and comforts himself with the thoughts of his being in a fair way of living which he prays heartily for she left a fine boy. Her family I am told will be home next week, but her father is altered his resolution upon her death and doth not come it is said they are much concerned. His relations are easily comforted.

Mr Wynne of Wern was married last week to Miss Williams of Llandegwning a pretty Lady of 17 they say with a good fortune. I hope Lady Longuervile's affairs are by this time in some sort adjusted. I heard she was at Chester my brother is gone to London from Bath and will soon be at home. He had not found any benefit by the waters as yet, but I am in hope he will as many doth after they leave the place. He is obliged to you and Cousin Owen for his kind enquiry after him. Mr Brynkir our Sheriff is given over by the bath physician and advised to come home, his father is with him, which is a loss in that family for his brother is but a loose young man. One of your players came here to act, but the company did not follow. I am sorry for poor Mrs Strudwick and Miss. I hope Master Owen is well and both young ladies and little Master. I beg my compliments to Mr Owen and that I am very grateful to Pretty Miss Margaret for remembering me for I often think of her smart replies and admire her with. Good Madam excuse this long letter and be so kind as to give my humble service to Mrs Margaret Godolphin with Compliments of Condolence for Lady Pendarves to her. Young Mr Griffith is a humble servant to you and Mr Owen he wishes he was able to write of him at Glynn, but we hope to see him here in his way. Mr Griffith hath not been well this 2 month he is gone thin with a continual pain in the breast and a cough which gives me great concern as has a very temperate liver and the weather fine yet it doth not leave him and he rides every day. I imagine you'll be glad I should not give you further trouble so will end it and ever be Dear Madam Your Most obedient, Humble servant to Command. Margaret Griffith Caernarvon June 1744.'

The 'Mrs Thomas' mentioned by Margaret Griffiths is Dorothy, the daughter of Thomas Wynn of Boduan and Glynllifon, who died in May 1744. She was married to William Thomas of Coed Helen.

William Wynne of Wern, Penmorfa, married Eleanor Williams, sole heiress after her brother and the daughter of the Reverend Griffith Williams of Llandegwning and Abercarn on June 8th, 1744. William Wynne bought Brynkir and Parc Llanfrothen from Sir Thomas Prendergast.

Then Margaret hopes that Lady Longueville's affairs are by this time adjusted. Lady Longueville was William Owen's sister, Elizabeth. She had married Sir Thomas Longueville of Flintshire, but there was trouble, and an acrimonious separation took place in 1735. She would barrage her brother to get a reasonable settlement for her. She complained, 'I am used as if I had been a common whore to be turned out in such a hurry.' Sir Thomas said he would cut his throat if I came under the same roof as him. Sir Thomas Longueville had decided to live with his mistress and make his sons legitimate. By 1740, the year

William Owen married Mary Godolphin, Longueville's affairs were in chancery.

Mrs Strudwick and Miss Strudwick were also in some financial difficulty. Henry Strudwick had married Mary Broughton when she was 14 years old in 1714 and was well off. They had three sons, Henry, Edward, and William, and lived in St Andrews, Holborn, London. Mary Broughton died aged 21 and Mr Strudwick fought the courts demanding part of her legacy, bequeathed through her parents. He fought many years and in the end Mary Broughton's legacy was left to her sons. Her husband died in poverty. Henry Strudwick the son married Mary Hanmer of Pantre-pant in 1740 and they had a daughter called Mary, but once he inherited his mother's money, he tried to divorce his wife and went off to Jamaica, married and started another family. His plantation was called Pantre-pant, a 250-acre farm.

It is obvious that Mrs Mary Owen of Porkington knew Mary Hanmer from her time in London. Her house was always open to those less fortunate until matters could be settled. Then Mrs Margaret Godolphin, known as Aunt Peggy, was a crotchety old dame who was the heiress to Abernant. She came from another line of Godolphins. She had married first Francis Hoblyn by whom she had a son, and then Sir William Pendarves who suffered from terrible bouts of uncontrollable temper. She was left with the upkeep of the Abernant estate. Mrs Griffiths sent Mrs Owen her condolences for Lady Pendarves, who had died on June 30th, 1743.

Porkington was obviously a very busy household, with three children, and Mr Owen busy looking after matters of the estate, as well as supporting William Price of Rhiwlas, Richard Lyster and Sir Watkin Williams Wynn when standing in the elections. Being left with a vast amount of debt when he became the heir was a tremendous responsibility for a young man just ten years of age. He was released from some of his debts by his cousin, Mary Tannant, between 1726 and 1729, and he proceeded to renovate Porkington, adding a whole new wing, which was not finished until 1735. Having to keep up with what was going on the country was also very important to them and they learnt that golf was very popular. It was also the year when the rules of golf were formed, 13 in all. There must have been rules dating back to the origin of the game otherwise how could players have squared off in competitions? What those 13 rules were, nobody knows. At least until the mid-18th century, when the first known written rules of golf were put together by the Gentleman Golfers of Leith, later known as the Honourable Company of the Edinburgh Golfers based at Muirfield. The rules were written for the annual challenge for the Edinburgh Silver Cup on March 7th, 1744.

Many interesting things were happening. Besides various countries declaring war on one another, this was the year that Sir George Anson returned having circumnavigated the globe. This was during 'the War of Jenkins's Ear' between Britain and Spain. Anson reached the Cape of Good Hope on June 15th, 1744, with only 335 of his men left out of 961. Most had died due to scurvy and the worn-out state of his remaining ships. He became Admiral of the Fleet and 1st Baron Anson and was elected Member of Parliament for Hendon in Yorkshire in 1744. His charts, which were captured on his ship, added many islands (and phantom islands) to the British knowledge of the pacific.

In London, in the library of the Madrigal Society, is the earliest Minute Book, dated 1744. This society was created by John Immyns at the Anchor & Crown, Whitefriars, London. He gathered a few people who had spent their lives practising psalmody. They were mostly mechanics, some were weavers from Spitalfields, while others had various trades and occupations. The Society lasted for 215 years.

Another sport which came to be very popular was cricket. It had started around the 16th century, having originated in the southeast of England and by the 18th century was regarded as a national sport. 'Early days in Kent', chapter two of *Barclays World of Cricket*, states that in 1719 Kent played London and it is claimed that this constituted the first county match. Frederick Lilywhite's *Scores and Biographies*, covering cricket from the mid-18th century to the later part of the 19th, records the first organised matches between Kent and All England, played in the artillery ground in 1744. Kent won the match by one wicket.

Emma was home again for the holidays and felt that really her time at this finishing school was not teaching her anything. Thomas and Mother Roberts thought differently. Thomas could see her behaviour was far better, but he doubted that anyone would be able to cure her temper. This time Emma accompanied Thomas and Mother Roberts to church, and once again Mother Roberts was able to explain how Emma's mother, Elin had, after her confirmation in 1713, presented the church with a large silver chalice. Emma became interested in learning about her family and their contribution to society. Her grandfather, William Roberts, Mother Roberts' husband, had been a high sheriff of Anglesey in 1712. Mother Roberts thought that at long last Emma was showing some recognition of her family's contribution to society and to the life on Anglesey. When most of the congregation had left, Mother Roberts walked to where her husband was buried in the floor of the church and Emma followed. Then Mother Roberts took her to where she had had a memorial put up on the wall which read as follows:

> 'In memory of William Roberts of Cayrey, Esq
> A person deservedly beloved by all who really knew him.
> He was a loving husband even to fondness,
> A Tender Parent A true Friend.
> A good neighbour, a kind Master.
> He was a man of extensive charity of a merciful and forgiving temper.
>
> And in all his dealings exactly just. To complete his character, he was not only punctual in his private and family devotion, but a constant attender on the public service of the Church and guest of the Lords Table.
>
> Having thus performed his duty to God and man and so done all the real business of life, he was permitted to change this for the better, on the 7th February in the 30 year of his age and of our Lord 1715, very much lamented, but by none more than his disconsolate relict, who caused this monument to be erected to the memory of one of the best of husbands.
>
> He married Emma the daughter of David Williams of Glan-Alaw Esq, by whom he left one daughter named Ellen.'

Emma had become very quiet. A cold shiver ran through her as she digested all that she had read. She looked around the church and thought how generous it was to have buried her grandfather inside the church and also for commissioning the memorial. Perhaps it was time to ask about different members of her family. She would have to learn not only of her Anglesey background, but that of Caernarvonshire too. Mother Roberts enthused about how proud her husband had been when Ellen, their daughter, was born; he had taken such a keen interest in her welfare and wrote to different members of his family inviting them to her christening. He wrote to his uncle and aunt, Mr John and Mrs Ann Owen of Penrhos. Emma, who had hardly known her mother, could not imagine what she looked like; and Thomas assured her that she was indeed very beautiful. They meandered down the road, with Thomas walking his horse alongside them chatting away until they arrived at Caerau.

After a delicious lunch, Thomas went to his study and Mother Roberts sat in a comfortable chair by the fire. Emma asked questions about various members of her family. Mother Roberts told her that Caerau was very old and that Gruffudd Llwyd who lived at Penhwnllys, Llangoed had bought the land and had Caerau built. He lived in 1375. During the Tudor reign, a descendant of Robert ab Ifan, from Beaumaris, and his wife, Margaret, who was the daughter of Richard Johnson Hen, a well-known merchant in the town, inherited Caerau and a grandson of theirs, Robert Roberts, was the first to settle there. He married three times. His son, Owen Roberts, married Catherine, daughter and heiress of Thomas Roberts of Castellior. They had six children and William Roberts, Mother Roberts' husband, was one of them. A descendant of Robert Roberts, known as Gabriel Roberts, was a prolific businessman and through hard work ended up owning most of the merchant shops at Beaumaris during those early times. He invested his money in land and established the Castellior estate. He died in 1614.

Mother Roberts went on to tell a little about her own father, David Williams of Glanalaw, who had married Ann, daughter and heiress of William Morris of Llansilin. He had a brother, William, who became speaker of the House of Commons in 1680 and 1681. He was also solicitor general to King James II. William became Sir William Williams and generations later his descendants became the Watkin Williams Wynns of Wynnstay. Mother Roberts's mother died the year Emma was born. She encouraged Emma to know about her family: she was an heiress in her own right and would be a catch for anyone, taking Caerau and Plas-y-Nant with her. Emma yawned as it was a lot to take in. Mother Roberts asked one of the maids for tea. When Emma had left the room, Mother Roberts went to Thomas and told him that she had explained quite a lot to Emma and instructed him that it was his turn now to inform her about his family, which he agreed to do when feeling better.

It was autumn and soon time for the balls, right up to Christmas. Emma was being escorted by Owen Meyrick, home again to see his father. It was no surprise that most of the nobility, seeing them together often, thought that they would marry.

Thomas was sitting in his study, contemplating what he was going to do once Emma married. He would be quite lonely. He thought about Owen Meyrick, a constant companion to Emma whenever there was a ball. Somehow, he felt that Owen did it out of duty. He felt perhaps Emma could do better. He was wise enough never to pass any remarks, but he would have been quite satisfied had anything between Emma and Thomas Pennant taken place. He knew Thomas Pennant's father, and both had discussed the matter some time ago. He then remembered Emma stating that she would never marry until she was of age. He would have to watch his finances as sometimes things did not work out as well as he had hoped for.

It was announced that Owen Meyrick was at the door waiting for Emma. Thomas entertained him until Emma appeared all ready for the ball. Thomas couldn't help but admire her. He thought that she had grown to be quite a beautiful young woman.

In January, when it was Emma's birthday on the 13th, there was a ball at Plas Newydd, a place that Emma loved going to. This would mean a stay overnight and a lazy getting up in the morning. She had been given enough money to tip the maids and anyone else who looked after her, which was usually the man in charge of the horses. She was now 17 and looked forward to life as a whole. She hoped that she would be able to leave Caerau and get closer to society. The person she did not want to hurt was her father. He was always looking after her and she loved him very much. Emma had already written to Mrs Owen of Porkington:

'Dear Madam,

For the second time I've taken pen in hand with an intention to make an apology for my last which I fancy you took for a piece of an Old Arabian Manuscript but as being very well acquainted with Madam Owen's ingenuity I was assured if anybody could construe the translation of it she must be the person I find by all account you certainly intend for Bath the ensuing season: will you marvel much at my impudence if I desire to bear you company thither in short this is a case my Papa has promised me a Bath journey when he met with a convenient opportunity and hearing of your expedition to that place I made a motion to him concerning it and he most willingly agreed to the expense if dear Mrs Owen would be so extremely kind to permit me under the shadow of her wing, but if I should be anyways troublesome I would much rather decline it than be an incumbrance to you however; as I flatter myself to the contrary, I hope my suit will be granted by dear Mrs Owen. You can't imagine how anxious my Grandmama is and has largely contributed to my hoped for jaunts dear Mrs Madam Honour me with a line next post as means of putting an end to this state of uncertainty I at present lie under, and let me know my doom if favourable or otherwise will ever obliged dear Madam your most obedient Humble Servant Emma Rowlands.

PS.
Pray my best respects and compliments to Mr Owen, and trust that he'll be a powerful advocate in this cause, that I so earnestly petition for, and as I've so often experienced his kindness, I don't doubt of his clemency in this case as to what has already passed. My Papa and Grandmama desire their compliments to you, Mr Owen, Masters & Young ladies and if you please mine to your Governante whom I wrote two posts ago.'

Now she had to be patient. The winter months passed with the usual stories of plagues or influenza, which carried off far too many people and children. The stories of six or eight coffins standing in the churchyards was very poignant and the constant plight of small villages when they lost so many to the various illnesses. It was cold and Caerau managed to keep a good fire going which helped, especially when people called with bad news about the death of someone both Mrs Roberts and Thomas knew.

Emma seemed pleased with life, especially if the news agreed that she could go to Bath. Now she was busy enjoying herself with the ball at Plas Newydd. At one ball it was announced that it was her 17th birthday, which went on for quite a long time. However, things would soon change. Owen Meyrick went back to London, and it was soon heard that he was to be betrothed to Hester, a wealthy heiress and the daughter of John Putland of London. Thomas felt that he had been right all along regarding the young Owen Meyrick. Emma felt that he was genuine though Thomas had always felt otherwise. He was glad to hear the news and it would give him time before Emma became interested in anyone else.

As the weather began to show signs of getting worse, Emma decided that she had to stay in to avoid catching cold or flu. She would sit with her father listening about his family. Emma learnt that her grandfather, John Rowlands, was a banker in Lombard Street, London. He was in a very good position to help many who inherited properties in Wales which they did not want. Many did not want to travel to Wales, especially North Wales, as the roads were very poor. Most of them brought up around London felt that they were at the centre of the universe. Therefore, John Rowlands did well, as he was able to purchase many of these properties, building up his own estate. He was born around 1645 and he married Frances Owen, the third daughter of William and Catherine Owen of Porkington and Clenennau. Frances was the granddaughter of the celebrated royalist, Sir John Owen of Clenennau, vice-admiral of North Wales and governor of Conwy Castle for Charles I. Frances was born on May 27th, 1665. John and Frances had 11 children including two sets of twins. He underwrote many debentures for land sales in North Wales and also purchased estates around Plas-y-Nant when the original owners either needed money urgently or had died, whereby the land had to be divided amongst heirs. Plas-y-Nant was built for John Rowlands in 1671, 11 years after the restoration of Charles II. He continued to enlarge his estate, buying more property around Betws Garmon and Beddgelert. He already owned a substantial nucleus including land up to the summit of Snowdon, inherited from his ancestors. He also purchased property in Clynnog, Llandwrog, Llanwnda, Nantlle and Caernarvon. Plas Puleston, Caernarvon appears frequently amongst his accounts when the Spicer family lived there. He was also the owner of Graeanog, Maesog and Bachwen in Clynnog.

Thomas told Emma that the Plas-y-Nant estate was his as he had inherited it from his brother, Richard, who had died at 23 years of age. The money collected for various properties in rent was allocated to his sisters and they never let him forget that. However, as Thomas pointed out, Emma would be an heiress one day. She would be taking his lands and her grandmothers into the marriage when it happened. Thomas had resided at Plas Maesincla, Caernarvon, which his father bought from Roberts Lawrence who had no issue. That was where he lived when Thomas met his wife Ellin, and in accordance with the marriage agreement, he left to live at Caerau. He had three sisters, one of whom was Emma's favourite aunt, her Aunt Margaret in Caernarvon. Elizabeth had married Hugh Davies of Caerhun. Catherine was married to Captain Samuel Wyn of Glan-yr-Afon Bach, who was a constant pain with his demands for money. He was always ready to take Thomas and Margaret to court. This feud went on for years.

The year came to an end and Emma had learnt about her family on both sides. She had never thought of herself as an heiress. But snob as she was, she certainly liked the idea that she was a very good catch. Before any further thoughts about her suitability as a wife, she wanted to enjoy herself and visit Mrs Owen at Porkington.

View of the façade of Porkington (later called Brogyntyn).

Exterior view of Porkington (later called Brogyntyn).

Chapter Eleven

Having been busy sorting his accounts out, Thomas realised that he had much to do, so that when Emma did marry everything would be in order. There were difficulties with tenants unable to pay their rents, many very late in doing so. Margaret was always very encouraging and had often been the silent helping hand when matters seemed tight financially. Both were annoyed with the constant threat of being taken to court by Captain Samuel Wyn. Margaret always asked her husband for a loan so that they were not taken to court. Both disliked this captain very much. Thomas felt that 1745 was not going to be a good year for him. He was quiet, not much fun, and Mrs Roberts was worried. She felt that Thomas really needed a doctor, but he would not accept the facts.

Thomas was thinking about the April sessions. It would be a change to visit Beaumaris and enjoy the company of many of his friends and be able to talk about various issues concerning the country. Mr William Bulkeley told a group, whilst having a drink, that a new hospital was being built in the Fitzrovia area of London which was to be called the Middlesex Hospital and that they were hoping that doctors would be walking the wards by 1746. It was to be a teaching hospital. This discussion went on for some time and Thomas was glad to rest and take his leave of his companions.

The usual bouts of flu were once again affecting many of the poor and the inevitable load of coffins was a sad reflection.

Emma learnt through a magazine sent to her by one of her friends that a new dance was fashionable in France, called the quadrille. This excited her and she hoped that it would soon be popular here. She made a note so that she could tell Mrs Owen of Porkington.

Having returned to Caerau, Thomas spent a few days entertaining Emma. She went with him to Amlwch where a boat had arrived with various wood. Thomas was looking for a some that was the same as Mother Roberts had in her part of Caerau. He needed it to be as near in colour as could be expected, then Mother Roberts's part of the house would be complete again. She felt very warm with her wood panelling around the room. Thomas bought a piece which he felt was suitable and then called at Llannerchymedd on the way back to ask the carpenter if he would call and fit it. They had a nice day together and Thomas had been trying to find out if there was anyone else that Emma might feel kindly towards. But try as hard as he could, Emma told him quite plainly that she wanted to wait until she was of age. They rode home laughing and singing.

Mother Roberts had been to the fair at Llanfechell and bought some vegetables and a piece of beef, ready to have the maids in the kitchen cook up some healthy food that would warm Thomas and Emma to keep them well and strong. Thomas continuously felt under the weather and his asthma played him up. Mrs Roberts and Emma were worried about him. Emma went off to stay with her Aunt Margaret in Caernarvon for a break which she enjoyed immensely. She was also very fond of her cousin, Hugh Griffith, and felt nearly as close to him as she had done to her brother, William. Her cousin, William, called home so that he could see her. She liked him but he was always quiet and studious, though they had a good laugh over a joke told by Hugh. In September, Emma wrote to Mrs Owen.

'Dear Madam,

I had the favour of yours this morning for which I return you a thousand thanks your being so expeditious in answering my letters is like fruits of your friendship and good nature. My papa is much better though a sort of invalid. He uses but little mortification and considers lent as carnival time.

There have been here a set of jolly bottle companions this week which I believe has undone the work of our physician. Doctor O endeavoured to complain about begins with a note as, Esquire Owen. I am very sick today and grunts woefully he hasn't received any answer about Mrs Povey. I had a letter a few days ago from Miss Williams wherein she mentioned Tom's death but no further particulars.

I hear by all hands Miss Tryggar is in a bad way but that her Mama intends going with her to Bath which I wish may be of service to her and now dear Madam Owen for your impossible imprecise suppose I told you a gentleman that it would not be agreeable to me to marry till I come of age, in answer Papa says "Phoo". I like you should sooner whose inclinations must follow for both I cannot and likewise suppose a gentleman should tell Mr Rowlands by mistake my affairs and I shall take the first opportunity of convincing him of his error and not do so and suppose a suitor promises to be in the country such a time and the next postpones the journey for perhaps a month or two according as it suits conveniences and last of all I should make an answer when father proposes another person, indeed Sir, I like Mr… much better and he immediately says, 'Why Em you seem to be assiduous about the matter than the gentleman for I haven't heard a word from him or nay of his friends that he intended remaining pessimist.

Must I tell him I was convinced he would deliver a Billie Doux by way of confirming what I had said and was what I had not concluded to do. I don't pretend to understand what method should be taken in such cases and if I do ungenerous notions I've for want of knowledge for my goodwill I won't say not use any gentleman especially Mr… whom you must know was not indifferent to me, you are welcome to believe what you please about the coronet. It is true I prefer the owner before Dr Owen, but would you be much surprised if matters fall out yet in the negative. I am sorry a suit of clothes should wrong me in good opinion of the honest party in King George's dominions but the other. I believe in my conscience your mind to try my matter here you accuse me of unsteady principles, vanity, no generosity, and Lord knows what. I wish I may be able to compose my temper and conclude as I ought.

Dear Madam
Your ever oblige and humble servant.
E. Rowlands. Papa and Grandmama join me in compliments to Mr Owen and your family.

I remember my Dear Mrs Owen you make many complaints that is some understanding person had been with your things perhaps might have been otherwise, but you find Mrs… whom I take to be persons of judgement in many disorders *as mistaken so oversight may be the subject to the most penetrating of all. I hope you are convinced on it whether Mr Griffith might not again be too confident. I cannot pretend to say but sure them informatory cases are horrible and may deceive the best. Colds and fevers sweep off numbers of the common people this way. Papa has lost three of his servants by this epidemical distemper which rages in our part. The death of Mrs Harri Powis a soon greatly surprised me by what I've heard of that lady I should... suppose the spirit would soon surrender. I must agree with you that even the gays and young are not immortal a few more instances of this kind will make- for fear of summons. I hope the giddy are excluded till better prepared.'*

Emma was obviously having difficulty in understanding the flirtations of men and she was also determined that she would not marry until she was of age. Now that she was 18, Thomas felt that she might find a suitor sooner and wasn't quite sure why Emma wanted to wait until she was 21. However, life went on and Thomas decided to write to William Owen at Porkington.

'September 18th, 1745.

Dear Sir,

The favour of your last ought long since to have been acknowledged and no excuse can be pleaded for my dilatoriness except an indolent aversion to writing and my imagining that the affair with Mr Meyrick would have over this have been one way or other determined but little or nothing hath been done and I can't resolve you as yet how twill turn out, but should it go on I hope liberty will be indulge me of nominating you trustee the settling of my daughter in the Country so advantageously joined with the prospect of rendering my circumstances very more be strong motives. I must ingenuously own that induced me to enter into this treaty which being so disagreeable to you and other friends gives me great vexation and concern from which without the greatest blemish upon my honoured good name and integrity do fear tis impossible for me to disengage myself provided them come up to the terms demanded am now sensible that sort of people I have to deal with therefore the more obliged for your kind caution which I shall endeavour to observe and call in some friend to my assistance for my own judgement I shall not venture to depend upon: since your business would not permit you to come over tis a great question to me if ever I shall have the pleasure of seeing you in my poor habitation where no person would be more sincerely welcome I hope that country air hath quite restored your health and that cousin Thomas Owen is upon recovery: with my compliments and best respects to Mrs Owen Master and Miss Owen I am sir Yours most sincere affectionate obedient humble servant,

Thomas Rowlands.'

Why Thomas was working so hard to try and marry Emma off leaves a question. Emma had found Mother Roberts far more understanding of her feelings and had long since decided that she was a better confidant that many of her friends. She had told Mother Roberts what Thomas had said over a certain gentleman and found Mother Roberts to be quite sympathetic. She listened to what Emma had to say and when Emma left her, she would sit and smile and thought she was lucky to be there for her. It should really be a mother's place and poor Emma did not have a mother.

As confused as Emma was about her relationship with men, she confided in her cousin, Hugh of Caernarvon, who thought it quite funny that she should need any support. He had felt that she was more than capable of handling her suitors from having met her at various balls. That, however, was not the point. How was a girl to feel when they accompanied her to balls and sometimes took her out, then they disappeared and even got married to other people?

Thomas was worrying as the year was not good for many farmers, and he wondered whether he could even afford a wedding for Emma. Through his worry he very nearly forgot Emma's birthday, but Mother Roberts had seen to it that he didn't. She gave Emma a beautiful brooch which she had bought from the travelling Jewish man who always had very beautiful items to show.

During October 1745, Thomas received *The Gentleman's Magazine*, where the words and music for 'God Save the King' were to be found. This was done of course so that the magazine would reach as many as possible in the hope that people would learn the words and music.

On January 22nd Thomas wrote to the Hon. Doctor Wynne at Bodewryd asking for a loan.

> 'Honoured Sir,
>
> *Tis with great regret and confusion that I make my application to you for the loan of a 150 pounds upon either my note or bond the interest I shall endeavour to pay punctually and also the principal sum upon proper notice given: if this my request can be complied with you will kindly oblige sir your most obedient humble servant,*
>
> Thomas Rowlands.'

He received a reply.

> 'Honoured Sir,
>
> Bodewryd, Jan 22nd, 1745.
> Hugh Hughes set out for Denbigh shire and will return next week. He shall wait upon you and accommodate you with the sum that you are pleased to make application for.
>
> Mr Rowlands. Jan22nd 1745.'

Soon Thomas would feel better knowing that he had £150 which he would hopefully put away in case there was a wedding. He couldn't wait for the year to end. Mother Roberts was full of hope that when Emma was ready, and at the age she felt comfortable with to get married, it would happen. She had gone through something similar with her own daughter. She well remembered the times when her daughter was distressed about some gentleman or other; then there was the laughter at all the funny things that happened until she met Thomas. The trauma of life that hit them with the loss of Elin and the baby, then Frances, followed by William. But Mother Roberts never let anything pull her down too far. She considered herself lucky that she lived at Caerau and was able to look after Emma to the best of her ability. Emma would always visit her grandmother in a hurry and spill out all that had happened until poor Mother Roberts's head was in a spin. She had to laugh at some of the things and how Emma described some of the gentlemen. Some, Mother Roberts felt, would have ridden away very quickly. They had lived with her fantasy about Thomas Pennant who obviously preferred his work to anything else but married in 1759. Then there was Owen Meyrick who had accompanied Emma to many of the Anglesey Balls, then went off to London without saying anything, later to get married to Hester, a wealthy heiress. No wonder that Emma was confused.

There were more deaths, and everyone felt saddened at seeing eight or more coffins needing to be buried. This affected Emma too. She couldn't come to terms with all this death, and she questioned herself and her father about it. Thomas asked if she remembered being born and Emma said, 'No'.

'Well,' he carried on, 'that is exactly what death will feel like.'

She questioned why so many died of these various plagues. Thomas said that it was a very sad part of life, but that with the news of doctors now able to find a cure for some ailments, it could only be hoped that they would find cures for these constant plagues and that the little children would have a better hope of living longer and into adulthood. Mother Roberts tried to explain that perhaps some families were so poor that they lived in very small spaces and that cleanliness needed more attention. Then the little children would not catch these plagues which carried them away. Emma tried hard to understand, always afraid that she would lose more of her dear friends. She went for a ride on her pony down to the sea, the air there would clear doubtful thoughts and she would also be able to think about someone else whom she might want to marry.

She was in a much better mood on her return and Mother Roberts suggested that there were still plenty of men around that she could marry. The best way was to make a list and tick them off should they not suit. Emma thought the idea was splendid and could not help laughing at the way Mother Roberts was busy trying to find her a husband. Mother Roberts was busy asking about eligible young men related to many of the families around Anglesey that she knew. She was determined that she would find someone.

Following the bad weather and the wind that shook everything in its wake, they all waited for the new year to come sooner rather than later.

Chapter Twelve

Several thunderstorms had created chaos over the island, and many felt disillusionment as they saw the devastation. Emma, however, had been singing each time the thunder clapped around Caerau.

Thomas was busy having to organise his plans for his estate in Caernarvonshire. He stayed with his sister who had always been a great support for him, and he loved the long conversations he had with his brother-in-law. He explained to his brother-in-law that he felt a sort of apathy amongst his tenants, as they seemed reluctant to try to pay their rents. One or two were always first to pay and even though times were difficult, they paid half until things improved. Thomas had gone along with this idea for some time, but he couldn't afford not to have an income. His brother-in-law was always ready to help, but Thomas felt that he couldn't keep asking him. He refused what help John Griffith offered and explained to his sister, Margaret, that he felt he had to manage as he was; things are bound to get better, he said. He had always tried to be fair to his tenants, but as the lack of full payments had gone on for several years, he felt that he had to persuade them that it had to stop or leave their abodes.

He visited many of them around Clynnog and Llanwnda only to find most of them with very long faces and their wives busy making food and grunting in agreement when their husbands complained. When he entered one of the farms, he was shocked to see that the farmer's wife was cooking a pheasant. He questioned them about it and said that the spread of food was like a banquet rather than an everyday meal. He told them that things could not be as bad as they pretended. Suddenly the farmer went to a chest at the corner of the room and settled his debt. Then he asked Thomas to stay and have some food. Having had a pleasant meal, Thomas excused himself, wanting to visit other tenants. One other tenant out of 13 offered to pay his debt; the others were reluctant and said that they needed time to see how the hay yield would be. Having argued for over an hour at one place, Thomas felt he had to leave and come back six months later, making clear that there would be no compromise then.

He returned to his sister's and told her and her husband what had happened. Later that day, he visited one or two tenants of houses in Caernarvon and of course Plas Maesincla which had been his home before he married. He had to return to Caerau the following day as he had business to see to on April 20th.

News regarding the Jacobites, was that Charles Edward Stuart was determined to regain the crown for his father. It was all the talk during the court sessions at Beaumaris. William Bulkeley showed his distain towards the Bulkeleys of Baron Hill, knowing that that they had supported the Jacobites. Many others were wary of them for the same reason.

Mother Roberts had been busy whilst Thomas was away. She had new curtains put up in his bedroom and that of Emma, matching the rug she had made for her previously. Her room looked better and cosier, and Emma made sure that she remembered it so that when she got married, she would have an idea of how things should be done. Mother Roberts was pleased to hear from Thomas and Emma that they were delighted with the new curtains. She made them a cup of tea and then said she was going out to the fair at Llanfechell where she bought some meat and some fish along with a variety of herbs. She always felt for those selling, especially when there were not many people bothering to visit the fair. It was a hard struggle for some of the sellers and she always gave something to the children, who usually hung around pretending to help. She had for many years tried to inform Emma of how lucky she was, having most things done for her and that she should consider what it was like to struggle, trying to grow things to be sold. Emma would just walk out of the room when Mother Roberts gave one of her famous lectures. She and Thomas clashed over Emma. He blamed Mother Roberts for spoiling her, and she would blame Thomas for not supporting her when she told Emma off.

Josiah Wedgewood was a well-known English potter. Pioneering mass production at his Etruria Works near Stoke-on-Trent, he became famous for his cream ware and best known for his jasper ware, which gave expression to the contemporary interest in the revival of classical art. The fashion for enamelling in colours and transfer work produced delightful bowls delightful punch bowls and jugs in Staffordshire ware, with portraits and inscriptions upon them. A punch bowl with the portrait of the Young Pretender must have been seen at many secret Jacobite meetings after the rising of 1745. Sir Watkin Williams Wynn was a great supporter of the Young Pretender and had been the founder in 1723 of the 'Circle of the White Rose', the Jacobite club which used to meet regularly at Wynnstay and other houses in the Wrexham district. His Parliamentary career was very important to him, and he kept his admiration of the Young Pretender to himself and his friends. He had promised many times that he would hide the Young Pretender. Sir Watkin was related to Mother Roberts. William Williams of Chwaen Isaf, Llantrisant, became Speaker of the House of Commons. He was the son of William Williams who was a brother to Mother Roberts' father, David Williams of Glanalaw, Llantrisant. The Bulkeley family in Anglesey were known to be Jacobites. In the inventory of Baron Hill in 1822, it was found that there were two busts of the two Pretenders, also secret letters addressed to the head of the family detailing Jacobites fortunes in 1715.

Mother Roberts began travelling to visit her family spread along most corners of Anglesey, asking about eligible young men and warning that Emma was not to hear a word of it. Several young men were proposed, and the funny thing was that most of them suggested the new Lord Bulkeley. Mother Roberts rode back to Caerau to think about the situation. After dinner, while Thomas was sitting, relaxed, she told him that maybe she had found the answer to Emma's dilemma. Thomas gave a little snort and wondered what Mother Roberts had been up to, but she was cute, she did not tell Thomas who she had in mind. She wanted time to sort it out and arrange for them to meet without Emma having a clue who it was that had arranged it. Months went by when suddenly Emma received an invitation to attend a ball at Baron Hill. The excitement this caused was not just between Mother Roberts and Emma; the kitchen staff and Thomas all cheered.

Having attended the ball and met Lord Bulkeley, Emma was in a dream. Shortly afterwards, she decided that she was going to Porkington. Her attitude was that if he really liked her he would have to wait, and he would have to show her that he missed her. Her father was glad as he had already arranged with Mr Owen that Mrs Owen would introduce Emma to local society, so that if she did happen to marry well, she would be well prepared. Emma went off to Porkington and the Owens introduced to her to as many people as possible. She wanted to continue her stay with the Owens but her father was anxious, and on September 8th, 1746, he wrote to Mr Owen.

> 'Dear Sir,
>
> My attending the Assizes and some other business detaining me abroad prevented me from sooner acknowledge the favour of yours which I thankfully obliged for and infinitely so for Mr and Mrs Owen's extraordinary kindness and civilities to my daughter such a favour I can no ways retaliate but shall ever remember them with the most sincere pleasure and gratitude: since tis Mrs Owen's and your desire if Emma should make a longer stay I shall most readily indulge with that satisfaction being fully assured that she can nowhere so much benefit and improve as by the so long a visit, conversation and example of such good company though really ashamed less a visit might prove over tedious and troublesome do heartily wish that Mrs Owen do not over hurry and fatigue herself in showing Emma the Country but if conducive to her health am greatly rejoiced that such company as Emma's doth in the least contribute thereto. When Sir you see Sir Watkin Williams and Mr Evans pay my respects and humble service; our harvest is very backward by reason of so great rains which have fallen of late: no news worth imparting: My best respects and honourable service attend you, your lady, masters, and Miss Owen's I am sir Your most sincere obliged Humble servant.
>
> T Rowlands.
> Pray my blessing to Emma.'

Mother Roberts went around her family announcing that Emma had met Lord Bulkeley and that if all went well, she felt that he might ask her to marry him. Her family teased her by telling her that Lord Bulkeley was already married in secret, which brought her down a little. She wondered whether it was a tease or not. If he was married, then she would have to carry on until she found a suitable husband for Emma.

Thomas was not keen to let Emma overstay her welcome. He wrote to her hoping that she would be back before her birthday on January 13th when she would be 19. Emma returned just before her birthday and Thomas arranged a very nice meal for her, also inviting Lord Bulkeley to join them. Everything went well though Emma seemed reluctant to show much interest in Lord Bulkeley. She was probably showing off and showing that she was spoilt. Lord Bulkeley was intrigued with Emma. She was very beautiful, he thought, and from that time kept asking her to attend the balls at various venues throughout Anglesey.

Thomas felt it best to leave matters and continue as though he knew nothing. He was soon off to London where he hoped to enjoy a little gambling. He was never a winner, but he enjoyed meeting the people he knew. The news was that there had been an execution of the Lords of Kilmarnock, Lovat and Balmerina for the part they took in the 1745 rising. Arthur Elphenstone was the 6th lord and William Boyd was the 4th earl, Scottish peerages. George II felt that he had been betrayed by them, when they showed their allegiance to the Young Pretender. They were executed on August 18th, 1746. Voltaire had produced a philosophical tale called *Zadig*, where the hero tries in vain to improve mankind. David Garrick was in *A Miss in her Teens*, a farce in two acts. Thomas Gray had written *Ode on the Death of a Favourite Cat*. This was Horace Walpole's cat, called Selima. Hogarth had produced satirical prints on 'Industry and Idleness'. Handel wrote 'Joshua' and 'Alexander Balus', which was an oratorio, with the latter containing music for the mandolin. Henry Flitcroft redesigned Woburn Abbey in the style of Inigo Jones. Flitcroft, the architect, was the son of a labourer who had trained as a carpenter. He was working at Burlington House when he fell from a scaffold and broke his leg. While recuperating, the young Lord Burlington noticed his talent for drawing and made him his draughtsman. This launched his career and brought him fame. When browsing in one of the bookshops in London, Thomas saw Hannah Glasse's book, *The Art of Cookery Made Plain and Easy*. He thought he should buy a copy for Emma, not for her to cook but as a guide to serving meals of a high standard. Should she not like it, then Mother Roberts could have it. He would think about it, and he walked back to accompany his friend to the theatre.

The following day Thomas decided to go back and revisit the bookshop and bought a copy of Hannah Glasse's book on cookery. He was looking forward to returning home if only to see Emma's face when he presented her with the book. London had been much warmer than Anglesey during his visit and that was the one thing he would not enjoy on going back. He knew that once again there would be coffins piled outside the churches, with many of his staff either ill or dead. He really found it difficult to cope with such difficult times. It was March and he looked forward to the following year. He did enjoy his visits to London. He was far more knowledgeable of the world after he had been there and met up with his friends.

Mother Roberts had a good old chuckle, she thought it was a good idea to give Emma such a book. During dinner, Thomas presented Emma with the book and as he had thought, her expression was total disbelief. It was meant to be for her benefit and Mother Roberts told her that she might find one or two more books like this, should she marry. Thomas joined in with Mother Roberts. He said to Mother Roberts that Emma could start choosing different dishes as a practice. Mother Roberts told Thomas that she well remembered receiving a list of all the things that she would need to prepare a house suitable to live in, but that she never found out who had sent it. She advised Thomas not to mention it to Emma otherwise they might have another storm of temper. They both retired and looked forward to the new year.

The year 1747 started rather dull, everyone had to sort out their year's list and moving money from one project to another.

A few days later Emma came in from riding and announced that she was thinking of going to Porkington. Her father had enough work sorting out his tenants, setting out what was to be planted in different fields, ordering seeds and various other things, besides his court duties, which he took very seriously. Emma would complain about the boredom of Caerau. She was restless and Thomas wondered whether he was right to have asked Mr Owen of Porkington to introduce her to important people in the area. He would talk with Emma and see if he could make her understand how difficult things were now but he promised that he would write to ask if she could visit Mr and Mrs Owen. 'Let me get the Assizes over with at Beaumaris,' he told her, 'then it will be nearly May, with the weather more favourable for you to travel.' She should by now have learnt how busy her father was at the beginning of each year. Now she was 20, she should behave more like a lady and have some understanding of the difficulties of life. Thomas thought of the times Mother Roberts had rebuked him for spoiling Emma, and in a way, he had to agree with her.

It was 1747 and he felt that It would not be too long before someone asked for Emma's hand. He sat and wondered how it would affect him; but then that is what every father wants for his daughter, he thought, trying to console himself. He asked Mother Roberts to send Emma in so that he could talk with her. Emma came and sat opposite her father and started to complain about Caerau. Thomas grew a little angry and told her that she had a group of friends and that she should either visit them or ask them over to Caerau. It wasn't all bad when she had all the comforts that Caerau could afford, plenty of good food and freedom to do as she wished. She had another year to go before she would inherit her mother's money and he would also make sure that she had enough. "What are you complaining about?" he asked her. Emma could not answer. All she could think about was to encourage him to write to Porkington, but Thomas was adamant that he would write when convenient to him and he walked out.

Emma left and decided to visit a cousin of hers. At least they could natter about various people they knew and have a laugh and perhaps a game of cards and she would return to Caerau later and quietly go up to her room so that she did not face Thomas after he had rebuked her that morning. She would just have to be patient and wait until he wrote to Porkington.

As promised, having organised the work around the estate, Thomas wrote to Mr Owen at Porkington. All they had to do now was wait for a reply. Thomas came and went, always busy, and then one day a letter arrived from his cousin, agreeing to Emma's visit. She was delighted and couldn't wait to go. Thomas told her that first they had to make sure there was a boat able to take her over from Beaumaris to the Lavan Sands, before she could take a coach to Wrexham and then another on to Porkington. She was so excited that Thomas felt a little hurt and again wondered whether he had done the right thing in asking them to introduce her to society. She left at the end of May with such a huge trunk full of clothes that you would have thought that she was moving house. Her grandmother wished her well and said that she would continue to try and find her a husband. Thomas was riding out here and there, trying to organise everything for her journey. He managed to pay for the boat and carriage to Wrexham and to Porkington. He gave her a bottle of special brandy to take to William Owen and advised her to go shopping and pick something nice for Mrs Owen and for the children. Emma did as she was told and showed Mother Roberts what she had chosen for Mrs Owen and the few toys for the children. Mother Roberts thought that she had chosen well and instructed her to pack them safely.

Thomas accompanied Emma to Beaumaris, saw her off on the boat and waited until he could see them reach the other side before he left and returned to Caerau. It was going to be quiet and when he got back, Mother Roberts said the same thing. She then busied herself visiting various people she knew and different members of her family in search of a suitable husband for Emma.

The usual court matters came and went, and Mother Roberts visited various fairs looking for material as she wanted to make Caerau look its best, just in case there would be a wedding. The months went by quite quickly and Thomas was rather pleased that Emma was down in Porkington enjoying good weather and would then be going to Bath and meeting various people there. The rain during the end of July was appalling and it caused many to stop working, it also brought about another epidemic of smallpox and measles and the coffins waiting to be buried mounted to eight or ten. It was custom after church service on a Sunday to bury them.

Thomas was also busy as he was trying to help with the new window tax brought in by John Owen, MP of Presaddfed, which many people disliked. However, it had to be done. During August, just when Thomas was wondering why he had not heard from Emma, Mother Roberts was taken ill. She was vomiting and couldn't think of eating. The doctor was called and gave her something to take which did her little or no good. One of the kitchen maids told Thomas that she knew what would help; Thomas told her to try it, if only to give her rest. The maid prepared three or four spoonsful of mint water with about the same measure of tincture of poppies sweetened with the syrup of damsons. When they administered it to Mother Roberts, she pulled a face but then put her head back and promptly fell asleep. Satisfied that Mother Roberts looked at rest, and grateful that the maid had been there to look after her, Thomas left her in peace. He was relieved that Emma was not there, she might have become quite upset to see Mother Roberts ill. He hoped that things would soon return to normal, and he prayed as he prepared for bed.

One day Lord Bulkeley paid Thomas an unexpected visit on the pretext of being on his way to visit Mr Meyrick of Bodorgan. When he asked about Emma and was told that she was at Porkington. A few days later he made his way down to Porkington. When he arrived, Mrs Owen and Emma were out and he was left with Mr Owen, who was not sure what he should be doing but decided to give him a glass of beer, much to Lord Bulkeley's surprise. He ushered him to the library and chatted with him about politics. Suddenly they heard the ladies returning. Mr Owen went to welcome them and tell them who was in the library. Shocked at what they heard, they scurried along to the drawing room so that they could discuss what to do. Emma was shaking and she explained to Mrs Owen that she had been to quite a few balls and had met Lord Bulkeley several times. Mrs Owen explained that everything was under control; and was not the right thing to show any excitement. Mrs Owen went to the library and welcomed Lord Bulkeley before calling in Emma. She was quite excited and asked him why he had come to Porkington. He replied that he came to see her. She found it very difficult to compose herself and thanked him for coming. The children were running along the hallway making a lot of noise. Emma asked to be excused, telling Lord Bulkeley that she always told them a story after their bath. Mrs Owen said there was no need for her to go and that the *gouvernante* would see to everything. When Mrs Owen moved towards the door, Emma went after her and said she didn't know what to talk about and why was he there.

At 6.30pm, the bell in the hallway went off, a sign that dinner was ready. They went into the dining room and Emma was seated opposite Lord Bulkeley. He told her that he had visited her father before coming, but did not tell him that he was going to visit Porkington. He also told her that Mother Roberts had been unwell but was much recovered. After dinner, Mr Owen along with Mrs Owen left and went into the library, and Emma and Lord Bulkeley went into the drawing room where they sat and chatted. Emma told him that she loved Porkington, and that life was better there than home at Caerau. Lord Bulkeley told her that he had not been able to forget her and that he constantly thought about her. Emma blushed and couldn't speak. In fact, she was so excited that she felt she might burst. It was time to depart from each other's company and Mr Owen, who had asked Lord Bulkeley to stay overnight, showed him to his room.

The next day after breakfast, Lord Bulkeley left for London. He would be away for three weeks before returning to Baron Hill. Then he would go and see Thomas Rowlands to tell him that he had found Emma in good spirits. Once he had gone Emma talked about nothing else, and she and Mrs Owen talked about marriage. A letter arrived from her father telling her that he had had a surprise visit from Lord Bulkeley, for what purpose he did not know. Emma smiled and thought that she was smarter than her father, but of course she would have to write to Mother Roberts to tell her that there was no need for her to look for a husband as she felt that she had found one. Lady Longueville, William Owen's sister, arrived to stay. There was so much to talk about, and Mrs Owen was most amused that

Emma kept talking as though Lord Bulkeley had asked for her hand. During the following week she busied herself with writing to her father and grandmother, telling them about Lord Bulkeley's visit. Mr Owen went about his business and was glad that his wife had company staying.

During August they went down to Bath and spent time meeting various people, many of whom they met each year. The conversation was mostly concentrated on Emma, who seemed to have decided that she was going to marry Lord Bulkeley.

When her letter arrived, Thomas, was quite shocked and felt that Emma must have known something before she went down to Porkington. He called Mother Roberts and told her that Lord Bulkeley had been to see Emma. How her grandmother laughed, excitedly rushing off to see members of her family to tell them that Emma was going to marry Lord Bulkeley. Thomas warned her to be careful as he did not know that it was true yet, but Mother Roberts wasn't listening. Two days later a letter arrived for Mother Roberts. She read it slowly making sure that she understood every word. She chuckled when she read, 'no need to find me a husband'. She waited for Thomas to arrive and showed him the letter. But he said there was no mention of marriage, it would therefore be dangerous to say anything to cause gossip. They would have to be patient until Emma returned. Thomas had to admit that it all sounded good, but why had Emma not said anything apart from 'no need to find me a husband'?

Emma took a fancy for a walk, and she wandered around the lanes near to a forest. She sat on a bank and thought about Lord Bulkeley. A carriage came along and stopped to ask if she needed a lift. The people were going to Shrewsbury and said that she was more than welcome to accompany them. Emma was delighted at the thought of shops where she could lose herself looking at the displays and thinking of marriage. She had been daydreaming for quite some time before her friends told her they were ready to return. It had been a nice day and Emma had enjoyed seeing the River Severn, with some people paddling along the edge, trying to feed the ducks and swans.

View that Emma may have enjoyed looking onto the grounds at Porkington (later called 'Brogyntyn').

Emma wanted to get out of the carriage before reaching Porkington, but her friend's husband said that he would take her all the way, which made her feel a little embarrassed. She should have told Mrs Owen that she was going with her friends to Shrewsbury, not just go off saying nothing. However, Mrs Owen had a guest who had called, so she was still busy when Emma arrived. Her maid said that there was a letter for her, took her up to her room and gave it to her. Emma found that it was from Lord Bulkeley, and she sat near the window to read it as the maid stoked up the fire.

It was now October and Thomas began to wonder if Emma was ever going to return home. He was, however, busy; concerns amongst the farmers had grown since no cattle appeared in the markets around Anglesey. The drovers were very wary in case the contagious disease which had spread rapidly throughout England had arrived on the island. It was ruled that if drovers bought cattle, they were required to obtain a certificate from the seller, attested by a justice of the peace. The farmers suffered much and many of the drovers were stopped along the roads and suffered great hindrances. When they were allowed to venture forth they were met with extremely poor markets. Those who grazed the land became fearful of buying cattle in case this contagious disease lasted for a long time.

Thomas was lucky as his foreman had taken to sheep for the year. He had bought some special breed from a farmer he knew, and the investment seemed to prove fruitful. On November 3rd news arrived that William Bulkeley's sister, Catherine Lloyd of Hirdrefaig, had died that morning. She was married in the year 1714 to Lewis Edwards, son of Timothy Edwards of Nanhoron in Lleyn, with whom (being a child of 12 years) she never cohabited, he being, at the time and to that day, mad. Her estate went to her rightful heir, her first cousin John Lloyd, son of her uncle Robert Lloyd of the county of Limerick in Ireland, who had lived with her in this country for the past four years. Where her personal estate would go was not yet known.

On November 7th, Thomas did his duty and attended Mrs Lloyd's funeral. The burial was to take place at 12 noon, but they stayed until 3pm before they went to the church. There were 12 bearers and nine who wore cloaks. The bearers were all people that Thomas knew. After the service, Mrs Lloyd's body was placed in the ground at Llanffinan Church.

It was becoming darker and wintry, the winds blowing high. Showers of hail were frequent and despite the bad weather Thomas rode to Llannerchymedd to see the saddler as he wanted a new bridle and girdle for his horse. During the afternoon it rained which helped to thaw the snow and hail and as he rode back to Caerau, he thought again that it was rather a long time since they had a letter from Emma. When he arrived home and after some hot beverage, he sat to write to a letter to Mr Owen.

'Dear Sir,   *Dec 2nd 1747*

My daughter's stay with you hath been some months longer than I designed when she left, and I still find her inclinations so strongly attached to Mrs Owen and to Porkington, that I believe she will part from you with the greatest reluctancy; I am infinitely obliged to you Sir and Mrs Owen for the extraordinary welcome and often repeated civility by hel..as also the long trespass a

great trouble given her and her maid, for all which I can only return my most sincere and unfeigned thanks. I fancy you have been through this informal by your lady of the cause of Mr Lewis Jones's journey hither and the purpose of my answer to therefore beg you to give me your advice and opinion freely in this affair which I shall esteem as a particular favour: ... Our occurancies in this corner are so trifling and insignificant that I shall not trouble you with them, want of money is the general complaint and I never knew tenants so backward in their payments. Your neighbour Mr Middleton hath ushered in Mr Manwaring's petition with a speech by which it may be easily questioned with the party who will espouse in the house. My most humble respects and service attend you and Dear Mrs Owen, Master and Miss Owen and I pray God comfort you. If Lady Longuervile be with you pray my respects and compliments to her.
Mother Roberts desires her compliments to you all.

I am your most humble servant,
Thomas Rowlands.'

When the letter arrived at Porkington, Emma was out with Mrs Owen visiting Mrs Sky and having tea. On their return, Mr Owen called Emma into the library and told her that her father had written, concerned about her and feeling that she should return home. Mr Owen said that as far as he and Mrs Owen were concerned, she could stay as long as she wanted, but he stressed that she was Thomas's daughter and that she had been with them for nearly six months. To go now would perhaps encourage her father to allow her to come again. Emma stood pouting, she was having such a good time and the thought of returning to Caerau was not encouraging. She accepted the situation and leaving the library went in search of her maid and explained to her that they were having to return to Anglesey.

Everything was arranged. A carriage would take them to Wrexham, change there for another carriage which would take them to Aber, and from the Lavan seashore they would cross in a boat to Beaumaris and be on their way home. On December 19th they began their journey. Emma found it difficult to say goodbye, she was very fond of

Mrs Owen and the children. It was a dark day, with signs of snow on the way and not wanting to be stranded in the snow, the carriage travelled at speed. Emma and her maid clung on for all they were worth, but once they were halfway the carriage began to ride at a more moderate rate. When they dismounted at Wrexham, they found an interesting eating house. They left their luggage on the pavement and went in to have a warm drink and something to eat.

Meanwhile, back at Caerau, Mother Roberts had been busy making sure that the maids had lit a fire in Emma's room, and another huge one downstairs where they could sit, with plenty of food waiting for them. Thomas was pacing up and down wondering how long they were going to be. It would be good to see Emma again and there would only be about three weeks to her 20th birthday. As the day went by, he grew more anxious. Were they safe? Did they catch the boat? Mother Roberts listened to him but was quite calm. She knew that Mr Owen would have ensured that they had got the carriage to Wrexham, and she felt sure that Emma would have been on the carriage to Aber. She had done it so many times and always enjoyed the boat ride across the Menai Straits to Beaumaris. The post carriage to Holyhead would have been waiting for passengers and she felt that any minute now they would hear them arriving.

The bailiff ran to the back yard, shouting that they were on their way and that he was going down the road to pick them up with their luggage. Mother Roberts was relieved and Thomas at last could take a breather and he walked through and stood in front of the fire waiting for them. Mother Roberts hugged Emma when she arrived. Then Emma went through to where the fire was and saw her father, who also gave her a hug and said how nice it was to see her again. He had thought she had quite forgotten about him and Mother Roberts. She blushed a little and then warmed herself after the journey, and soon they would eat. Mother Roberts had managed to get some beef and they had plenty of vegetables, Thomas opened a bottle of wine in celebration of the homecoming, which made Emma feel extra special. But she couldn't quite understand why they were having wine.

After dinner they were sitting talking about various things, Thomas asked if she had any special news to tell them, but Emma shook her head and said no. This gave Thomas the opportunity of enquiring after

Lord Bulkeley, though he had met with him on several occasions in Anglesey and nothing had been mentioned about Emma. She told him that she had written telling him that Lord Bulkeley had visited Porkington and that was all there was to it.

On December 30th Lord Bulkeley was giving a ball and sent Emma an invitation. She quickly decided that she needed to go to Dublin to buy a new dress. She pressed Mother Roberts to ask her father for money as she wanted to look good for Lord Bulkeley. Mother Roberts didn't ask Thomas, instead she gave Emma the money and told her to go to Dublin and buy the best dress she could find. On December 23rd Emma ventured over to Dublin. She knew of several good shops where she would look. She went to one and explained what she wanted and to her delight they had several dresses to show her. There was one dress that Emma loved, but when she was told the price she shrugged away explaining that she could not afford it. She was about to leave the premises when the lady who owned the shop came to her and asked how much she intended to spend. Emma told her how much money her grandmother had given her and that she was hoping to find something for that amount. The lady walked her back into the store and looked at the price of the dress Emma liked and told the assistant to wrap it up. She took what Emma had and wished her well. Emma couldn't get over it and didn't know what to say, apart from thanking her several times. The fact was that Emma was very beautiful with her dark curly hair and she would look lovely in anything.

Arriving back at Caerau she told Mother Roberts what had happened which left them both wondering why this lady had been so kind. Mother Roberts said that it sounded like a good omen and that she couldn't wait for December 30th to arrive. At last, the day arrived, and Emma spent most of her time indoors, busy getting ready with the help of her maid. Mother Roberts remembered how her daughter used to get ready for balls in just the same way, dressing and redressing in anticipation of what the young men would think. Now it was Emma's turn. Thomas was busy in his study, but Mother Roberts knocked and went to tell him that he should show a little more interest in his daughter knowing that she was going to Lord Bulkeley's ball. Thomas said that when she was ready to go, he would wish her well. Thomas heard a knock at the front door and went to answer it, and who should be standing there but Lord Bulkeley. Thomas welcomed him and he said to Thomas that he had brought the carriage from Baron Hill so that Emma would not be too cold. When Emma appeared coming down the stairs Lord Bulkeley looked at her in wonder and Thomas could not help but think how beautiful she looked. The dress stood out and he admired her taste. Lord Bulkeley took her hand, and they walked outside to the awaiting carriage. Thomas thought it was lovely to see them, Emma looking like a queen. He thought that the fact Lord Bulkeley had been down to Porkington and was seeing her back in Anglesey bode well for the marriage prospect.

When Emma returned in two days, she told them all about the event and about the people she had met and how nice and kind Lord Bulkeley had been. He was, she said, very attentive towards her and he had also suggested that perhaps he should see her father soon. She then went on to tell them how the drive up to Baron Hill was lit up when they arrived that evening. She told them about the lovely glass ware and the beautiful dresses. She had a lovely room which looked over the Menai Straits and many there wore beautiful dresses. She liked Baron Hill.

Thomas called into the drawing room and told Mother Roberts that Lord Bulkeley was coming to see him soon, assuming that he was coming to ask for Emma's hand. They were both delighted and as it was the end of December, they would have to think of Emma's birthday on January 13th. Thomas ordered all the fires to be stoked up, as it was exceedingly cold with a heavy frost.

For the next two weeks the weather was bad but as the month moved nearer the 13th of January it seemed calmer, although it was dark and the air was raw and cold. Emma was too excited to feel the cold and insisted on going for a ride on her pony down to the beach, which made Mother Roberts shake her head. She was on tenterhooks waiting and wondering when Lord Bulkeley was going to come.

Thomas had arranged for them all to go to Beaumaris to celebrate Emma's birthday. She would be 20 and just the right age to marry. He made sure that he invited Lord Bulkeley to join them. He wrote out the invitation and then rode to Llannerchymedd to post it. Emma was very chatty as they sat having dinner and Thomas was thankful that she was the only daughter. The chatting and talking about Lord Bulkeley as though she were already married to him was more than he could take. Mother Roberts joined in and told Emma that she would have to spend a day with her, to see all the things that she had quietly collected for her in anticipation of her marriage. Emma was getting more excited by the minute, but Mother Roberts said there was much to be done before a wedding could take place. The next day she called Emma to her and went with her to William's old room. In there was a cupboard. Mother Roberts took a key and opened it, while Emma stood on tenterhooks. She couldn't believe her eyes. There was nearly everything that any bride would need. Some of the stuff had belonged to her mother and Emma wanted to touch those things. Mother Roberts told her that when she was 21, she would inherit her mother's money, which has been safely kept for her. Mother Roberts was extremely kind, Emma felt, and kissed her cheek. During the afternoon, when the two were sitting by a lovely fire, Mother Roberts told Emma that she should make a list of all the people she wanted to be at her wedding. Emma said that there weren't that many, and she wanted a quiet wedding. It had to be held at Llanfairynghornwy, so she would have to visit the vicar. As the church was small, she would be careful to invite only those whom she felt should be invited. Mother Roberts asked what month she would choose for a wedding, and without hesitation Emma blurted out July.

When it came nearer her birthday, Thomas checked all his arrangements and on the morning of her birthday Emma was greeted by her father who gave her a lovely, lace shawl and Mother Roberts who gave her a new dress. Emma had been complaining for some time that she needed something new. Everything was set for a marriage but not just yet.

Having finished preparing themselves they left Caerau and arrived at the Red Lion at Beaumaris around six in the evening, so that they could book themselves in and tidy up before Lord Bulkeley arrived to join them. They all met downstairs in a room kept for people who came for dinner or parties. In two minutes, Lord Bulkeley arrived wearing a wig which made him look better. Emma thought how smart he looked. They had a lovely meal and sat talking until it became quite late. He asked when they were leaving, and Thomas answered that they would be heading back to Caerau in the morning. Lord Bulkeley said that he would see them before they left.

True to his word, Lord Bulkeley was there to see them off, still holding on to Emma's hand, and with Mother Roberts' eyes twinkling with excitement. They were glad to be back if only to get warm in front of a lovely fire. Thomas found it rather funny that Lord Bulkeley did not mention anything about marriage. He felt that they must not read too much into the fact that he was paying Emma attention. He discussed the matter with Mother Roberts once Emma had left them and warned her not to talk about marriage until they had something firmer to go on. 'I mean,' said Thomas, 'we were all together and then he came to see us off and never once mentioned anything about wanting Emma's hand.' Mother Roberts said that perhaps he wanted to feel the atmosphere between us all before saying anything. Thomas again said, 'But he never said anything.'

Emma was a little upset. She really had hoped that he would have asked her father for her hand. This was the second time it had happened and Emma felt that she did not understand men.

An epidemic spread around the island. At first the people thought it was a mere cold, but many became sick with fever which caused pleurisy, diarrhoea, and smallpox, from which many died. Mother Roberts was busy as usual when such things spread, putting lavender around the house and various spices which were to stop anything from affecting them at Caerau. Thomas, however, suffered quite a bad attack of asthma and one of the kitchen maids had whooping cough. The weather did not help, what with snow, sleet, and hail. Then waiting for it to thaw and hoping that they had enough to keep the animals fed during these difficult times.

During February the government appointed the 17th to be a day for fasting and humiliation for everyone's sins and to crave a blessing upon our arms against our enemies. Many felt that that this mocked God as it was a well-known fact that the lack of success was owing to the conduct of the ministry.

Emma had been to see her cousin and learnt that Mrs Frances Warmingham, the daughter of Mr Owen Williams of Carrog, had gone on an East India voyage. She thought it was wonderful that people had enough courage to travel and thought it must be exciting to see all the places one only read about. Arriving back at Caerau, Emma went up to her room and sat looking through the window watching the men smashing up cattle dung and spreading it over the field. She was only disturbed when she could hear her father coughing and thought she had better ask about his asthma. She loved it when you could smell the lavender and the spices throughout the house and thought it should be made law to keep lavender and spices in the house to reduce the risk of catching colds and fevers. She had not seen Lord Bulkeley for a few weeks and felt that perhaps like Owen Meyrick he was only using her as a companion to go to balls. Because of his importance, he probably had someone more suitable than her to become his wife. It was the last day of the year 1747 and she felt that it was an apt ending, as she had heard nothing.

Chapter Thirteen

On March 28th, 1748, Thomas decided to send Dr Wynne of Bodewryd interest on the loan which he had received from him earlier. He felt better, and now he could concentrate on the estate and then his Caernarvon property.

> 'Sir,   Cayrey March 28th 1748,
>
> I have by the bond sent fifteen pounds your interest for two years for which I pleased to send me a receipt. I have promised to send you a letter some time since received from Sir Thomas Prendegast which I desire you'll pursue, as the design is good and commendable and if perfected will be greatly beneficial and advantageous to the whole Island, but more especially to head. I don't doubt Sir that you and Mrs Owen will favour me with a liberal contribution and that Mrs Hughes's mite will not be deficient a list of subs and the money paid into my hands you will likewise receive.
>
> Mother Roberts and daughter join in their compliments and respects to you and Mrs Owen and Miss Owen and Miss M Hughes with.
>
> Honourable Sir
> Your most obliged
> Humble servant
> Thomas Rowlands'

Emma was in her room reading a magazine when her maid knocked and came in saying that there was a gentleman wanting to speak with her. Emma asked what sort of gentleman and ran down the stairs, her maid following close behind. Much to Emma's surprise it was Lord Bulkeley's chief man, saying that Lord Bulkeley was sorry that he had not been over or written, but he had been rather ill and was only just getting over it. Emma asked at once whether he wanted her to visit him, but his handyman friend said there was no need, and that Lord Bulkeley would come over once he was well enough. He took from under his riding cloak a package and then he left. Emma was in a dizzy state not knowing whether she should go and see Lord Bulkeley or not. She stood there holding the package without looking at it. Mother Roberts said that by all accounts there was no need for her to go and as the courts were about to take place soon, she could ask her father if he would call and see Lord Bulkeley to make sure that he was better.

Oh, the excitement of it all which only made Emma more discontented than ever! She wished in a way that she was at Porkington enjoying walks through the forests. Her maid pointed to the package which she was still holding. Emma came in and unwrapped the package only to see a beautiful handkerchief, the nicest that she had ever seen. She ran around showing it to everyone and when she got to her father, she burst in through the door much to his surprise. He asked if she had forgotten her manners and that no one should enter his study without knocking first. Emma nearly ran out again but apologised to her father and explained that she wanted him to see what Lord Bulkeley had sent to her. Thomas was surprised and asked who had brought it, Emma explaining that it was his handyman and that she felt she ought to go and see him as he had been ill. Thomas explained that as the sessions were due to start, he would ride out the day before and stop at Baron Hill to enquire about Lord Bulkeley. Emma seemed to accept the situation though she would have preferred to have visited herself. The sessions started on April 18th, so Thomas left home on the 17th. He called at Baron Hill and was met by his main helper and the man who looked after Lord Bulkeley's affairs. He enquired about Lord Bulkeley and was told that if he came in, he would see for himself. Thomas followed and indeed was welcomed by Lord Bulkeley who did look a little under the weather but sounded very well. He had been administered some medicine and was much better he informed Thomas, who said that he was on his way to the sessions but had promised his daughter that he would call In and enquire.

Thomas left and went to his digs where many of the other members were staying. They saw to the sessions which lasted two days and when he got back to the digs, there was a message for him from Lord Bulkeley, asking him to join him for dinner. This Thomas did and as they were sitting after dinner enjoying a drink Lord Bulkeley asked him about Emma and whether Thomas would agree if he asked her to be his wife. Thomas was most surprised, but Lord Bulkeley said that he thought Emma quite beautiful and felt that they would make a fine-looking couple. Having received Thomas's permission Lord Bulkeley decided that they should open a bottle of special wine, which they kept for celebrating. Thomas said that he would prefer it if they celebrated when the event had taken place. Lord Bulkeley agreed, and Thomas left to return to his accommodation. The following morning, he was up dressed and ready to ride back to Caerau. On his way he began to think about many matters concerning the marriage of his one and only daughter. He would have to write to Mr Owen of Porkington, as he and his wife were the ones chosen by Thomas to introduce her to important people in the area.

When he arrived back at Caerau, Emma was pleased to see him and was waiting for him to come in and have something to eat. He wanted to retire to his study and promised Emma that he would talk with her later. Emma joined her grandmother, and they went to a fair held at Llanfechell, where they bought some fish and some beef, which was cheap. Emma was busy with looking at various materials and found some lace that she rather liked, and Mother Roberts having examined it, encouraged her to buy some thinking that it would make a nice veil.

They both enjoyed the fair and felt that it was time to return. After having tea Emma knocked on her father's study door and went in. Thomas told her to sit down, as Emma wanted to hear about Lord Bulkeley. Her father explained that Lord Bulkeley was much better and that he would soon be calling to see her asking for her hand as he had already asked Thomas for permission to marry her. He then went on to explain that he would have to write to Mr Owen of Porkington to make the announcement as he had been the one to introduce her to people. Emma was so excited that she wanted to run out and tell everyone, but Thomas cautioned her and said that now she could say nothing; she would have to wait for Lord Bulkeley to come over and see her.

Emma said that she would do as asked, which was unusual for rather a wild girl. She forgot to tell her father that a letter had arrived for him from Porkington. She waited until the afternoon and went and knocked on his door and handed him the letter. She said that she was going out for a ride and left Thomas to it. Thomas was in the middle of writing to Mr Owen but decided to stop and read the letter just received. It was dated the 9th April 1748 and Thomas found that it had been written by Mrs Owen's brother and couldn't understand why it had been sent to him until he read it and found the reason.

It was a letter written to Mrs Owen from her brother, Francis Godolphin. He had inherited the title after his cousin died and became Baron Godolphin of Helston. He made his home in Baylies–now Baylis Park–an enormous house in Buckinghamshire, where he tended his garden and entertained his friends. He and his sister, Mary, were close with shared interest in music and theatre. He was married twice. First to Barbara Bentinck but she died after just three years of marriage which left him grief-stricken. His second wife was Lady Ann Fitzwilliam who brought with her a great fortune. He was interested in politics and the letter he wrote to his sister at Porkington read as follows:

'Pall Mall, April 9th, 1748.

I received yours yesterday Dear Sister and am very sorry that poor Lady Williams suffers so much, as I am that Mrs Jenkins is like to dispose of herself so much to her disadvantage, but that is her affair. My Aunt has been much indisposed this week with her old complaint but is at present much better again. Lady Anne has got a cold, but we hope to go to Baylies on Tuesday for a week if the weather is tolerable if not being warm, yet this wind is changed. The person that makes the speech that I sent you is Mr Grenville who has been the occasion of all this bustle to please his borough of Buckingham; and all that can be said for him is that he was not the aggressor. The aggressor is gone to St Asaph and the chapter is appointed to elect the Bishop on Thursday next. Dr Hume succeeds the Bishop of Exeter as Residentiary of St Pauls, and Dr Crane succeeds him at Westminster.

I cannot inform Mr Owen very exactly of all the alterations in the Window Tax, but the chief is that Brew Houses, Wash Houses, Stables, and the like are to pay and that the windows that are stopped up must be done with the same material as the house is built with and not with boards. I received Burgon's Paper but believe there is no money paid yet. One of my Quanton tenants lost eleven cattle out of twelve, but we hope to get him the allowance from the Treasury; it was six weeks ago, and I do not hear that any of the rest were sick. I don't know why you thought poor Mrs Ely was dead. Gregory was 78 and has left 800 Pounds behind him to his niece. Mrs Hawtrey is gone again to Bath having been ill again since she went home. Lady Anne desires her compliments with mine to Mr Owen and yourself from Dear Sister

Yours F.G.

I hope Mrs Skye's October proves good.'

Thomas sat reading the letter carefully. It had been sent because of the window tax which had caused many to block their windows up in the attempt to avoid having to pay. He would have to have another discussion with John Owen MP who introduced this tax in parliament, and tell him that he must make sure no one blocks their windows with just board in case they get into trouble. The window could only be blocked with the same material from which the house was made. Everyone in Anglesey was of course cross with John Owen for having introduced this tax, especially as he had had someone block many of his own windows to avoid paying. John Owen thought that this was a very good tax, but it made many enemies around Anglesey.

On April 27th Thomas attended the funeral of Mrs Ann Wynn, widow of the late Mr Robert Owen of Penrhos. She was buried at Bodewryd, her brother's home, and she had six bearers who were all priests.

William Bulkeley called and went through to sit with Thomas in his study to discuss various matters. He told Thomas that Evan Pierce of Beddgelert had been very good and caught a dozen moles and that he was glad Thomas had recommended him. He stayed and had dinner at Caerau and Emma loved to talk about his horses. He found her an interesting person to talk to; had the conversation been with Mother Roberts it would soon have turned into church matters.

The following day Thomas felt that he should write to Mr Owen at Porkington. No sooner than he had started writing than there was a knock on the door. When he went to answer it there stood

Lord Bulkeley. Thomas welcomed him, asked him in and told the maid to call Emma. Emma couldn't believe it! She went in and told the maid that she had to change and make herself look grand. She was running around in excitement, nearly falling over herself several times.

Eventually she came downstairs and went into the drawing room where her father was entertaining Lord Bulkeley. He stood up when she joined them and then led her to a chair. Her father said that they had something to tell her. Thomas explained that Lord Bulkeley had asked him when he visited Baron Hill for her hand and that he had suggested they celebrate when he was well enough to come to Caerau. And now he had come. Thomas got up and left them, thinking that they would feel a little more relaxed. Half an hour went by when suddenly Emma opened the door and shouted in glee that Lord Bulkeley had asked her to marry him and that she had agreed. Thomas joined them, and Mother Roberts eventually arrived having been to Llannerchymedd fair. They had a very good dinner and Lord Bulkeley stayed quite a long time. Emma asked to be excused when it was time to go to bed knowing that her father and Lord Bulkeley would probably be drinking her health until the early hours.

The next day Thomas called her into his study and told her that he was writing to Mr William Owen, his cousin, to tell him the good news and then he would await suggestions from him as to what would happen next. As William Owen had been the one to introduce Emma, which Thomas could not afford to do because of his debts, Thomas would have to abide with whatever William Owen told him. Emma understood, but she was hoping that she would be allowed to go to Porkington. She busied herself while waiting to hear the news from Porkington by going through all the things that Mother Roberts had put away for her and making a list of them. That way she would soon be able to see what else was needed. Her father would need several talks with Lord Bulkeley about what they were putting into the marriage, and what agreement could be arranged and accepted. First, he would have a discussion with Mother Roberts so that they knew exactly what they were doing and what Emma would be bringing to the marriage. The most important point would be that Emma would be taking quite a dowry to the Bulkeley estate. She was the heiress of both the Caerau and Castellior estates as well as the Plas-y-Nant estate. They deliberated for hours and when they were satisfied Thomas took many papers to his brother-in-law, Mr John Griffith at Caernarvon, to make sure that all was in order.

When he returned, Emma was ready to travel to Porkington and said that she would stay for May and half of June before returning. Thomas felt that there was nothing he could do, only wish her well. She began her journey two days later having been to see Lord Bulkeley to explain to him that it would the Owens who would be preparing her for marriage. She left a list with Mother Roberts of other things that she felt she would need when she was married. Mother Roberts was very pleased that Emma was at last going to get married and to such a good match. She busied herself going around her family proud to show off the fact. Emma has done very well for herself, she kept telling them.

When Emma arrived at Porkington she was very excited to be able to tell them that she was to be married to Lord Bulkeley, not that anyone liked the man. Mr Owen assured her that he had received a letter from her father and that he would do his duty and see to it that she would meet all the people who might be included in her circle of friends. Mrs Owen would polish her manners and teach her how to behave when meeting important people in society. Oh, there was going to be so much work to do, but then they knew Emma well and she was extremely fond of Mrs Owen. Emma loved the children too and would often tell them stories which helped to keep them quiet.

Mr Owen called for her to see him, and he explained that they would have to sit and work out the details regarding the marriage, when it was to take place and how many people would she want there. Emma explained that they would also have to ask Lord Bulkeley, and so Mr Owen wrote to him asking him to come to Porkington.

Lord Bulkeley replied that he was more than willing to travel to Porkington which he did the following week. Emma was delighted to see him and after two days Mr and Mrs Owen sat with them to discuss matters. Emma wanted a July wedding as it was probably the time of year when the chances of rain were minimal. It was then decided that the Owens would start with their first wedding dinner in July which was really to announce their engagement. Mrs Owen had written out a list of all the things that Emma would need, and Lord Bulkeley agreed with everything. At the end of that week Lord Bulkeley returned to Anglesey, promising Emma that he would be going to Caerau to see her father and Mother Roberts to tell them that things were moving ahead for the wedding.

Her stay at Porkington was filled with shopping, visiting people, and playing with the children. Time soon passed and she had to return to Caerau, before coming back again later with Lord Bulkeley. It was usual in those days before a marriage, rather like the banns in church, that those who were in charge gave a dinner to announce the engagement followed by two more. The first dinner was in July as Emma had chosen July for the wedding which meant they would be married after a 12-month engagement. They travelled together and were welcomed at Porkington.

The first dinner took place two days later. Mrs Owen had arranged for help, and the dining room was full of flowers and there were place cards for each guest. Emma and James took their places opposite one another, and the other guests took theirs. The evening was full of chatter and at the end of the meal the men went to the library where they could smoke and drink to their heart's content. Emma had never dreamed of having such a wonderful event and it was all for her. How was she going to repay them? She had never seen such splendour. She was so fond of Porkington and the Owens, and wanted to stay on and let Lord Bulkeley travel back, but Mrs Owen encouraged her to go with him. They were now engaged, and James would probably want to have a special dinner for them at Baron Hill. Mrs Owen was right to advise her to return with James and she would, of course, be able to tell Mother Roberts and her father all about her engagement dinner.

When she arrived back in Anglesey, it was late and James invited her to stay at Baron Hill, as Emma was feeling rather tired she accepted. The following day she rode back to Caerau and was given a tremendous welcome by her father and Mother Roberts. Emma spent the rest of the day telling them all about what was going to happen, and that she and James would have to go back to Porkington and have their second engagement dinner there. Emma asked her father whether he could join them at Porkington to which Thomas agreed.

The weather for the rest of June was extremely good and Thomas – who was interested in reading the news about cricket – noticed that it was now a legal sport according to the court of the King's Bench. Cricket was played illegally until 1748 under the 1710 statute of Queen Anne. The first recorded codification of the rules of cricket was in 1744. Something else for everyone to be happy about.

Suddenly it was the beginning of July and Lord Bulkeley and Emma were on their way to Porkington, with Thomas following a few days later. Once Emma and James had settled in, they met Mr and Mrs Owen in the library where they had to make final decisions about the wedding. Mr Owen felt that it would be good for them to marry in a church near Oswestry, but Emma was adamant that she was going to get married at Llanfairynghornwy Church. She had been dreaming about this for some time. Thomas arrived two days later, and the house was full of chattering so that you could hardly hear what was being said.

Print of Llanfairynghornwy Church designed by Margaret Jagger R.G.A. who created the logo for WH Smiths in the 1930s.

The exterior of Llanfairynghornwy Church.

The interior of Llanfairynghornwy Church.

Stained glass window inside Llanfairynghornwy Church.

The font at Llanfairynghornwy Church where Emma was christened on January 23rd 1727.

The special dinner was to take place on the Saturday and Mrs Owen had to see to the people who were arranging everything. Emma would listen and watch how they set the tables and where the cutlery was placed. She hoped that when she was married, the maid at Baron Hill would be able to set a table in the same manner. The dinner was a huge success with entertainment afterwards. At long last Thomas could sigh a relief now that his one and only daughter was engaged to a peer. It felt good. Two days later Thomas returned to Anglesey. Emma would follow in a week with James so that they could have another party at Baron Hill.

Mother Roberts was waiting and wondering how things went. When Thomas arrived, he was hungry. He ate a good meal and then sat telling Mother Roberts about the dinner and the entertainment. He said that she could tell everyone now as Emma was formally engaged to Lord Bulkeley. Mother Roberts was delighted. She said they would have to sort out papers and make sure that their money would be going to Emma and not to her husband. It was nice, Mother Roberts felt, that Emma would be 21: she had always maintained that she would not marry until she was of age. She would be 21 in January and married the following July. It was all getting so exciting.

The dinner at Porkington had a mention when Mrs Owen's brother, Francis Godolphin, wrote to her:

'Baylies July 11th, 1748.

I thank you for your letter dear sister and should not have troubled you till next post having little to offer, but willing to let you know that Mr Leadbeter [Leadbetter] had sent me the money for the bill which I thought you would be glad to know. I am glad to hear that you have had the trouble over of the first dinner of the wedding folks and think you did very well to call in help, which saved you a great deal of trouble and other wise one can never be sure how things will be performed. It is now grown much in fashion at London on extraordinary occasions to hire people to perform a great entertainment, which makes it more expensive but then one is sure of it being done well.

The provost is come home a Complete Doctor in Divinity and left his nephew Jack Harris settled at King's College. I have bought a load of Hay at a guinea and 22 shillings, and the rick will be finished this afternoon. I went to see Mrs Cook last week who lives near Dr Carters chambers which have lent them by Mr Burton, she has left her two girls behind her in Dorsetshire with a sister of Mr Cooks, but she begins to be impatient to see them, but I suppose they will stay till after the election. Your boy Jack Evans drinks hard at King's College and is rather too full of politics for a scholar of the College. With lady Ann's compliments to Mr Owen and yourself and mine to him I must conclude this from Dear Sister.

Yours affectionate brother.
F. Godolphin.

Mr Crewe has let his house at Bristol and is gone to Cheshire for the present, his lady is lost to this neighbourhood by.

whom she was very much esteemed.'

Once again, Emma was home and many things had to be sorted out. Mother Roberts did her best to tell her what had been going on locally, including telling her that Mr William Bulkeley's dog, Ranter, had died. He had been with him since the 10th December 1730. He was 17 and eight months old and had followed a horse from Gleidion in Flintshire to his house at Llanfechell. His master felt that he would have carried on living, if he had not been carried off by a distemper as his teeth were better than in many a dog half his age. Mother Roberts also went on to talk about itinerant charity schools for neighbouring children held in a Caban house. They taught in Welsh about the meaning of the church catechism and about the New and Old Testaments. The charity was run by South Wales English gentlemen, but the clergy were against them and called them nurseries for Methodists. However, these schools held their ground despite the resistance.

Emma went for a walk in the garden and called her dog, Rŵan. They sat in the garden. Emma loved the roses as she had loved the daffodils earlier in the year. After a while she rode her pony down to the beach with Rŵan running alongside her.

Mother Roberts thought how calm Emma was, taking things in her stride and not worrying about anything. It was quite different when she herself married years before, and also with her daughter's wedding to Thomas. They checked that they had everything that was required of them and would visit the church several times practising how long it would take them to walk down the aisle. But Emma seemed to think that everything was going to appear from the air. Mother Roberts shook her head. She was pleased though that Emma was now secure, and she looked forward to the day of the wedding.

Everyone Emma knew welcomed the news and many came to help her with her clothes. She had ordered some things from Dublin and hoped that they would be suitable. Every other weekend she would visit James and they had a good time together. He would show her around Baron Hill and take her for walks around the estate. She would then return to Caerau and organise things to do with the wedding. She was shocked when she realized how quickly the time had flown. They had been invited to William Bulkeley's house to hear the harpist from Pwllheli play for them which Emma loved. It was lovely entertainment. He earned two shillings for the evening's entertainment.

That January was a very wet month and was followed by sleet and the wind was raw. It got worse and brought trees down. Jamison, a Scottish pedlar, called selling stockings and cloths. Emma bought enough to keep her going as she needed them for her wedding. As the weather seemed calmer, she ventured down to the seashore. She could hear the green plovers or the lapwings crying more like the way they cried when they were ready to build nests and hatch, which normally happened in the month of March. Emma felt it rather unusual. William Bulkeley mentioned that he, too, had heard the same thing and thought it was unusual.

Emma visited the fair at Llanfechell where there was plenty of cloth both woollen and linen. Shoes were plentiful as were hats. During March she went to see the garden again and found the gardener sowing peas, beans, savoy cabbage, prickly spinach, white broad spinach, parsley, and celery. It was the last day of 1748, and she was beginning to get a little nervous, thinking about everything.

Chapter Fourteen

On March 28th Emma heard that the swallows had arrived, which was very early for them; they usually arrived around April 19th. Emma took it to be a good omen and believed that everything would go well for her forthcoming marriage. She would often sit with Mother Roberts playing cards, making sure that she would be able to entertain her guests well when they visited her at Baron Hill.

It was soon time for Thomas to attend at Beaumaris with the rest of the jury. On April 11th an express was sent to Lord Bulkeley informing him that Sir Watkin Williams Wynn's wife was taken to bed and had given birth to a son on April 8th. Lord Bulkeley drank the baby's health. He ordered a bonfire to be lit and the bells rung all evening and night. This seems to have been a custom when boys were born to important families. The Williams Wynns were also related to Mother Roberts as Sir Watkin was a son of her father's brother. He was recently been married to Miss Fanny Shackerely who had produced a son, hence the celebrations.

Emma – who had received a dowry from her mother, which Mother Roberts had been looking after safely for her – decided that she would clear her father's debts before she married James.

Lord Bulkeley came over to Llanfairynghornwy to announce their wedding through the first of the three banns which had to be announced at church. Emma was more nervous than ever and glad that they had attended church. They dined at Caerau before James returned to Baron Hill. All that was left now was the wedding. We can see in William Bulkeley's diaries where he states, July 11th, 1749, *'This day James Lord Bulkeley was married at Llanfairynghornwy Church to Miss Emma Rowlands daughter and sole heiress to Thomas Rowlands of Caerau Esq.'*

According to the church register, the marriage is dated July 15th, 1749. The church had been beautifully decorated with flowers which scented the air and made it a wedding to remember. The people of the surrounding area had all helped with the decorations and Thomas was most proud to lead his daughter down the aisle to marry James. There was dancing and harp music all around the church and children shouting their good wishes and singing. Emma had to admit that it was just like a dream. There was eating and drinking and lots of fun, and everyone seemed jolly. At long last she was married and now the task of moving all her things was to take place, with Thomas hoping that they had enough room for it all.

Mother Roberts, despite being proud that Emma was married and to a peer, missed her. The house felt oddly quiet. She had spent the last 21 years looking after Emma and protecting her and trying her best to instruct her in readiness for marriage.

Thomas saw to it that all her things went to Baron Hill, though he mused to himself that perhaps James would have to build new quarters when he saw all that she had. Her maid at Baron Hill soon took a liking to her and they got on well.

Everything was fine for the first six months, and then James showed signs that did not please Emma. He brought a group home from the inn and shouted in his drunken state. Emma tried to ignore it all by disappearing to her bedroom. When things were quiet in the morning, she would sit and talk with James and tell him that she was not happy that he brought back such a menacing crowd to the house. She felt she should be considered as she was now the mistress of the household. As someone of standing, she expected that they would entertain similar people. James, because he was sober, agreed with her and promised that it would not happen again.

They attended church and invited members of their families over for meals and everything seemed better. During September news came that Sir Watkin Williams Wynn of Wynnstay had been thrown off his horse, broken his skull and died. It was a shock to both. Emma was soon to discover what being married to James was all about, as this was another excuse to go drinking.

During September, Emma went back to Caerau, pretending that she needed a change. Mother Roberts went to Llanfechell market and bought a side of mutton for 20d, and had it cooked for their evening meal. Emma spoke to her father about James and his debt. That night they all sat in the study trying to understand how he could be so indebted. Emma asked her father if she was right in suggesting that some of the smaller farms should be sold off. They brought in little rent and were worth more if sold. Her father agreed and said it was sound advice. She returned to Baron Hill in a few days and spoke with James and said that she would go through the list of all that he had and work out a solution. Thomas knew that she was pregnant and that the baby was due early the following year.

Thomas decided to ride out to Baron Hill to see how Emma was. She told him about James and how he was often debauched and brought women home and taunted her. She usually disappeared to her bedroom but felt that it was not the way she believed her marriage should be. Thomas stayed so that he could face James and warn him that he was getting tired of the way he was behaving and that if he was not careful, he would expose him and his debts so that all the people would know. James was shocked but promised that he would refrain from such behaviour if Emma was there.

In November, Mother Roberts had gone to Bodior, the home of her niece, Emma Roberts, to inform her that Emma was pregnant. During her stay she fell and broke her arm. Thomas wasn't sure what to do as Mother Roberts kept on about wanting to come home. He wrote to the Honourable Dr Wynne at Bodewryd.

'November 18th, 1749

Dear Sir,

Poor Mother Roberts having had the misfortune lately to break her arm by an unlucky fall at Bodior is very desirous to come home but dares not venture on horseback for fear of any further accident. Therefore, she begs the favour that you will be so kind as to lend her your litter with horses and all proper equipage for the purpose. If you will suffer one or two of your servants to attend lest it should be anyways damaged. She will be obliged to you. It will not be wanted till Monday the 27th instant.

I am infinitely obliged to you Sir for your most kind and generous present. I have often designed myself the pleasure of waiting upon you which I must now defer till after xmas and shall then bring the interest of two years together; my compliments pray to little Miss. The favour of an answer will oblige.

If you can't spare Horses I do fancy I can provide with my neighbour Mr Lloyd to lend me two of his.

Sir Your Most obliged obedient Humble servant.

Thos Rowlands'

The 'little Miss' referred to by Thomas was Hugh and Margaret Owen's little girl. Her father had died after going to Bath, so mother and daughter were staying with her grandmother Mrs Owen of Penrhos at Dr Wynne's home, Bodewryd. She later grew up to become Lady Margaret Stanley of Holyhead.

Thomas sat in his study. He would be glad when Mother Roberts returned. It had been oddly quiet, and he wasn't used to it. He read much and saw that Georgia had become a Crown Colony. The world was growing, he thought. Handel's firework music was written and Halifax, Nova Scotia was founded. A novel by Henry Fielding was published in February 1749, which sold out and everyone read it though it was intended as a comic book. It was called *Tom Jones*. My grandchildren will be brought up in a world with far more knowledge than I had, thought Thomas. Books were often printed and published now so that children everywhere could enjoy reading.

He had written to Emma explaining why he could not come over as he was waiting for Mother Roberts's return from Bodior. When she returned on November 27th Thomas had had the maids clean out her room, making sure that there was a fire lit. He looked forward to their conversations once more. He gave her a warm welcome and soon they had dinner together. She asked about Emma and Thomas and he thought it was time that he told her about Lord Bulkeley's behaviour. Mother Roberts was shocked and announced that she had better come home at once. But Thomas said that he would talk with James and tell him that if his behaviour continued, he would do something about it. He had already warned him.

Christmas came and it was the first time they did not have Emma with them. They attended church as usual, then came back to a feast of food and later rested. Mother Roberts was worried about Emma. Now that she was pregnant, she would need more care.

Thomas made a point of taking them out for a meal when Emma's birthday came along on January 13th just to make sure that James was behaving himself. He spoke of issues that were of interest to James as he was an MP for the borough of Beaumaris from 1741. They discussed the window tax which had caused much consternation, and that some employers were too slow to allocate people to mend the roads, especially as there was plenty of rubbish from various quarries to do the job. Later that evening, having dined well, Thomas felt as they left that James was not as bad as had thought.

On February 20th 1750, Emma wrote to Mrs Owen of Porkington:

'Dear Madam,

I am in much better temper than when I wrote last to you as you may perceive answering your long looked for letter soon. I was in some apprehension that cold weather had contracted your fingers to such a degree as to prevent your friend having the pleasure of your correspondence. But now to my no small satisfaction I find contrary you are dear Mrs Owen quite on it in your supposition regarding my wedding apparel. The enclosed is a direct list so pass your judgement accordingly. Lest you should be too severe a critic I must tell you one agreeable recommendation they are very cheap if not t'other part of the story. I shall likewise disclose I am now about little affairs a Grand Christening suit which I cannot possibly afford so these will be some long performance. I hope you will not tax me now with privacy and I am extremely sorry you should imagine I could be so to you of all people. A person whom I always look upon worthy of the greatest confidence thought perhaps in some less trivial matter I might not care to trouble you with. I had not provided but not Lady Baileys that I fancy you heard. Old Mother Cleaton will bring her old bones once more to Anglesey she has promised me. I must contradict you again I do assure you no one in the world is easier about males and females than I am being thankful for providence for – still mighty resigned for the hair positively, madam your notion is not right. I had seen for the hair positively. I had seen Abseay, who lately told me several ladies of premier fashion walk in the park with their locks flowing and I did not understand by him that any spectators imagined they were inhabitants of the infernal regions and perhaps I was in London I might attempt marching part of the fag end of those ladies with my curls dishevelled and I fancy I might pass without molestation don't think I would differ from all the world nor above appearing like other folks but you will allow people the smallest rank to be obstinate in an opinion especially as the conceit may not be harboured in themselves, besides I have seen when creation wore their locks down some of my acquaintance tucked it under a hat, but that looked might pretty to be sure and not at all remarkable. However, if dear Mrs Owen will favour me with her company in a few months' time you shall then regulate of myself or any other part that you see most neglected. I am glad to hear Mr Robert Williams reaps so much benefit by the death of his sister. How come he wrong dated the wills of Mr Wynne Glyn designs disputing all points I am told. How does poor Esquire Owen do after his fatigue in Meirionethshire? I believe everybody is plagued with bad servants in their farms I condole you for the Lady Williams of Mount, I suppose she is gone by this as the brother has given her over. Mr R. Williams danced at Esquire Lloyd's exit I have been confined this last seven weeks with the toothache and never free from pain. You must consider blunders holding my head down too long always brings a toothache. Lord Bulkeley is upon the road downwards I expect him in the country next week. Lady Bulkeley Williams plays the devil and refuses to sign the Act of Parliament for selling the timber upon her jointure which is an extreme hardship on our side. Surely Mrs Owen will venture next summer to Anglesey if not sooner. You will be considered exceedingly unkind if you don't. My best wishes and compliments to your family in general Papa and Grandmama desire theirs I must beg to be remembered to good Mr Owen when you see him from.

Dear madam, your obliged and affectionate servant.
E. Bulkeley'

It was soon time for Emma to give birth. Bridget was born and christened on March 15th. Though she was weak she managed to survive. Emma was named Emma Bridget Rowlands before her marriage. This gave James another excuse to mock her and he brought his group of debauched friends along to toast the baby's head and make fun of Emma because she had produced a girl and not a boy. The following day he lost his temper and ridiculed her for having produced this little girl. He shouted that she was useless and made Emma very upset. She had not witnessed such behaviour before.

Emma returned home to Caerau with the little girl and her grandmother was glad to see them both. She liked the name Bridget and made them both comfortable and warm. Mother Roberts was concerned about her and had never thought for a second that James could behave so badly.

At the end of 1749 it was announced that a year of Lord Bulkeley's estate was to be sold at 25 years' purchase to different people. Thomas knew that this is what Emma had worked out to reduce his vast debt of £40,000. No consideration was shown. Many people bought these properties, but James's mother would not consent for them to sell some of the woodlands which would have brought in a substantial amount.

Mother Roberts was much better. She had been pampered, with the maids and Thomas looking after her. Dr Lloyd of Rhosbeirio had called a few times. Dr Lloyd had matriculated on March 17th 1723-4 at Jesus College, Oxford. He married Catherine, daughter of Williams Wynne of Wern. Mother Roberts had been binding her arm herself and saw no need to have a doctor. She knew many things about medicine and looked after herself well. She wished that she could be at Baron Hill looking after Emma and the baby. She did not like what she heard about James.

Thomas had been busy sorting things out for Caerau and travelling to Caernarvonshire to see his tenants and reminding them about their rents. He was now sitting in his study catching up on news and what was going on in the world. Many new countries had been found and proclaimed and he appreciated how big the world was becoming. He then read that Lancelot Brown (Capability Brown) had designed the gardens of Warwick Castle. He was doing well for himself and travelled from shire to shire designing gardens which amounted to 170 before he died. The English Jockey Club was founded in London and the first Westminster Bridge was finished.

During August, Thomas wrote to Mr Owen at Porkington.

'Dear Sir,   Cayrey August 9th 1750.

As you were not pleased to give me any direction where to write to you at Bath, I do not sooner thank you for the favour of yours for it was but accidently that I heard of your return home. I hope and do most heartily wish that you have received the desired benefit by the waters and your ailment in your hand perfectly relieved thereby that you'll have no occasion for a second journey there upon the same Act. If I thought, they would recover a dejected and almost broken heart I should struggle hard for little money to spend some few weeks there with my poor daughter who since her lying in has had terrible sore breasts frequented and violent fits of the cholic and by too much vexing and frothing at the most undeserved, barbarous brutish ill-usage; she hath for some months and does still receive, seems to have a jaundice hanging upon her and is really in all respects in dangerous, miserable way. You will I hope pardon me for giving you a short detail of our afflictions, which are in some measure alleviated by being disbursed to friends, in which number I have found you and Dear Mrs Owen to be the chiefest. I thank you a thousand times for your expensive favour to poor Emma. We have very rainy, stormy weather of late which is very unseasonable for our harvest. Mr Griffith Tan-y-Bwlch is dead as I just now heard. I am glad to hear that, Lady. Longuervile is much better. My most sincere and best respects and compliments attend you Dear Mrs Owen, both Master and Miss Owen. Pray my compliments to Lady Longuervile.

I am dear Sir your most obliged affectionate Humble Servant.
T. Rowlands'

Thomas felt despair regarding his son-in-law and worried about what might happen if Emma chose to divorce him. For now, however, they would look after her and the baby, feed them and keep them warm. Emma enjoyed being back home at Caerau and rode her pony down to the beach which she always enjoyed. Her dog, Rŵan, accompanied her and she let the wind flow through her hair. She felt much better when she returned and ate a good meal which pleased both Thomas and Mother Roberts. Mother Roberts had managed to get a nurse to look after baby Bridget so that Emma could get better and have plenty of sleep.

At midday the following day, Mother Roberts went to Emma's room, and she was still fast asleep. The noise of her bedroom door woke her, and she was surprised to see Mother Roberts standing there. She was shocked when her grandmother told her that she had slept deeply and that it was now past midday. Emma couldn't believe it and apologised but her grandmother said there was no need and that she was glad that she had slept well which would help give her strength. Emma told her grandmother some of the things she had endured at the hands of her husband. Her grandmother was shocked and said that she could stay at Caerau as long as needs be. Emma had been very ill, and her husband cared little, so that it was best that she remained at Caerau.

At the end of the week there was a knock on the door and the maid answered. There standing was Lord Bulkeley. The poor maid was not sure what to do knowing that there wasn't much welcome for him. She asked him to stand in the foyer and ran to the dining room where Thomas, Mother Roberts and Emma were having a meal. The maid told them who had come. Thomas stood and said that he would see to him. Emma was shaking. Her grandmother encouraged her to continue eating and leave matters to Thomas.

Led into the study, Lord Bulkeley immediately sat down. Thomas told him that he had not asked him to sit and that he should stand then Thomas went and sat in his chair and looked Lord Bulkeley up and down him which obviously made him feel uncomfortable. He asked what was going on. 'Going on?' said Thomas. 'There is nothing going on, only your bad behaviour to my daughter.' Lord Bulkeley laughed, and Thomas told him to get out of his house. Understanding that he was wrong, Bulkeley did not move and once again Thomas told him exactly how he felt and that he was keeping Emma with them at Caerau. He told him in no uncertain terms that his behaviour was disgusting, contemptable and that the aggression he had used against poor Emma had caused her to be very ill. He could not forgive such behaviour against an innocent woman. James stood there trying to make excuses, but Thomas was having none of it. He called his bailiff and asked him to escort Lord Bulkeley from the premises. By now, Lord Bulkeley understood that he was in a corner and said that things would improve. But Thomas would not move from his stance. Realising that he was not going to get anywhere with his father-in-law, James left.

Two days later he was back again and pleaded to be allowed to speak with Emma. Thomas stood his ground and told him that he could only see her after he had explained what he wanted from her. James pleaded that he loved Emma and that she was his wife. But Thomas did not give way. He told James that when his own wife had given birth to a girl, he was happy and pleased, as no one could possibly know whether it was going to be a girl or a boy. He continued, 'There is plenty of time for you to acquire a son, but you do not badly treat your wife when the baby is a girl. You must nurture her until you have a son.'

James realized that his father-in-law was quite right. He had been through it and he apologised to Thomas for his conduct. After some further time, Thomas took him to where Mother Roberts and Emma were sitting in front of the fire. As was expected, Emma's grandmother left them together. James pleaded with Emma to return and said how much he missed her, held her hand and continued begging. Emma, who since the birth of Bridget knew that she was in love with James, agreed that she would return in a few days' time. Thomas joined them and told Emma what he had told James. Emma asked her father not to be too cross with James because she loved him, which left Thomas standing shaking his head.

James left, kissing Emma before he went. Thomas couldn't quite make up his mind whether to tell Emma that she was being foolish or just let the matter ride. Four days later, Emma was ready to travel once more to Baron Hill where she was met by a very excited James. Everything, it seemed, had calmed down. Life continued as normal, and they busied themselves entertaining friends. By the end of the year, it was known that Emma was pregnant again and James thought that this time it would be a boy.

They both took a trip to Caerau so that they could tell Thomas and Mother Roberts, who were naturally delighted. They enjoyed a meal and returned to Baron Hill as James had to be away for a week in London. Thomas prayed that things would be better, and Mother Roberts referred to their squabble as sorting themselves out rather like wedding jitters.

In May the following year, 1751, Emma gave birth to another daughter, Elinor Maria, born on May 22nd. When James heard it was another daughter he well and truly lost his temper and called Emma many derogatory things. He started his drinking and womanising again and for a fortnight after the baby's birth had a party every night with his debauched friends until Emma could take no more. Once again, she waited until all was quiet, took her two babies, got her horse out of the stable and rode back to Caerau in the dark.

When Mother Roberts heard the knocking on the door, she was shocked to see that it was Emma, Bridget, and the baby. She quickly put on some water and stoked up the fire and thought it best if Emma went to bed rather than disturb her father who was fast asleep and heard nothing. Everything was quiet once more and Mother Roberts was first up the following day making sure that the maids understood what extra help was needed for the baby. She prepared herself for when Thomas appeared, and he was shocked when he heard the news. He was more determined than ever that Emma should not go back to James. If James should turn up, they would hide Emma, Bridget, and the baby. Mother Roberts took her and the little girl to her part of old Caerau. Emma used her own first bedroom and an old cradle for the baby. James had never seen that part of the house so Emma could hide well.

It was four days later that James called at Caerau. Thomas, well prepared to greet him, said that he knew nothing of where Emma was. He pretended to be shocked when James told him that Emma had gone and asked, 'Gone where?' James was now baffled. If her father didn't know where she was where could she have gone? Thomas advised him to go back to Baron Hill and ask around Beaumaris to see if anyone had seen her. To convince James that he knew nothing, Thomas suggested that he ride out with him part of the way. James accepted this and told

Thomas that he would do everything in his power to find her and he continued without Thomas.

Thomas arrived back and was met by Emma who hugged him. He saw his second granddaughter for the first time. She was a delicate little baby and Emma worried about her. Thomas asked her to come to the study later so that they could talk about what she was going to do. He was more worried about her since he had learnt of the deep debt that James was in. He couldn't really afford to keep Baron Hill by all accounts. His mother was still getting a share which caused some difficulty, and his sister-in-law was getting another share. Emma said that they were selling some of the smallholdings which did not bring in much rent. At least the proceeds would yield some sort of income. Thomas' natural reaction was to suggest that she moved back to live with him and Mother Roberts. Emma did not seem keen on the idea. Whatever anyone thought, she loved James and forgave him his tantrums. She stayed a month at Caerau. James visited several times begging her to return, with Thomas refusing to have anything to do with him. Emma wanted to see the situation for herself and returned to Baron Hill with Bridget and the baby, who was still very weak. Once again everything seemed quiet and well. They continued living and enjoying various parties and visiting friends around Anglesey, both hoping that their financial affairs would improve.

In August, Elinor Maria became very ill and nothing could be done to save her. She died just three months old on August 13th 1751. Emma was distraught and found James's behaviour terrible. He couldn't appreciate what the loss of this baby meant to her. Once more she returned to Caerau. She felt safe there.

Thomas sat reading the news and learnt that the British calendar was to be altered by an act of parliament. January 1st was to be the beginning of the New Year. This is recorded by William Bulkeley in his diaries:

> *'By Act of Parliament passed in April last for regulating the commencement of the year and correcting the Calendar – there are among other things enacted that the old computation of the year by which it begins on March 25th is not made use of throughout the whole of British Dominions – after December 31st, 1751. January 1st next following is to be reckoned the first day of*

the year 1752 and every year for the future to begin January 1st instead of March 25th and several days each month after to January 1st are to go in the same order as usual till September 2nd in the said year inclusive – but the natural day next immediately following September 2nd instead of the third is to be called the 14th of September - omitting only for the time 11 intermediate nominal days of the present Calendar and the several natural days that shall follow the said 14th September are to be reckoned forward in numeral order as usual and so on continually.'

It must have been a shock to many as January 1st was upon them. On December 14th 1751, Margaret Griffith wrote to Mrs Owen of Porkington and in it she refers to Emma.

'Lady Bulkeley I am told is as cheerful as ever, she has got over her afflictions, it helps that she has good spirit, and the Lord lies in bed all day gets drunk every night by 4 or 5 o'clock in the morning which is better than to be in the way he was half a year ago regarding her. She is with my brother at Caerau and is much better since she went there.

Dear Madam
Pray is Lady Longuervile at Chester, she bid me not.
Write to her till I heard from
Her the letter
Was dated 12th of September.

Your most Obedient humble servant
Margaret Griffith'

It appears that James had misbehaved again. Thomas did not care that he was drinking but he was furious at the way he treated Emma. He became determined that she should divorce James for her own safety. Emma enjoyed being back with her father and grandmother, and little Bridget kept smiling at her grandfather, Thomas. He thought she was wonderful and played with her whenever he could. Emma wrote to her cousin, Hugh Griffith at Llanfairisgaer, told him about Lord Bulkeley and asked if he could perhaps visit him to make sure that he was well in himself. Hugh wrote back saying that he would call once a week to see how sober he was. This went on for quite a while. Whatever her father said she loved James. But her father had seen the effects on Emma and how badly bruised she was. He couldn't allow it to go on.

Thomas was busy now that the year had changed. It meant that they had to bring their accounts to an earlier date. He sat himself in his study and Mother Roberts and Emma only saw him in the evening looking worn and cursing the paperwork.

They lived peacefully and carried on going to the fairs and various places and Emma had quite a few cousins call to see Bridget. Then one day they had an unexpected visitor, her cousin, Hugh Griffith. He had called to see Emma and during tea he told her that he was extremely worried about James. He realised when he had a bad turn that he was suffering badly and thought there was something wrong with his health. Emma asked if she could do anything, and Hugh said that he felt that James rather soothed his pain by drinking and having his women friends around. Emma felt totally deflated. There was nothing it seemed that would heal James. As Hugh was calling again at Baron Hill, Emma asked if she could accompany him and the following day they left Caerau.

When they arrived, the place looked empty but when Emma went up to their room there was Lord Bulkeley fast asleep having thrown himself onto the bed. He was still too drunk for them to get any sense out of him, so they left him and sat downstairs, Emma called the maid who made them some tea. Emma felt that she should stay with James until he was sober at least. Hugh said that he too would stay until James woke up and sobered up and if everything was fine, he would leave and go back home the next day. Emma was conscious that things could get bad if she questioned or rebuked James, so she chatted as though things were normal and fine. She occupied her time writing letters to various members of her family. At this time, her aunt, Margaret Griffith, wrote to Mrs Owen of Porkington.

'Dear Madam,   March 12th 1752.

Your letter always gives me infinite pleasure which I acknowledge as a great favour done me whenever you can and are so good as to confer them. I did not hear of your indisposition long after and while you are recovered, at which I was much rejoiced, and to hear that cousin Owen and both misses are well. Mr Griffith and I are much obliged to you both for your kind reprimand for my apology in sending my son and civil reception and extraordinary generosity to him and for your recommendation to Mr Robert Owen whom Billa writes is so good as to take notice of him. Pray Madam hath he passed the smallpox? I hope your family may have it favourably if ever. My mother never had it nor brothers, my sister Wynne though she had a girl who suckled her and died of it. I take freedom to enclose this for Mrs Godolphin, we cannot hear of any place for her money. The family of Glynllifon are so rich that they purchase and supply most people here under 5 per cent. I suppose you heard that Sir Nicholas Bailey has bought about 4 or 500 of Lord Bulkeley's some of the very best of the old family estate.

I had a letter from Lady Bulkeley, she says that they go on in the same disagreeable way. He drinks and sleeps to 2 or 3 days after a night's debauch. He is I am told to her, ably good humoured. Pray Madam when you write to pretty Miss Owen let her know that I am her humble servant. Mr Griffith and self our compliments to you and Cousin Owen and our best wishes attend Master Frank and Miss. I fancy Lady Longuervile longs for Miss Molly that letter I had from her; she was in raptures of her. My little Granddaughter has had fits but is better. Miss Bulkeley begins to walk but speaks little. This place affords no news. We have a lady that lives next door to us, she is with child. She is a sister to the Earl of Bute and a niece to the Duke of Argyle. When Mrs Wynne comes to town, we shall be polite, their house is fitting up for their reception in all haste. Lady Bailey miscarried 2 months ago and is not well. Yet, they lost a fine boy that died of fits. He had them ever since he was half a year old and was 3 years old when he died. The family do not go to England I suppose to help the Lady. I think it high time to end my scribbling.

Dear Madam,
Yours most Obedient and
Obliged humble servant.
Margaret Griffith'

Chapter Fifteen

Thomas' concern grew each day over the condition of James, who made no effort to curb his dreadful behaviour. Emma left him to his own devices and went out and about. She felt she was a good wife to him, putting up with his behaviour. She also sorted out his money troubles which he never once thanked her for. Part of the estate was now sold. Had his sister-in-law allowed them to sell even part of the woodland it would indeed have helped his present situation. Thomas took it upon himself to stay at Baron Hill for two or three days at a time, returning to Caerau then back again.

Towards the end of April there were definite changes in James. He kept falling over and lost a lot of strength. Hugh Griffith passed remarks about it and it was decided between Thomas and Hugh to call a doctor to him. The doctor had prescribed medication and Emma encouraged James to try it, but he carried on by going out and drinking until he could not stand up and some of his debauched friends carried him home. He then slept for two or three days at a time. Emma was already pregnant again and was worried that the child might not have a father. What would she do? There was no love lost between her and her sister-in-law, the Dowager Lady Bulkeley, and even when she remarried, she would never agree to sell the woodland.

During May it was apparent that James was showing signs of consumption and found it very difficult to breathe. His strength was diminishing. Hugh became a very good friend to him and only had a respite when Thomas came. James was agreeable to Emma, and she was most despondent when she tried to make him eat and saw just how thin he was. He still called his friends in and had a jolly time with them. On May 21st he looked emaciated, and Hugh was more concerned than ever. James was also weak and told Emma that he felt that he couldn't last much longer. Emma fed him nutritious soup and managed to get him to eat a little. On the 23rd he was weaker still and quite unable to sign a letter. Thomas and Hugh were anxious about him, but it was always, 'Give me more wine'. Friends called and he laughed and joked with them and drank white wine though he could hardly move about due to his weakness. Then he fell asleep, and Hugh went to him and realised that he had died and ushered his friends away. It was 5pm on Saturday May 23rd.

On May 25th Margaret Griffith wrote to Mrs Owen of Porkington.

'Dear Madam,
May 25th, 1752,

I am sorry to hear that you have been indisposed and hope that you are over it quite and that your family are well. My Lord Bulkeley died on Saturday at 5 o'clock in the evening. He had taken to his bed 6 weeks but forced up to make a will. He died in a fit which continued for an hour and a half. My lady and all about her are much shocked for they did not apprehend his danger, but my son gave me such an account of his weakness that anyone that had seen a person in a consumption must imagine he could live but a short time. He was the night before many a drinking and jollily with him and his white wine given him in turn for, he could not frank a letter, then he endeavoured it. I hope this frank will come uncharged as it is last post that will come, so I am afraid a great many will suffer by his death. It is talked here that his lady nor child will get a farthing from him. My poor brother will be greatly embarrassed if what they say be true. He was not of the art of saving or the knowledge of business to manage confused affairs. Mr Griffith was not to come to Baron Hill; we have just now had notice that he is to be buried privately. I beg Madam you be this hasty service.

From Madam,
Your most Obedient Humble servant
Margaret Griffith'

Thomas was not sure what to do, but he knew that he would have to arrange a funeral. None of Lord Bulkeley's family came or offered any help. James's brother before him had a great send off. He was well thought of by the people of Anglesey and his political interest had introduced him to many people on the island. It was feared, however, that James had a very bad reputation even though throughout his life he had been Chamberlain for North Wales, Constable of Beaumaris

Castle, and member of parliament for the borough of Beaumaris. All these positions he had acquired after the death of his brother, which had been given under authority of the king.

Thomas rode back to Caerau for some suitable clothes and returned bringing Mother Roberts with him. She wanted to be there to comfort Emma and Bridget. She understood the predicament that Emma was in. Days passed, and in the end Thomas arranged that Lord Bulkeley would be buried privately as there was little money and none now that they could get their hands on. Mr John Owen of Presaddfed came to give Thomas support. They took James as far as the court gate and then they returned to the house. Servants accompanied James to the church, but many were shocked when they saw but four halfpenny candles taking him in, though there were many neighbours waiting to attend him. There were no scarves or rings to be given to anyone, which made his funeral look sadly poor against that of his brother.

On June 3rd 1752, Mrs Owen's daughter, Molly Owen, wrote to her mother:

'Dear Mama,

I am sorry you thought I expected an answer so soon, it was Friday fortnight you wrote to me. I was glad to hear of Lord Bulkeley's death. I fancy few people are sorry. I hope you received the bit of silk I sent you the same as my robe, you will be surprised when I tell you Lady Anne and I had a race half round the garden last night her ladyship won. I was sorry to hear Mrs Humphries has been ill, I am afraid my aunt will be a great while without a maid. My uncle and Lady Anne send their compliments to you and Papa. My uncle has had a letter from my Aunt Ellen, she says Lady Bulkeley has written to Mrs Williams to buy her mourning. My uncle wants to know how many children she has. I have eaten strawberries yesterday and cherries today. The provost asked me whether I loved to browse a strawberry bed. Pray my duty to Papa and love to brother and sisters. I am dear Mamma your dutiful daughter.

Molly Owen'

William Bulkeley had written in his diaries for May 23rd 1752: '*Lord Bulkeley died last night 23rd, so that the male heirs of that house are quite extinct. He is leaving only a daughter behind him, a child 2 years old weak and sickly.*' This was a dilemma for Thomas, who was not sure whether he could manage to look after Emma and her daughter. After the burial and wake, Thomas spoke with various lawyers. They consulted the Bulkeley family, and it was said that neither Emma nor Bridget would get anything, which upset Thomas and Mother Roberts. Bridget was a Bulkeley.

On June 8th Elizabeth Longueville wrote to Mrs Owen mentioning several people:

> '*A lady came to visit me and gave me account of Lord Bulkeley's funeral. Cousin Rowlands and Mr Owen Presaddfed attended him as far as the court gate and went back to the house. Two servants went with him no lights to bring him there but 4 halfpenny candles in the Church. A great many of his neighbours waited to attend him. Lady Bulkeley is 4 months gone with child will have her thirds of what he has in possession of.*
>
> *Elizabeth Longuervile*'

Mother Roberts was adamant that Emma and Bridget should stay at Baron Hill. Thomas decided that he would have to look after the Castle and the town of Beaumaris for the time being and with a court's permission. Most of all, should the baby be a boy, he was duty bound to carry this out until the child was of age.

June disappeared quickly, and Thomas made several appointments with the people in charge of the Baron Hill estate, so that he knew what was there. He knew that Emma was pregnant, hoping that it was a boy this time. He had to make sure that she was safe and had been given a list of properties recently let out for 25 years, which helped to bring in some money. Emma had marked those properties that she felt should be better sold. She certainly proved her worth in working these matters out.

Emma had been in turmoil. She had never expected to lose her husband after just three years of marriage. She loved him despite his bad behaviour, and she could only hope that the baby would be a boy.

That is why she was so determined to stay at Baron Hill until the baby was born.

Mother Roberts returned to Caerau and Thomas stayed. Emma had dismissed James's servants, keeping only one maid plus a cook and one maid to help look after Bridget. She called the rest of the people employed and spoke with them explaining that as she was to receive next to nothing, she could no longer keep them. Should things improve, she would call them back. Sadly, they left wishing her well.

Thomas was enjoying himself and was very pleased that his cousin William Owen had sent him a newspaper full of things going on in the world. Manchester Royal Infirmary was founded and was opened on July 17th 1752. A Doctor Charles White started it in a house in Garden Street off Withy Grove, Manchester. Claydon House was built by Earl Verney who became Viscount Fermanagh (it is now owned by the National Trust). Benjamin Franklin invented the lightning conductor and demonstrated the identity of lightning and electrical spark. For Thomas the world was improving all the time, and his grandchildren would see a very different world from what he was used to.

In September, and as from the 2nd, 11 nominal days were omitted in conformity with the Act of Parliament for correcting the calendar. Thomas felt that he had seen a great change himself, but it appeared to him that it was going to get much better. He played with Bridget every night before she was put to bed, then he sat with Emma discussing what she would do should she have to leave Baron Hill. Emma would have none of it, she was staying there until the baby was born. Thomas accepted that. He felt her very brave in the circumstances and understood why she was occasionally cross with the Dowager Lady Bulkeley, her husband's sister-in-law, who was married again and had children with her new husband. Had she allowed them to sell the woodland, things would be much easier to sort out now that James had died. They were allowed to touch nothing. They kept receiving orders as though they were children. They lived and worried about what was going to happen. How were they going to cope? The difficulty was that as her husband had been a viscount, his business affairs had to go through Parliament. No one asked how they were going to live in the meantime.

It was now December and everyone in the household knew that it would not be too long before Emma gave birth. She decided to stay in the parlour, then she started with her pains which went on practically all night. At noon on December 12th, she gave birth to a fine and healthy son. A messenger was sent to Caerau to give the news and the town of Beaumaris was so excited and overjoyed at hearing that Baron Hill had an heir that they lit the town up and cheered loudly so that Emma could hear. This went on for days. They were so pleased for her. Margaret Griffith wrote to Mrs Owen of Porkington.

'Hon Madam,   Thursday December 14th 1752

Tho I writ so lately to you, I will not apologies for writing to let you know that Lady Bulkeley was delivered last Tuesday of a son. He and his Mamma were as well as could be expected. My Brother's servant left Cayrey, my lady had been far from well for a fortnight last but supped in the parlour the night before. Her labour was sharp and quick but imagine the joy of bringing a son makes amen (as the scripture tells us) for the great pain and where it was much corrected. The town illuminated seemingly much rejoiced for the heir to Baron Hill. He is a lusty boy. Pray God make him a better man than his father was. Poor Miss Bulkeley fares the worse of it, she must be taken care of by her Mamma.

I wish the scheme they impose may benefit my lady and her by the Act of Parliament, which they are preparing. I do hope Mrs Owen all your family are well and that you continue so. Mr Griffith and myself join our compliments to you and cousin Owen, he bid my servant tell me to let him know that Lady Bulkeley was brought to bed which I know will be agreeable to you all. I expect your commands about cloth daily which I will be glad to receive and am.

Dear Madam,
Your Obedient Humble servant
Margaret Griffith'

It was a relief to all her family that Emma had safely given birth to a son. It was now that Thomas would have to be busy making sure that things were put to parliament and that they would get good results without too much of a delay. He was very proud of Emma and when he asked what she was going to call the child, Emma replied, 'Thomas James Bulkeley.' That made Thomas even prouder. She gave the baby Thomas's name because he had been there for her, especially when things got so bad that she had to leave James. On December 15th Thomas wrote to Mr Owen of Porkington:

'Dear Sir,   Caerau 15th December 1752

You will excuse the freedom I hope that I take in acquainting you that my poor daughter was safely delivered of a boy last Tuesday at noon. They both are as the women tell me, in a fair way doing very well and trust in God will long so continue; the hurry and confusion that commonly folks are in, prevented my writing last post, which designed you will overlook and attribute it not to the least neglect or disrespect not writing to you as often fully intended, hath been occasioned by the multiple of distresses and difficulties that our affairs labour under. The two distant and slender prospects of being extricated out of them; besides I am far from being free of aches and pains and complaints being seldom with a cold and much afflicted with the piles, which do not agree with riding. The gelding Mr Henry Jones bought me doth not at all please, for the previous and errant jade and a stumble and cant mount him without some dread; but if I live and do well and some of these and heavy clouds dispose, I will endeavour to wait on you next summer.

    My daughter and Mother Roberts join in Compliments and best wishes for the health and happiness of you, good Dear Mrs Owen, the young gentlemen, and ladies,

With Dear for you most sincerely,
T Rowlands'

Difficult times lay ahead and once the new baby had settled and the house ran to suit everyone, Emma found that she had plenty of time to sit with her father going through mountains of paperwork. Thomas started visiting people who understood parliamentary law and managed to receive a few signatures. Emma went through as many papers as she could each day and found that they were tied to many places. Perhaps as some of the nobility rented many of their larger houses in parts of Cheshire, it was time to ask them whether they would like to buy them before they were put up for sale.

Thomas felt that he had achieved something when he returned. He had to make a list of people whom he knew within court circles and get as many signatures as possible. He was glad of a few minutes to relax and have a look at the newspaper. He read that land tax was to be two shillings in the pound for England and Wales. He shook his head then continued reading, when he came to read about the British Marriage Act, which forbids weddings by unauthorized persons. The British Museum was granted a Royal Foundation Charter. On another page he read that by Act of Parliament in England the naturalization of Jews was permitted. The fire was roaring away and when Emma came looking for her father, she found him fast asleep in his chair.

During the year 1753, Emma and her father worked hard on getting signatures and working on the petition and in July they heard that Emma's mother-in-law was very ill. She died on July 11th 1753. She was known as Lady Bridget Bertie and was the eldest daughter of the 1st Earl Abingdon. When her husband, the 4th Viscount Bulkeley died, she became known as the Dowager Lady Bulkeley and her allowance was £800 per annum. Emma, on learning the news and finding what the Dowager Lady had been getting, was fraught, thinking how she had been left with nothing. Besides, she learnt that her sister-in-law was to get her mother-in-law's allowance added to hers which meant that she would be receiving £1,400 each year. All Emma's husband, James, had received was the title and the estate and under these encumbrances a debt of £40,000. Emma, who had decided to do away with her widow's outfit, was having to wear it for a longer time out of respect for her mother-in-law—which she felt was ridiculous as she was the one suffering.

Emma was inconsolable. As Jane, her sister-in-law, was the daughter of Lewis Owen of Peniarth in Merionethshire, and had remarried to Edward Williams and had several children, how could she be so cruel and still be demanding her allowance? What hurt Emma the most was the fact that she had refused to allow James to sell the woodland. That, on its own, would have helped his and Emma's situation. How could she leave her in such dreadful circumstances? Thomas too was quite upset and felt that things needed to be sorted out sooner rather than have to wait for the petition to go to parliament.

Thomas knew that he would have the support of people like Dr Wynne of Bodewryd, Mr John Griffith of Caernarvon, Mr Owen of Porkington, John Owen of Presaddfed MP, Mr Nicholas Bayley of Plas Newydd, Mr Price of Rhiwlas and many more people whom he knew through the court at Beaumaris. He continued the long process of getting enough signatures and Emma sorted out the papers into neat piles of documents with information about most of the properties that the Bulkeley family owned in Cheshire. Thomas wrote to each one explaining Emma's position and those who felt that they could buy the houses that they rented were to be given enough time to sort the matters out. He enjoyed writing to Emma's sister-in-law referring to her cruelty. He also wrote to her husband, who seemed to understand the situation better than his wife.

Emma was also involved with choosing a candidate to stand at the 1753 elections to keep the seat for her son when he became of age. She decided to ask Hugh Owen, the son of Sir William Owen of Bodeon, to stand against Mr Meyrick of Bodorgan. She was fed up with all the squabbling about who should stand and who should vacate their seats. She was determined to try and keep the seat for her son. It would be 1774 before he was of age.

In 1755, a great friend, Dr Edward Wynne of Bodewryd, died. He had helped so many people and Thomas would certainly miss him. He had been allowed to take various books home to read and Thomas liked the fact that whether he wanted to look up ecclesiastical books or agricultural books, he could be sure that Dr Wynne would have a book on the subject. Edward Wynne was a very clever man who had completed a distinguished career at Jesus College, Oxford and secured the office of chancellor of Hereford in 1707 from his uncle, Bishop Humphreys. He was also a progressive landowner who turned his findings in agricultural developments in Hereford to good use in Anglesey. He was reputed to have been the first man to grow turnips successfully in Anglesey. He was well respected throughout the island and now Thomas would feel a little lost. Dr Wynne was always at hand when Thomas wanted to raise money and he always tried to pay back on time. He told Emma that he would return to Caerau and attend the funeral. Mother Roberts wrote to her niece who was also a niece to Dr Wynne to ask about the funeral.

> 'Dear Niece Owen,
>
> I send this on paper to know when Dr Wynne is buried, and whether a public burying or what them call a private burying. We design poor Maggie a very private but would not choose it on the same day. Pray write a line Pr and your much obliged.
>
> Your affectionate Aunt E Roberts.
>
> I shall not let anyone know if you desire not'

It was obvious that Thomas felt bad at the loss of Dr Wynne. He sat quietly in deep thought and was not eating as well as he should. Mother Roberts was quite concerned. She would ask him many things and he just sat as though he was in a trance. She resorted to write to Emma and ask her to ask her father if he could go over, as there was a matter she wished to discuss with him.

Eventually Thomas decided that he had better visit Baron Hill to see what Emma wanted to discuss with him. Bridget was so excited when she saw her grandfather and he swept her up in his arms and made her laugh. He tickled her which she loved and then they had to behave as dinner was ready to be served.

Thomas was taken aback when he saw the amount of post that Emma had received, all supporting her with the petition. Thomas sat during the rest of the evening going through them and shouting out names of various people who were supporting Emma. Thomas was more than pleased and all he had to do was make sure that the wording of the petition was correct, and have it checked before they could send it. Emma had been extremely good and faced her difficulties gracefully. She had sold much of her jewellery to raise money to buy things that were needed, believing that no one would want a dowager with two children to bring up. Some pieces she had inherited from her mother, and some had been given to her on her birthdays by her grandmother. She knew Mr John Nangle, an Irish silversmith who had come over from Ireland and married Margaret Lloyd; they lived at Llwydiarth outside Llannerchymedd. He spent his time in London where he ran his business. Emma trusted him and in return he would gather all the things she ordered from various merchants and deliver them to the Bulkeley house in London. This meant that life could carry on, which was a great relief.

Emma wanted one copy of the petition to go to the Prime Minister, so that he could see the extent of her deprivation. But it was not until January 19th, 1756, that the petition was heard, as follows:

> *'Lady Bulkeley & al. Petition referred to the Judges.*
>
> *Upon reading the petition of Emma Lady Viscountess Bulkeley of the Kingdom of Ireland, Widow and Relict of James Viscount Bulkeley deceased, for and on the behalf of Thomas James now Lord Viscount Bulkeley her only son, an infant; and also the petition of several Persons whose names are thereunto subscribed, being Purchasers of the estates of the said James late Lord Viscount Bulkeley, in the Counties of Lancaster and Cheshire, praying leave to bring in a Bill, for carrying into Execution certain Contracts therein mentioned for the sale of certain Estates in the County of Chester, by such Ways and Means as shall be thought proper.*
>
> *It is ordered, That the Consideration of the said Petition be, and is hereby referred to the Lord Chief Baron of the Court of Exchequer and Mr Justice Clive; who are forthwith to summons all Parties concerned in the Bill; and, after hearing them, are to report to the House the State of the case, with their Opinion thereupon, under their Hands, and whether all Parties who may be concerned in the Consequences of the Bill have signed the petition; and also that the Judge, having pursued the Bill, do the same.'*

Emma was very anxious, but an Act of Parliament was passed, and Thomas James's Cheadle estates were sold to raise money for his education. This was already in court after the death of Richard Viscount Bulkeley, who had inherited the land in Cheadle from his aunt Frances Bulkeley, who had in turn inherited it from Humphrey Bulkeley. After his death they passed to Frances Bulkeley, and on her death, they reverted to the Beaumaris branch of the family. In 1702, Richard Bulkeley, afterwards Viscount Bulkeley, on his marriage to Bridget, Lady Bertie, acquired for himself and his male heirs the manors of Cheadle Bulkeley, Timperley and Whatcroft, and other lands in these and various places in Cheshire which had been in the possession of Frances Bulkeley.

In 1731, after the death of Richard Viscount Bulkeley, his eldest son, Richard settled his Cheshire estate in trust to be sold for payments of his debts. An advertisement appeared in the London Gazette of 16th January 1732 announcing the sale of Cheadle, Timperely, Edgeley and Whatcroft and the advowson of the rectory of Cheadle to be held on the 5th to 7th March. Richard died in 1738 without male heirs and was succeeded by his brother James. In 1747 the Cheshire estates were ordered to be sold by decree in Chancery of 1st March 1745, but the death of James prevented the sale from being completed. In 1756, an Act of Parliament was passed in which the manors and lands in Cheadle, Timperely, Edgeley and Ashley were vested in the trustees,

Sir William Meredith, Bart., of Henbury, and Robert Williams, Esq. In September of the same year the manor of Cheadle Bulkeley was sold to the Rev. Thomas Egerton, clerk Rector of Cheadle.

This came out of a paper on 'CHEADLE' which was reduced as it came out of a book called *East Cheshire Past and Present* by J.P. Earwaker, London 1877.

Emma sighed with relief for herself and her young children. They would be cared for now. Emma would see to it and control the estate to make sure that it made money. Thomas was also relieved; it had indeed been a very traumatic time for them all and waiting four years had been long enough.

Once back at Baron Hill, Emma decided that she wanted to make the place as homely as possible. She used her time to make the children's bedrooms comfortable and then decided to change the colours of the drawing room and other rooms. She felt that this was her home for the time being and that she had to keep it in good order for her son. She wrote to Mrs Owen of Porkington who sent her information about how to use paint so that she could improve Baron Hill.

Several gentlemen visited her father asking for her hand, which seemed to annoy Emma. She had told him it was too soon to think of another marriage. She was cross with Thomas for listening to them. He had however felt that she would be better off with a companion rather than face life alone. He arranged without her knowledge for one or two of the gentlemen to visit her under some pretext or another.

There was a very nice gentleman from near Worcester who had a large house and plenty of land and another who had a castle up in Scotland. Emma found their time wasted upon her, she did not like any of them. Another came and he was an earl with a handsome house in Buckinghamshire with plenty of land. He was twice widowed, and was willing to give her time to get used the idea of marriage. Emma, however, had different ideas and thought she would wait and see what would happen. She believed in meeting someone herself without having to be introduced. If she met someone, she would know whether they were right for one another. Months passed by and they enjoyed themselves. Bridget was growing. She loved Thomas and they both loved watching the boats going along the Menai Straits. It was a wonderful sight to see. The young viscount was also pleased to see his grandfather and wanted to know what had gone on in court and how he knew the way from Caerau to Baron Hill. 'Oh,' said Thomas, 'this is the stage when questions are more important than food.'

During the summer months, Emma became aware of a gentleman who kept walking along the lane parallel with Baron Hill. She knew that it was where most people took a walk on a sunny Sunday afternoon, but this gentleman seemed to have an penchant for often walking there. She would watch at certain times of the day just to see if she could see him. This went on for weeks. The trouble was that she thought he was very handsome. She questioned herself because it had become apparent that she wished to meet with him.

Emma had become acquainted with a lady from Beaumaris called Mrs Jane Williams, and she had told her about this handsome chap she kept seeing walking along the lane. It was therefore arranged that Mrs Williams would visit Emma on a Sunday and see him as he walked past. Mrs Williams was intrigued and walked with Emma around the gardens. Then Emma became shy and hid behind a tree whilst Mrs Williams pretended to tend to the roses. She was shocked to see who the gentleman was. She ushered Emma inside Baron Hill to tell her that she knew him well and felt that it would indeed be a wonderful match. Mrs Williams recommended him highly, and could not wait to return home so that she could write to Sir Hugh and tell him that Emma wished to meet with him. She then thought that if she walked along the lane, she would be sure to meet him on his return, and could usher him back with her to Baron Hill and meet Emma.

The excitement was tremendous. Mrs Williams met Sir Hugh and brought him back with her. As far as Emma was concerned, she saw nothing in front of her, but Sir Hugh's face, which she thought was like an angel's. Molly Owen and Mrs Williams disappeared and went to play with Bridget. After a long introduction and talk of many things. Sir Hugh departed, and Mrs Williams and Molly returned to see how things had fared with Emma and Sir Hugh. Emma was in raptures, and they chatted away until Mrs Williams left.

The following week went by quickly with Emma still in a dream, they laughed and chatted, and they heard that Sir Hugh was going away. Then Mrs Williams thought it was time she wrote to Sir Hugh to instruct him as to what he should do if he wished to keep his acquaintance with Emma. This letter is dated July 25th 1757, and is full of comments by Mrs Jane Williams. She tells Sir Hugh that her description of his character to Emma had quite won her heart but that, personally, she (Mrs Williams) could never be in love with a man if he looked like an angel...

> *'For I would only look at him as I would a picture: if he had nothing but his beauty to recommend him: but it is his character. I regard her ladyship gave you free liberty to write to her and to declare your passion. She said to me I have every confidence in you and friendship for you my dear Mrs Williams that I give free liberty to manage this affair as you think proper. She fixed upon a friend to command.*
>
> *Jane Williams*
>
> *You must enclose Lady Bulkeley's clergyman to perform the ceremony, which is cousin Molly Owen's lover and I do answer you; we have fixed upon a place where you are to be made one of the happiest of men, which is the library. You are to bring*

down with you a special licence, but this you are not to give her the least hint of my telling you.

Now all you are to do is to write to her as a lover with passion and how fond of her you are and press her with great vehement to make you quite happy in every letter, you will write to her truly first noon. My Dear Sir Hugh, you must batter her ladyship with loving letters. Your paper war cannot last alone a fortnight at furthermost, for you will not want ammunition to besiege her. I will answer for her being won and taken and then it must end in a long honourable peace.

She asked me a great many questions about your temper, and I told her that I knew you ever since you were six-year-old and that there never was a better tempered person in the world; and that you were free from vice and had all the good qualities that a woman could desire a man to have. I laid before her your tenderness and duty towards your mother and your humanity and generosity towards all your fellow creatures and your great sincerity to your friends. She was charmed and in quite high raptures with you. Now my Dear Sir Hugh, you are to think yourself just upon the brink of happiness, with a woman of quality and great fortune and one that has a thousand charms in her own person. If you had been my own son, I could do no more and I write to you just in the same way without any sort of form, for all I tell you is the sincere truth. I hope to God you will make her Ladyship a good husband for I wish her extremely well and there is quite a sincere friendship between us: and we are never happy if we do not see one another everyday of our lives. If I had a son that she really liked to marry, if I thought he would make her a bad husband upon my honour, I would do all I could against him. In your letter to my Ladyship, you must say some girly things to Molly Owen, or in my letter which is your will for she knows all and there is a great friendship of yours. You must thank her, for her good will towards you. I hope you will be so good as excuse this shocking female the pen is so bad that I really cannot write anymore. This affair must be kept a grand secret for if it once comes out before the knot is tied, we are all demonised, so you are to hurry her as much as possible towards it. *You will have a very good excuse to do it, as you are to go abroad. I am resolved not to let Mr Williams, nor brother, nor sister know anything of it until the ceremony is over. My Dear Sir Hugh I hope you don't think that it was selfish of me that I thought of this affair, I do assure you upon my honour I had no other motive than a sincere affectionate friendship for you and if I could make you a Prince I would think nothing a trouble that I could do towards compassing it, so my Dear Sir Hugh, I beg you will believe me to be your very sincere and affectionate letter in mine and tell her Ladyship how to direct to you, in London. You should write to her from Chester as well as Conway.'*

The affair between Emma and Sir Hugh started in 1757, three years before they were married. Sir Hugh Williams was born at Ariannws, Llangelynin, Conwy. He was born in 1718, the son of Colonel Griffith Williams and his wife, Mary Williams. Like his father, he was an army man, entering in 1739 and becoming a Captain in the 34th Foot in 1744. His uncle was Sir Robert Williams, 7th Baronet and Sir Hugh became the 8th Baronet of Penrhyn on his death in November 1745. His cousin, Ann Williams of Prendergast, inherited the house of Marl and Prendergast, along with Park and Llwyn. In 1756 he was a Major in the Sixth Foot and was at Minorca when the garrison was attacked. Then he met Emma, and he was trying to be careful even though his old friend, Mrs Jane Williams, was busy advising him how to behave and how to woo Emma. In her second letter to Sir Hugh dated September 29th 1757, she says:

'I acknowledge with the lightest gratitude the favour of your agreeable friendly letter, and ten thousand thanks to you for your benevolence towards my poor Boy. May the great God reward you for it, with health and prosperity in all your undertakings shall be my constant prayers. The poor boy leaped for joy as soon as I told him of your goodness and said, 'God Bless Sir Hugh forever and ever.'

My dear Sir Hugh I am really surprised that you did not enclose a letter in mine to Lady Bulkeley. She expects to hear from you with the greatest impatience imaginable for she is really quite in love with you, in short whenever I am with her, she cannot talk of nothing but you. I do assure you it is all our discourse, and then she says I wish to God I had Sir Hugh here, that I might talk it over with him and then you and Molly should leave us and then by the time you would come to see us, you would see us in such good humour, so fond of one another that would make Molly and you quite happy and she proposes a great deal of pleasure to herself corresponding with you at Gibraltar. She says that she will write all the news that is happening in the County and that her letters should be little histories to you. She said she would be very cautious what she wrote about her long affair for it is impossible knowing into whose hands one's letters might fall into, but if he was with me, I would not say anything to him that would give encouragement to think that I thoroughly loved him: as I have such a high opinion of his honour.

There is a gentleman of three thousand a year from Hampshire that has a fine house and Park within ten miles of Winchester that is vastly in love with her Ladyship and has proposed to her Father to make what settlement they please, that he desires nothing more than her ladyship and he would not hurt my Lord's interest nor future in the least point, but would do all he could to improve both his proposals. I saw myself from under his hand to Mr Lewis of Llandyfrydog, his name is Sir William Hanam, he is a member of Parliament in the country interest, but she has rejected his proposal upon your account I assure you. I persuaded her at last to have a very favourite opinion telling her that you were in such a hurry in writing about poor Bob for fear he would be disappointed that though the ship was under sail you could not forebear writing about him as really his bread depends upon it, and that I was sure you had not time to answer her ladyship's letter properly so you would not attempt it. I then told her, nor did he indeed answer a word of my letters, but just that part relating to Bob's affair. I then told her that I knew you to be a man of honour and sincerity and that I would lay down my life if you would forfeit either and that you had so much business in your friendship to weave in your love affairs and especially as he has so fine a person to deal with as your Ladyship, as he is desperately in love with you, that at last she smiled and said 'Dear Mrs Williams, we shall soon see that by the letter you will receive from Gibraltar; then said 'I will answer for him, that he will make it his business to convince your Ladyship of his constancy himself as soon as he arrives in Gibraltar. Last night I supped at Baron Hill with Lady Bulkeley's Father and Mr Lewis of Llandyfrydog, and her Ladyship and Miss Molly Owens. Most of our conversation was upon the power of Love. Mr Rowlands said that nothing was surpassing true love in his opinion that he would sooner choose to see his daughter married to a man of one hundred a year that had a thorough affection for her and she for him, than if she was married to a man of four thousand a year if she could not love him. here must be equal love of both goes before a couple can be happy. I do not know that there ever happened a cross word between your Mother and me and if I was to begin my life again, I would choose her in her smock sooner than any other woman in the world with a hundred thousand pounds and then his Tears dropped very fast, he carried it so far as to say, 'Nay, my dear I would rejoice to see you quite happy with a man you loved if you had but bread and cheese with him if he returned your love for love and was a gentleman.' Now this way of thinking of Mr Rowlands made Lady Bulkeley quite happy though she pretended to be quite against it and joined Mr Lewis and Molly Owen. I was strong with Mr Rowlands all that Lady Bulkeley and the other two went upon was that it was impossible to find out whether a young fellow was sincere if he was not an equal fortune to the Lady, he made love to, for his motive for making love might be fortune or interest. Yes, said Mr Rowlands you might find out that by his perseverance if he was sincere, he could think of no person but you. It was one o'clock when I came home. Lady Bulkeley brought her boy down to the lowest gate and told me. I am sure my father would be reconciled to me in a week's time. If I married Sir Hugh, I do assure my dear friend his sentiment from the occasion has made me quite Happy. As well as her Ladyship, Mr Lewis told him that it was a very foolish doctrine before his daughter. Poor

Molly Owens was quite rejoiced to here Mr Rowlands opinion of matrimony. I beg for God's sake you will burn all my letters as soon as you have read them, and do not let any person living know anything of your love affair. I am sadly afraid Captain Jones will find it out and if he does, he will let everybody in the Country know it.

My Dear Sir Hugh I wish I had you here only for one week and I am sure in that time her Ladyship would be all your own. Adieu My Dear, Dear Friend adieu and may the great God protect you and keep you from all harm, shall be my constant prayers, for you my dearest best friend I have in the world, and I may safely say you cannot have a more sincere friend than I am to you. I would think nothing too much that I could do to save you if I was to lay down my life for you. I am in great dread for fear you should not enjoy good health abroad. For God's sake let me know in every letter you write to me. Molly Owens desires her best respects to you and says that she would have written to you long before now but that you desired her not to do it till, she heard from you: she expects a letter from Gibraltar. I hope there will be a letter from you to her Ladyship before you receive this drool, but if not write immediately to me and enclose a letter to her Ladyship in mine. Do not pretend that you have had a letter from me till after you have written to her. Be sure that I had not written to you to acquaint you that I had received your bill for poor Bob. Pray let me know in a loose scrap of paper that you have received it for I shall be very uneasy about it, for fear it should fall into anybody else's hands. Lady Bulkeley says that she would give a hundred pounds to see all my letters to you. I forgot to tell you that Lady Bulkeley's Father scolded her most heartily at the end of the argument and said to her My dear Child I am surprised how you can be so covetous as to prefer a man of fortune to a pretty young fellow that thoroughly loved you tho he has not a groat. He said My Dear you should never forget the woeful experience you have had by marriage for interest and fortune. Adieu, once more my Dear Sir Hugh. Her ladyship had only a mind to try her father, it was not her way of thinking no more than it was mine.

> *Her father's sentiment about matrimony rejoiced her most extremely well as well as it did me. As much as I hate writing I believe I could write to you forever. Jane Williams'*

It appeared that the love affair was developing with the help of Mrs Jane Williams. She was the daughter of Edward Holland of Conwy and Elizabeth, daughter of Owen Anwyl of Park, Merioneth. She married Robert Williams of Pwll-y-Crochan in 1738. They had eight children but only three survived. She now lived at Beaumaris and had become very friendly with Emma and was in fact her confidante. Life was very sweet, thought Emma, and she busied herself with writing to her friends telling them about her life at Baron Hill, though never mentioning a word about Sir Hugh.

Sir Hugh Williams was in Gibraltar due to the Seven Years War of 1754-1763. Britain emerged from the war as the world's leading naval and colonial power, having gained several new territories at the Treaty of Paris in 1763. This was under the leadership of the Prime Ministers, the Duke of Newcastle and William Pitt the Elder.

Mrs Williams wrote again to Sir Hugh, this time to tell him about the letter he had sent Emma.

'October 20th 1757,

My Dear, Dear Sir Hugh, As the post is just going out, I have only time to tell you; that I received your long-expected letter which came in hand in about a week after I sent you my last. I never was as much rejoiced when I found a letter from you to her Ladyship, as she was impatient about having one – she told me that it was your most loving, pleasing she ever had from you and you may assure yourself that she is as much as a woman can be, that is not married to you. Baron Hill has been crowded with company that she could not possibly write to you till today; it was but yesterday that all the company left her ladyship.

I am sorry that her Ladyship of Marle knows anything of your love affair for I am sure she will blab it, to all the world. I do assure you upon my honour Mr Williams knows nothing about the matter, it was I that sent you some of her Ladyships hair; though I told her Ladyship that I would do so and she did not desire me to do so, but now she says that she is determined to deny it, for fear you should think it to forward in her and she says that she would sooner choose: that having a good opinion of her: than all the world besides and she charged me not to own it to you upon any account. So do not take any notice that I have if you write to Molly Owens; enclose it in mine for if you direct a letter to her certainly would be found out at this post office, that there was a love affair carried on between her Ladyship and you. I showed your last friendly letter with the ten pound bill to Mr Briscoe and he admired your generosity vastly, but my main reason for doing so was that he should not think it too odd that I wrote so often to you: and in your letter he saw that you desired me to write immediately: then he said to me, indeed Madam I think it is your duty to write as often as you can, to so good a friend and it must be very agreeable to him to have letters from any of his acquaintances while he is abroad. I must say that I was glad to hear him say so. Poor Bob is to go up with my Cousin Watkin Wynn of Voelas to stay at his house in London till he goes to the Academy. My boys are all well and cannot tax myself in misbehaving towards him and I thought Sir Hugh was Hugh desire there love to you and their best respect – be sure to mention Molly Owen in all your letters to me or to my Ladyship in a very loving manner.

At Baron Hill is one Mr Price making hot love to her Ladyship, but she despises him most heartily. He has five and twenty hundred a year and they say he will have twenty thousand pounds in money. He is a member of our borough. She tells me, that she is determined not to give any person living the least encouragement to think of her till she sees you; and that she would not for the world guilt you if she thought you were quite sincere to her and that you really loved her. I really think her a most desirable woman and I am sure she would make you most extremely happy; for she has excellent sense, and good nature; and has a hundred good qualities; She is worth her weight in rubies. She is vastly jealous of Lady Young; she is sadly afraid that you have some liking towards her. I beg for God's sake that you will write to Lady Bulkeley as soon as possible and declare *your passion in a soft loving style. If you do not, I shall think you guilty of a crime that you always abhorred, which is the sin of ingratitude to a most charming woman. I dare not tell her that I received a letter from you for fear it should alter her way of thinking about you and cool herself towards you. Molly Owen is really your sincere friend and I beg you will always mention her in every letter you write to me with respect. Yesterday I received your letter, if you have altered your mind concerning my Dear Lady Bulkeley, I beg you will let me know it as soon as possible, that I might by degrees tell her of it. Charity and friendship will demand my actions in that manner with her Ladyship. All or children's Tickets came up blanks pray let me know in your next whether you have had any prizes. Sister Peggy is gone to a grand concert at Denbigh, there is to be balls and I do not know what there. I wish you would be so good as to write to her she really expects a letter from you, and she is a very good friend I do assure you. Brother and Sister Holland are now at Mold, the smallpox continues still very fatal at Conway. Mr Williams is at Marle. Mrs Farrow of Pablo told Lady Bulkeley that you were favourite there. I believe it is no great loss to you. Lady Prendegast is to up to London this winter, Sir Thomas has taken a house for her, he is to winter in Dublin by that I imagine there is no good understanding between them. Lady Dowager Bulkeley is just come to town with a grand carriage. The Lord Lieutenant travelled through this country with a very pompous retinue, he had six coaches with him. The boys are all well and desire there love and best respects to you. Believe most affectionately and faithfully your sincere friend to command till death.*

Jane Williams

This moment Lady Bulkeley came into this room and caught me writing to you so, I was obliged to discover my having a letter from you for I was afraid to deny it; as she might easily found it out at the Post Office that I had one from you, and then it would have had much worse with you and sadly vexed at her being disappointed in you, and then she said, I am sorry I have shed so many tears about him; I shall no more about him: nor talk of him anymore. I wish I had never seen him. I think I was too polite to be guilty of so great a fault as not to answer a Lady's letter for all young fellows reckon that a woman gives encouragement to her while she continues to write to him: but for all that my Dear Mrs Williams, I cannot help wishing Sir Hugh Williams as well as anybody in the world can wish him, though I always thought that his passion was too violent to last long. Soon hot and soon cool. I really had vanity to imagine that he would have persevered for some time at least and would not have thought of anybody but me for I thought of non but him. All I have told you about her Ladyship upon my honour are her own words. She desired to see your letter to me and then she read it thrice over and admired your generosity to poor Bob and then she said, he has not sent me the least compliment, no more than if he had never heard of my name and then she begged it as a favour my not mentioning her name to you upon any account, and I promised her I would not. My friendship for you made me guilty of a vile fault which is a breach of promise; but I could not help having your well fair at heart and was loath you would lose so great a prize by your own need that made me discover the whole affair to you. I must it to your honour that you will never disclose to her that I told you how dearly she loves you will mess if you were to give her the least hint of it. It would ruin our friendship.

My Dear best friend, I am surprised how you can think me so miserable a wretch as to keep account of the money that I will lay out in sending letters to you, after your proving to me, one of the best and most generous Friend I ever had in this world, and you may be assured that you will never meet with a sincere friend than I shall be to you as long as I have breath. Last Friday Admiral Mostyn was buried in a very pompous manner in his family vault at Llanrhos. He left Sir Thomas's the eldest son: Master Roger Mostyn sixty thousand pounds- what a charming fortune that young fellow has now – I wish to God, you had it.

Sir William Hanam has written two letters to Lady Bulkeley, but she does not intend to answer either of them. What you said of Lady Young to Lady Bulkeley quite charmed her for she said no man could behave with more gentility than you did upon the occasion; I do assure you she was in high raptures with you and said that she could trust you with anything as you were a man of such strict honour. She said she only did it to try him and said she, how many men in the world would have been glad to have sacrificed the character of one woman to please and humour the vanity of the other. Adieu my dear Sir Hugh – and I entreat you to believe me to be very sincere.

Your affectionate Friend and humble faithful servant to command

Jane Williams'

When her father next called, he found Emma somewhat subdued. He asked after her health and if she was well enough to talk with him. Before Thomas had a chance to say much, Emma gave him the two letters that had come from Sir William Hanam. Thomas read them and asked if she had replied; Emma told him that she had not. She warned her father to leave her alone, and that it was not his place to suggest her to anyone or try to marry her off. She went on about her duty to her son and that she was trying also to make sure that Bridget would be looked after.

Mr Price of Rhiwlas was a frequent visitor during 1758, he still called when he was in town and assured her that he would wait until the time was better, so that he could talk with her. Emma had been very kind to Mr Price and allowed him to stay when he was on business in the borough. Unfortunately, Mr Price was thinking further than just holding the seat for Emma's son, he thought he was in with a good chance of being able to propose to her. However, it was found he had a very bad temper, and he would lose his temper quite often if Emma showed him that she had no interest in him. Molly Owen said of him according to a letter from Mrs Mostyn to Mrs Owen of Porkington, that Captain Price was well huffed by Molly Owen who branded him of a venomous temper. *'It's a fine life when such trollops are suffered to abuse gentlemen.'* Mrs Mostyn then goes on to say that she wishes Captain Price was married but not to Lady Bulkeley, so far, she went on without stop. He has some friends left to battle for him. The lady was tough in his interest I'm sure and spoke of things as they might have been not as they are for people degenerate. Emma did not worry about Captain Price; she was more than convinced that she had met the person with whom she would spend the rest of her life. It was more than enough to write daily when she could to Sir Hugh Williams giving accounts of all the events that occurred. At times she was very excited and couldn't wait to see Mrs Williams and tell her what she wanted her to know and how pleasing it was to hear from Sir Hugh and that she wished he could come home, but she was always aware that men had to serve their country for the King.

Chapter Sixteen

After the attack on his garrison, Sir Hugh began to feel unwell. He suffered for quite a while, and he wrote to his uncle. His uncle answered him and suggested that he asked for leave so that he could come home and visit Bath for the waters. That was in December 1756. He explains that it was the only letter that he had received from Sir Hugh that did not give him pleasure, *'for to hear of my best friend's welfare and happiness always gives me satisfaction.'* He goes on to tell Sir Hugh that the Bath waters saved his life and if he managed to get leave then he must go to Bath.

Sir Hugh mixed in a good circle of people, those whom he knew would support his promotions to better himself within the army. People like the Warburtons and the Youngs, who wrote and recommended him to the King as did the Duchess of Argyle. As the son of an army colonel, he was used to living an ordered army life. Unmarried, and at 42, he thought that the army was to be his mundane life until he was too old for anything else. He became unsettled. Having read his uncle's letter, he arranged leave for himself.

During the summer of 1757, he was on leave at Bath for his health. On his return he stayed at Friars outside Beaumaris. He walked daily to strengthen himself, until he met Emma, Viscountess Bulkeley, and fell in love. Knowing Mrs Jane Williams, her companion, and that he could trust her, he received many letters informing him how he was to behave and what he was to do to woo Emma. When he had gone back to Gibraltar, he carried on a clandestine love affair with Emma. By 1759, he was a major in the volunteer battalion.

There is a letter from a Mr E Harrison, who wrote to Sir Hugh on April 30th 1757. He refers to a young woman at the tea rooms in Bath whom obviously Sir Hugh had fancied and was only known as 'H--t—y'. He then sent Sir Hugh Mr and Mrs Andrews' compliments. There is also a letter from his relation who lived at Coetmor, dated March 21st, 1757.

'Dear Sir,

The reason of my writing to you when abroad, I must attribute to the superior genius of my better self for who'd presume to be senile, when such a charming sentiments of exalted mind, and only proud from such a one as your Aunty, which is the only thing I have to move in my own defence: But joking apart it was not out of any disregard or want of friendship, but a diffidence in myself that occasioned it. We are vastly glad to hear that Dear Sir Hugh is so well and that the Bath waters have had so good an effect, and at the same time much affected with the thoughts that we are not to see you at Coytmor.

Now for Occurancies.

We have lately discovered a lead mine by Coytmor Mill, just by the river side, and the prospect is so far, that a company is forming to carry on a trial to effect: between our farm and the share we reserve to ourselves as adventures, will amount to better than one 4th of the work: who knows what strange mountains you may see at Coytmor when we shall have the honour of seeing you here.

On Tuesday last 3 ships were castaway on the Lavan Sands, and another drove ashore at Deganwy, all bound for Liverpool with grain and malt. The crew saved except three, but cargo lost. I am ashamed that the money for the wine, you were so kind as to send me, is not paid. I must entreat you to send word, which way you would chose to have it paid, either by return to London, or to Mrs Williams your good Mother, whichever it be, shall be complied with by return of Post, since we can't hope for the happiness of seeing you at Coytmor; Pray since fate has so decreed it to be so kind to let us know from you as soon as possible, which will give the greatest pleasure to him, who with the greatest truth is most sincerely.

Dearest Sir Hugh
Most affectionate relation
Obliged Humble servant.
Edward Philip Pugh.

Your Aunt writes.
So, you'd have the best respects and I hope you accept mine and the children.'

Whenever Sir Hugh was on leave, even for a short time, Emma would make the effort to travel to London, Plymouth, and Cork to see him. She wrote to him practically every day and filled him in on her position as a mother whose duty it was to keep the Baron Hill seat for her son, the young Lord Bulkeley. It created in her an interest in politics, although Sir Hugh did not agree with some of the people she thought suitable to stand. She also had to think about the education of Thomas James, until it was decided that he should go to Westminster like his father. On July 17th Emma wrote to Mrs Owen of Porkington.

'Dear Mrs Owen,

I had the honour of a letter from my dear Mrs Owen some weeks ago, and I should have returned you a speedy answer did I not fear consequences would have been profound silence as the punishment for plaguing you. Jimmy, I settled about a fortnight ago at Westminster and I have the pleasure to find him very tractable and complying to the rules of the school and as ready to return there as to come home.

I had no objection to Eton only his father and most of his relations were brought up at Westminster and his friends here strongly recommended to me to bring him up there as Doctor Markham pleases extremely so that entirely followed their advice and hope the best.

The town now is immoderately hot and empty. General Clive his immense wealth is the chief topic, he gave the captain of the vessel that he came over in seven thousand guineas and a Colonel who was upon the same service as himself though not so successful he gave him five hundred pounds a year. Mrs Clive has as many diamonds as will cover a yard square table and garnets and pearls in the like number. There has been bad news from Germany, Prince Ferdinand flies before the French is overtaken it is feared.

I was at Vauxhall a few nights ago and I could have wished Miss Owen of the party for I do believe by that sprightly look of hers she is no enemy to society and jolly I had high persuasion. I shall go to the country within a fortnight's time it would be nothing for my lively Miss Owen to fly over to Baron Hill how glad and happy I should be to see her, and her brother can show her the way. It is commonly said that Miss Williams Whitlock is to be married to Mr Vaughan of Hengoed, pray, is there anything in the report. I met Mr Peter Davies at Mr Egerton's we talked our Bath expedition over, and he declared solemnly that pretty Mrs Merchant jilted him fairly when you did see her. I hope you would be able to prevail on good dear Mrs Owen to winter here the best receipt in the world for gravel. My compliments attend Mr Owen and the young ladies, I am always and in places dear madam.

Your ever obliged servant
Emma Bulkeley'

Emma and Sir Hugh wrote to each other practically every day. Emma travelled to see him when he was in this country, she had even travelled down to Portsmouth, she was so much in love with him. She also went to Cork so that she could see him, and that is why she was always asking where to send her letters, whether to Cork or Portsmouth. During September 1757, shortly after their meeting, Sir Hugh questioned her after Mrs Williams had informed him of other suitors trying for her hand. She wrote and signed her letter to him, *'I now reckon myself firmly yours'*. In 1759, Sir Hugh received a letter from the War Office.

> *'It is His Majesty's Pleasure that you cause the Companies of the Royal Volunteers under your command at Chester to march by the shortest and most convenient route to Newcastle under Lime, Macclesfield and Stone, where they are to be quartered and remain until further order. Wherein the civil magistrates and all other concerned are to be assisting in providing quarters, impressing carriages and otherwise as shall be occasion. Given at the War Office this 30th day of October 1759.*
>
> *By His Majesty's Command*
> *In the absence of the secretary at war*
> *Thomas Townshend*
>
> *To the officer Commanding*
> *The companies of the Royal Volunteers*
> *At Chester'*

Sir Hugh was a major in the army, which he disliked immensely. He was keener than ever now that he was married to Emma to leave the army. He wanted a life and having written and told Emma how he felt, he thought it was her duty to think of him rather than those her father had suggested for the different posts of Constable of Beaumaris Castle. Her father had held after the death of Emma's first husband, and he felt that she should consider him when an election came along. Several people felt that she should – and Sir Hugh certainly thought so, if only to prove to his stepson that he was interested. The difficulty was getting out of the army.

So, their clandestine love affair continued until 1760 when Emma felt easier. Her son Jimmy was now settled at Westminster and her daughter Bridget was at school in Chester. Emma went up to London and felt that this was going to be the most exciting year of her life. She devoted most of her time to thinking about her wedding attire without telling her father. Her choice of colour rather shocked many and especially Mrs Owen of Porkington. Her choice was scarlet, and she wrote and assured Mrs Owen that it was a fashionable colour. When everything had been sort out and Emma was ready, Sir Hugh called as he was on leave and staying with a friend.

On June 28th 1760, they were married at St George's, Hanover Square, Westminster, London. Sir Hugh thought her scarlet dress was wonderful and suited her well.

Emma felt that her world was perfect now. But she knew that she had to be careful due to her position. Therefore, they decided that they would keep the marriage secret for the time being. Sir Hugh felt that Emma had too many decisions to make with the elections and he sent her various ideas he had. The trouble was that her father had quite an influence on her, and she therefore did not always agree with Sir Hugh. However, on November 27th 1760, Sir Hugh received a letter from Mr Warburton.

'St James's Coffee House
London
November 27th 1760

Dear Sir,

I would not willingly be the last in wishing you joy and much happiness in your present situation which I was not acquainted with till two days ago, since I came to town. I have another reason for troubling you with this which I hope you will ensure Lady Bulkeley both understand and will bring you into Parliament if agreeable, but as I am not acquainted with your inclinations as to that, I hope will ensure the proposal I am going to make. I have one thousand pounds I would lodge in any friends' hands, and to be at your disposal. (Pay you in case you do not choose to be in Parliament yourself) if you will remember me to her Ladyship to represent the Borough. I flatter myself you will pardon this proposal and believe me.

Dear Sir
Your most faithful Humble servant
H. Warbuton

If this letter comes to your hands, I shall be very glad, as I find it unsure whether you are upon this expedition or not.'

This unsettled Sir Hugh more than ever and he now tried again to leave the army, but somehow, he had to stay. He was very interested in becoming a husband and listened to Emma when she related all her duties and her responsibilities. He had told her of a few that he had, one being his mother. Emma wrote to Sir Hugh's mother in December 1760, and received a reply on the 11th. She also assured him that now they were married, should anything happen to him she would look after his mother financially.

'Honourable Madam,

Yesterday the Reverend Mr Roberts favoured me with your Ladyships letter himself. I received a letter from my son by last Friday's post, in which he informs me of the Honour of being married to your Ladyship, he begs pardon for not acquainting me sooner, as it was necessary to be kept a secret because of your Ladyships private affairs required it should be so. Tho acquainted of being obliged on the expedition, but I was in great hopes he would not go abroad anymore. I am very much obliged for your Ladyship's kind offer of your services in his absence so am with affectionate compliments your Ladyship and most obliged humble servant.

M. Williams'

Emma received a letter dated December 13th 1760. This was from the lady who looked after the young Lord Bulkeley.

> 'Madam,
>
> I have the pleasure of informing your Ladyship that Lord Bulkeley is quite well. I do not wonder at your Ladyship's uneasiness about his Lordship, the distance and my being a stranger to your Ladyship must greatly add. But I do assure you I pique myself upon taking very particular care of my young men, when they are ill and your Ladyship may depend upon it that they have not common school nursing.
>
> I took to everything material myself, but as it is impossible to be always present with them, I have a careful person I can trust to do as I order them; and I do assure your Ladyship that I often put myself in a tender Mother's place.
>
> Your Ladyship is vastly good to think of cash, which will now be very acceptable to me, having at this season, so many bills to pay for the gentlemen, therefore if your Ladyship will order your banker to let me have twenty pounds on account, it will be of great service to me, and when my Lord's half year is up, then we will settle the accounts. I am glad to hear of some new shirts, these we have are pretty good, but my Lord has grown out of them so much that I have been forced to lengthen the sleeves.
>
> I can give your Ladyship a very satisfactory account of Lord Bulkeley as to his behaviour in every particular at home and at school. He goes on extremely well and his French Master told me the other day that he was sure that he should have great credit from Lord Bulkeley and that he thought his pronounced it better for the time he had learnt it than any he ever met with. I fear I have quite tired your Ladyship, so will only add that I am
>
> Madam
> Your Ladyship's
> Most Obedient
> Humble servant
> C Porben'

Sir Hugh had for some time been advising Emma to tell her father that they were married. She kept putting it off, as she believed her father did not approve of Sir Hugh as a husband for her, he did have some rights such as taking over the political aspect of the family on behalf of his stepson. He also wanted to be Constable of Beaumaris Castle, a position held by her father after the death of her first husband, Lord Bulkeley. Sir Hugh wrote to her from Southampton.

'Southampton 20*th* October 1760

My Dear Dearest Emma,

I have just time to tell you of my arrival here last night after a troublesome experienced journey; you know my order was dated Saturday night, and I set out on Sunday about 4 o'clock, after seeing the Ceremony of Proclaiming the Young King which was performed at Savill House upon the steps. Your house was very convenient upon that occasion, found there Lady Ann Hamilton, Mrs Taylor, Miss Middleton, and many others.

The honour of your house in the last manner I could. I gave them chocolate coffee, my only reason for taking the liberty in your house that I happened to be the only male being, in the room. Pray is her ladyship your acquaintance, she seems very witty and sensible, and I am told she is the thing for 'Proper diva'—

I hope all my epistles are come up to your hand and you will continue giving me the only satisfaction I can have makes me happy; let me know your free thoughts of what I have said about the borough.

I must beg you will avoid all thoughts of favouring the present member-for be assured if he is elected, it will be a certain loss to the family; besides I don't see how you assure him a present of fifteen hundred pounds. Write immediately and direct here, Gosport, excuse my haste for the post going out.

I remain my Dear Lovely Emma
Your faithful affectionate husband

H Williams'

In a letter of November 26th 1760, Sir Hugh wrote to Emma, he mentions how pleased he was to hear that she was on tolerable terms with her father, who had so little reason to be displeased with her conquest. *'You did very right to make your submission in person, for I was certain your agreeable behaviour would prevail'.* Further along... *'I hope he'll find no difficulty in giving me a qualification to be the member for your Borough'.* He goes on about her choice of candidate to stand in the election and tries to get her to make her father understand why he is so keen to come out of the army and stand for Beaumaris. Further in the letter he asks about her new chaise and four bays, and then he tells her that it is no secret within his regiment that they are married. *'I have told it public... When can I direct to you properly or are you ashamed of your new name?'*

Emma went to London to enjoy herself. She felt alive and excited there and would be nearer Sir Hugh should he be allowed any leave. He had just been made a lieutenant colonel by the King at the beginning of the year. Emma was very proud. On January 15th 1760, a letter came from her father.

> *'My Dear,*
>
> *I received both of your letters wherein you gave a pleasing account of your safe arrival in town, without any other accident, but which you met with near Abergely, which hath twice been fatal to your carriage which greatly rejoiced me, for by the blind accident I had received greatly dreaded lest some hurt had befallen either of you and not quite free from some apprehension lest the highwaymen mentioned in the papers might have attacked you; but thank God you escaped all danger and are likewise free from colds, and dear Butty performed your long journey so well.*
>
> *What of your cousin Kyffin in your opposition. Sir I W. Certainly some pretended friends, have bamboozled and cajoled this wild thoughtless road into this idle delusive scheme will prove abortive and injurious to this fortune if they pursue it; be pleased to recollect that my scarily chiefly proceeded from hearsay was to Mr William Owen's will. I do upon*

recollection verily believe that I've heard Mr M L saver what he mentioned. I have not yet soon nor heard a word from my candidate; certainly, you are always in a hurry when you write to me for both your last came upon to me besides the expense of double postage, pray when you favour me next with a time to be more careful in the sealing up and write a long hand. I fancy that your boxes and luggage may forever this came up, also you and the dear girl must be greatly confined; the harp lies here still and I've no servant that I can trust to carry it to Pencraig. I wrote to you which I hope you've received this day 7 nights: which I hope you've received. In your next be so kind as to inform me how the Dear Buck and Butty first greeted; that God may bless and preserve you and them is a hearty prayer and wish of.

My Dear your most affectionate poor father
T. Rowlands

Your Grandmother desires her blessing and compliments to you all'

Sir Hugh received a letter from Nicholas Bayley of Plas Newydd, sent from Bond Street, London on January 15th 1761.

'Sir,

I have had the honour to wait on Lady Bulkeley to make my compliments of congratulations on your marriage and was in hopes at the same time to have paid them to you – and now my desire your acceptance of them in the best manner. I can make a tender of them at so great a distance.

I should have thought myself much honoured to have had your approbation of my being candidate for Anglesey, but if Lady Bulkeley is otherwise inclined, I will urge the subject no further.

I am with great regard Sir.
Yours most obedient humble servant

Nicholas Bayley'

During February 1761, Emma wrote to Mrs Owen at Porkington.

'February 28th 1761

I had the unexpected honour of a letter lately from Dear Mrs Owen, whenever you take up your pen, you make ample amends for your silence. I have been in town this two month, on my arrival Lord Bulkeley was taken ill of the measles at a Mr Courdeneby's, about forty miles from here, where I immediately posted. I found him in a fair way of recovery, on his return to town he was well physicked and so got over his disorder, he's now again at Westminster.

I think without a mother's partiality I may pronounce him a fine boy. My poor little girl is rather sickly, I have just placed her at Mrs Sheebs's in the hope that a regular school life may be of service to her.

Now my dear Mrs Owen I am ready to dispute a point with you, you say I thought purple and yellow tawdry colours, as I hope to live, I deny it, for I well remember that it my poor heart so fluttered at the agreeable mixture that I thought no rainbow like it—

Well, to be sure you have lived to good purpose these years in the country, I don't believe that there's a living woman under three score that can think or at least within three score that can think or at least within a hundred miles of London. Scarlet, blue dowdy colour, quite the reverse, Nay can I ever that since these have been in my esteem. I am a thousand times the decent woman, you know sent me the last in valuables, I am sorry to tell you that I wear them in my meridian of gaiety, I am sure every friend of mine will be rejoiced to see the good effects that the powerful colour scarlet has had on me.

After this prelude I may venture to tell my dear Madam Owen, what the world knows already, that I am married, and to a soldier, the King was pleased to make him Lt Colonel some weeks ago, and I believe if you knew how prudent, good, and decent my husband is, you would not condemn my choice.

I can't say tho that he comes up quite to my honoured fleet. Doctor Owen in these worthies accomplished but really very near it.

> *The account of your Shropshire widows shocks me, what a mercy it is that they're prudent in other parts. I am sorry you did not come up to town for I flattered myself I should meet you here. I hope dear good Mr Owen enjoyed his health to whom pray my best compliments. Don't forget me to Mr F.G Owen who I regard much tho we sometimes disagree. I am Miss Owen's and Miss Molly's very humble servant. Have you any commission here, I should be proud to do anything for you.*
>
> *Sir Hugh Williams and I go soon to the country where I should be happy to see anyone from Porkington.*
>
> With purest regard & respect
> Yours ever
> Mrs E. Bulkeley Williams'

Sir Hugh was a prolific writer of letters and had many friends whom he kept in touch with. He was by now very keen to be made Constable of Beaumaris Castle, feeling that it would be the first step towards being allowed to stand for the borough, and being allowed out of the army. As there was to be an election various people wrote to him and on February 5th 1761, he received a letter from T Kyffin.

> 'Dear Sir,
>
> *The great approbation and encouragement I have met with in canvassing the county is the reason of taking the liberty of soliciting your vote and interest in the county of Caernarvon in favour of Dear Sir*
>
> Your most humble servant
> T. Kyffin
>
> Maynan. Feb 5th, 1761'

Emma was travelling back to Baron Hill and Sir Hugh returned to his regiment, the 53rd Foot. Next time he was travelling to Baron Hill he would be collecting Lord Bulkeley and looking after him as he travelled home. They both got on very well and soon Sir Hugh's wish to be made Constable of Beaumaris Castle materialised in July 1761.

He was elated at last he felt part of the family. Bridget was not as well as expected, she had never been strong, but at least now she would have plenty of rest during her holidays. Emma was grateful that Bridget had received an inheritance from her father, as she was at the time his only child.

Emma entertained as usual and had various friends to come and stay at Baron Hill where she was pleased to show them her wonderful view of the Menai Straits with its sailing ships. Life, she believed, could never get better than this.

Sir Hugh was glad to have conversations with Mrs Jane Williams, explaining to her how important it was for him to leave the army. He became more involved with all the economics of Baron Hill. Emma was very careful with all the accounts and had inherited a mind akin to her grandfather, John Rowlands, a banker in London. Every Michaelmas, one of the four quarter days of the financial year, she would sit and go through all the accounts and decide what was more important to buy or sell. She would examine each expenditure until she was satisfied that they could continue to live a good life. A rental of the estate descended to the Hon. Miss Bridget Bulkeley, daughter and heiress of the Rt. Hon James 6th Lord Bulkeley deceased, in possessions upon her said father's death. This is the time when Emma, having done the accounts, would order items to cover the following year, including food for the horses and dogs, of which she always had plenty.

Unfortunately for Sir Hugh, who thought that he would not be called back, a letter from the War Office arrived, dated December 12th 1761.

> 'Sir,
>
> *Major Lindsay being returned from Gibraltar I do not think it proper to move his Majesty to prolong your leave of absence, and therefore I hope you will take the first opportunity of joining your Regiment. Sir Hugh I am sorry if this notice should be very inconvenient to you, but General Parslaw's remonstrances, with the critical circumstances of the situation of his Kingdom as it relates to Spain makes it necessary, I should give you this order in my justification, and for your information.*

I am Sir your most obedient.
Most humble servant
Lt Col. Sir Hugh Williams of the 53rd Reg of Foot.

C. Townshend'

In April again, Sir Hugh received a letter from Nicholas Bayley, being solicitous because he was hoping for a vote. Sir Hugh was important now simply because he was married to the incomparable Lady Bulkeley. She may have been spoilt and perhaps she was a snob, but she certainly showed them how accomplished she was with figures besides her many other qualities. She made sure that she could account for every penny that was spent, and when she had finished looking at the accounts, she would then send them to an auditor. It was a shame that the recall order came meaning that Sir Hugh would now have to travel down to where his regiment was based. Another letter came for him from Emma's father.

'December 16th 1761.

I was agreeably surprised by my daughter's letter just received with the account of your unexpected return and leave of absence from your regiment; for so many months longer, and greatly obliged for the favour of yours, which I should have immediately answered, but I concluded your stay in town would be very short and were for hurrying down to Plymouth to overtake the Conway. Since it otherwise happens, will you venture with my daughter and dear Butty, M Wynne & co, to eat a xmas pie and partake of such fare with sincere welcome as poor Cayrey affords, if you will favour us with your company, we shall be extremely glad to see you all. I wrote to my daughter yesterday the pleasing account; she gives of the health of my dear child rejoices my old heart and hope she will excuse punctualities, but if you and lady will come over here, shall expect the favour of a line per first post.

God Preserve and bless you all.
I am dear Sir your most obedient and affectionate servant.
T. Rowlands.

Love to M. Wynne.

Mother Roberts desires to be remembered to you all'

With many people writing and assuming that he would be elected for the borough it must have affected Sir Hugh, as it seems to have been the cause of the discord that arose between them. On the day of King George II's death, Sir Hugh wrote to Emma:

> 'Lucky is he who gets this present Parliament, for it be the seat of promotion... I am very sorry to find you inclined to continue the present Member (for Beaumaris). If you regard your son's future interest and glory, and your husband's satisfaction, you must not hesitate to endeavour to turn out Mr Richard Price, even at the hazard of a poll... if you don't do it now, you never will or can have at least right to call that borough the property of the House of Baron Hill, and it must be looked upon as lost by your bad management.'

Emma's father, Thomas Rowlands, had a great influence and being a zealous Tory, wished to have Mr Price for the election. At that time, he disapproved of Sir Hugh, as their marriage had been kept a secret. Regarding this, Sir Hugh wrote to Emma:

> 'Your concealing our marriage from your father, I am afraid disqualifies me from serving the borough – which should be your natural dependence and interest at present. But if I cannot be qualified, let me recommend a person who will give me the Duke of Bedford's interest for promotion and ensure me a Lt Colonelcy immediately and a thousand pounds in ready cash.'

Emma was in a difficult situation, her husband was away in Gibraltar and her father, who felt he oversaw certain things regarding Emma's son, favoured Mr Price and disapproved of the secrecy surrounding her marriage to Sir Hugh. Sir Hugh had kept the pressure on her to tell her father about their marriage and how best to secure both borough and county for her son when he came of age.

In her reply to Sir Hugh, Emma said, 'Nor do I despair of seeing you, my dearest Baronet, mighty snugly established in the borough of Beaumaris, then Price may hang himself if he pleases... To now talk of party, whatever my real opinion is, I shall keep it to myself, only I must *be excused from drinking to the... memory of either Georgites or Old Will'*. In a way, Sir Hugh felt that she was being uncommunicative to him on this subject, especially when Price was returned, and he had failed the 1761 election.

She had of course by now told her father that she was married to Sir Hugh, who was requested to re-join his regiment by Charles Townshend, the Secretary at War. On December 12th. Sir Hugh appealed to Townshend to be allowed to change to a company in the Guards, so as *'to get out of this vile climate where I have been eleven years'*. Life, however, went on and although Sir Hugh hated the climate of Gibraltar, he occupied his time doing his job and answering many letters that he received from various people like the Youngs, the Warburtons, Nicholas Bailey, his uncle at Coetmor, his cousin, Ann Prendergast, Mrs Wynn, and many other members of his own family.

Ann did not write very often to him. She and her brother, the children of Sir Griffith Williams and Catherine Annwyl, were the ones who had inherited Pant Glas, Marl and Park, Llanfrothen. She had married Sir Thomas Prendergast, whom George II called 'a blockhead', but who continued to bombard his cousin's husband, Lord March, with applications for a seat in Parliament until he gained one. He later gained the position of Postmaster General for Ireland. He married Ann Williams on January 11th 1739.

It was not a happy marriage, and they divorced. In September 1760, Sir Thomas Prendegast died, having gained and sold part of his wife's estate. In 1761 she married her husband's cousin, Captain Terence Prendergast, and separated from him in 1762; he again sold off part of her estate. Ann Williams was known to be so extravagant and had such bills that Sir Thomas had to sell off part of the estate to clear her debts. She had been a lady-in-waiting to Queen Caroline and rumour had it that she was the mistress of the Duke of Cumberland and had a son by him. However, the register of the parish church at Conwy claims that he was the son of her brother, Sir Robert Williams, by his mistress, Margaret Roberts, and that Ann his sister brought up the baby.

There is no evidence to suggest that she had a child by the Duke of Cumberland, and only one letter from him was found and that was on business – not romantic – matters. When her brother, Robert Williams, died in 1745, the baronetcy went to Hugh, Emma's husband, but he left his property to his sister, Ann. She was for some time the wealthiest heiress in North Wales but lost much of her estates. She lost Parc and Llwyn and she and William Roberts went to live at Pant Glas, her grandmother's old home, leaving Marl to her husband, Captain Terence Prendergast. She died in poverty at Nant Gwilym, Bodfari, on 15th December 1770.

In January 1762, Ann Williams wrote to Sir Hugh, laying out everything to him as regards her situation and telling him that she did not think that he would get any further in the army, as she had seen a similar situation in Ireland when she lived there with Sir Thomas Prendergast.

On January 21st 1761, Sir Hugh received a letter from Silence Holland, sister to Mrs Jane Williams, who had been busy arranging a match between him and Emma.

> *'Dear Sir Hugh,   Leicester Square.*
>
> *I found myself not a little mortified when calling on Sunday morning at the Red Lion to find that you had set out for Portsmouth in order to sail for old Gib: without calling upon me to take leave, the only thing that has made me able to bear this unexpected neglect is that I hope you are to be recalled to raise the Welsh regiment so much talked of which would give me no small joy, but whether this may be the case or not I most heartily and sincerely wish your health and every other happiness and prosperity your heart can desire. Lady Prendegast was favoured with a letter from you by yesterday's post and writes this day to you herself so I say nothing from her to you as she can have her own say which I am sure will be more agreeable than anything I can say at this time. I have bought yesterday for Roberts, so I hope that he'll be time enough at Portsmouth to sail in the Newark for Gibraltar.*
>
> *Captain Griffiths of the Gibraltar is so well spoken of that Colonel Taylor and many more advise me not to have Roberts changed but to let him take his chance on board the Gibraltar and Colonel Taylor said he would try to have him rated board Gibraltar. The man that was kept being exchanged for Thomas*

has fallen ill of the smallpox, so that I am disappointed again in getting Thomas discharged but shall try other means to get the poor lad his liberty.

I don't believe, but if you would wait upon Admiral Holborn and tell him Thomas's story (and inform him that he is the young gentleman whom Admiral Townshend wrote to him about, some months ago) but that Admiral Holborn would give Thomas his discharge: if you are still at Portsmouth and would take this affair in hand. I do believe that it would be the quickest way of getting Tom discharged: the gentleman whom I got to beg Admiral Townshend to write to Admiral Holborn in Thomas's favour is not in town else I should have had Thomas here with me.

Were this without more trouble than to say that the union is come to Portsmouth Dock.

Let me hear from you if you can on this subject and try to find out what condition Thomas is in as to clothing and health. If I could but get him once discharged from his present dreadful situation. I make no doubt but that I should be able to have something done for him so as he might be enabled to get his bread as a gentleman.

Thomas is now on board the Guard ship for it seems all impressed men when the ship comes into port are sent on board the Guard ship – Captain Risdale is come to town but where he is or when he leaves London, I cannot tell he and Miss Parry called here this morning, but we were not at home. Mr Roberts desires his most respectful compliments to you and wishes you every happiness and does dear Sir Hugh your most affectionate friend.

Humble servant
Silence Holland

I shall often trouble you with hearing from me and I shall send you the chit chat I meet with from time to time and all little news I can pick up for such. A voyage that to old Gib.'

Sir Hugh's cousin, Lady Prendergast, wrote to him again in March. In reply, he said that he could get a cash buyer for Marl, which she was trying to sell as she was in debt. In April more letters arrived:

'Conway Thursday April 27th 1762

Dear Sir Hugh,

Though I have been at the brink of the grave and am still so feeble that I can hardly hold the pen, nor have not had it in my hand for five weeks, but my spirit is today revived and raised to the highest pitch – by the good news I had about an hour ago of Dear Lady Bulkeley being safely brought to bed last Tuesday night of a fine girl. Her ladyship has had a very good time she and your daughter, which I wish.

Dear Sir Hugh joy of in both as possibly can be expected. I likewise about nine days ago had your good news of Lady Bulkeley's hearing from you and that you was in health and safely at Gibraltar, which I give you my word Dear Sir Hugh, comforted your poor friend in my great weakness and will further do – if I have the pleasure to hear from you – tho I would not in this weak condition pretend to write to any person in the world but your dear self-acquainted.

Now that I have been in bed some while I think you could expect I should give you some account of my illness which was a severe fever, that knocked my down at a very unlucky time of the affairs happening to be here on the third day of it when the Young's was here, and the house full of company. I was taken so ill that my life was thought in danger by all that saw me. There was an apothecary sent for to Denbigh, which attended me but did no service. It was my dear neighbour Mr Davies of Caerhun who came to see me and brought with him as many doses as she thought proper of Dr James's powders – and he carefully attended me whilst I took them, which with God's blessing and I spared my life, which was mighty gone, but I cannot express my weakness.

Our neighbour Mr & Mrs Holland are gone to London with Mr Wynne Llanuchan and his daughter to bring her to school – they are all there with a severe cold – Miss Jones of Caerhun was married at Chester last Saturday night to Mr Ralph Griffith which her brother does not approve of, nor anyone else – as to point of fortune his estate being settled.

This good news, which to be forwarded home by the same pen from Baronhill – and likely will have it sooner as her Ladyship had your direction how to send it which I am at a loss for and know not how to convey this to dear Sir Hugh the speediest way.

I have a friend in the navy office who will venture to send it to – and believe me he will take care to forward it as soon as possible. I give him charge to pay for me what the postage is required. God send you luck with it is I believe all I can say, for I must go and lie down which I have done often since i began this letter.

It is my whole days' work again tomorrow's post I shall only add that my prayers for ever attends you with affectionate compliments from Sister Nelly and myself to dear Sir Hugh from your poor relation that dearly loves you and am your obedient obliged servant.

N. Coetmor'

Sir Hugh received another letter in April 1762 from Emma's father.

'Caerau

I received yours dated March 21st last Monday, am obliged for your favour and very glad that you safely arrived at Gibraltar; after so tedious and disagreeable a voyage, for an idle rumour was spread by an Irish gentleman: in his way to head that an express vessel had been dispatched after Sir P. Brott with orders for him to sail directly for the West Indies without putting into any Port, so it was imagined faster there was not the least account: of you ship or squadron in the papers, that you might have gone thither but t'is more agreeable that it hath otherwise proved: I now have the plessure of congratulating you upon the birth of your little girl on Tuesday last, and by the account received from Mr M Wynne my poor daughter had an exceedingly good time and was attended by Mr H Wynne of the town, Mrs Lewis and Miss A. Langford were there likewise, so I trust in God that by care and good nursing tending she will do well in a short while, & that I shall find her in good spirits & fair way of *recovery about the 9th or 10th of May when I now fully intend seeing her, if not prevented by the asthma & other complaints that I am tormented with. Mother Roberts intends that way very soon; nothing new transpires in this solitary corner but that the flux & fever have carried off many of the lower classes of people in this Isle, the sickness begins now to abate & tis hoped as warm seasonable weather may be expected that it will entirely go. I've lately heard from Mr I T Evans wherein he informs me of your dear little Buck's being in perfect health, & that the militia must be raised forthwith in this and your two neighbouring Counties or 400 a year must be paid for the three ensuing years by each to the Government; and that a report prevailed our troops (which is likewise hinted in the papers) are to be recalled from Germany to withstand the invasion threatened by our enemies; do suppose it will prove only a rumour to saddle us with more taxes; Dear Butty enjoys good health stretches a littlee in her height but fear she suffers for the time lost in schooling: I can't recollect any news worth imparting; my best wishes attend you. Mother Roberts desires to be remembered to you, pray my compliments to Major Jones.*

I am Dear Sir Hugh Your most affectionate humble servant
T. Rowlands'

Sir Hugh was doing well for letters all full of family news while Emma kept him informed on the political side of things. However, he became a little worried and he wrote to Emma on June 6th 1762.

'Gibraltar 6th June 1762.

My Dearest Lady Bulkeley,

You may well imagine how much I am distracted by my not hearing the least intelligence from or off you since your letters in February. I take it very unkind of those about you at your lying in, that they would not give a few lines agreeable to my desires especially to Molly Wynne and Mrs Williams, that if they had been kind enough to write by way of Lisbon I should have had it before now, for I reckon its above two months since you was brought to bed Pray God send me good news from you by the next packet from Portugal. I shall now only trouble you in acquainting you that this is the tenth letter I have wrote to you since my arrival here. I hope they all came safely to hand, for fear they have not, I must repeat the directions if writing to me. Lt. Col to 53rd Regiment at Gibraltar, to be left at Messer's Mayne, Burne & Mayne at Lisbon, Portugal. That house has my orders to forward my letters to this place. I hope there is no occasion for me to beg of you to write immediately upon receipt of this letter: in my last I requested of you to pay my Mother twenty pounds by the 24th instance and I now repeat that desire with the first opportunity after I have heard from you, I shall send you an order upon Mr. Ross to receive my subsistence upon you with please to pay yourself. I have the pleasure to tell you that yesterday the active Man of War Captain sawyer and the favourite Captain Pawnhill brought into the harbour a Spanish Man of War homeward bound from Lima in the South Seas, loaded with money. They compute her with one Million sterling, there is found Registered Seven hundred thousand pounds in spirits. The Spanish Captain owns she is the richest ship ever to come to Europe. She is three times as rich as Lord Anson's prize. They had the good fortune to take her without ten largees of Cadiz where she was bound: the captains share will amount above one hundred thousand pounds: They are brothers in law, and both married very lately in this place to Merchants daughters from Lisbon. Lucky ladies – we continue very peaceable with our neighbours, but they threaten to disturb us soon with besieging our Garrison: but in my opinion they have neither skill, courage nor resolution to put their threats into execution.

Pray God send me a speedy peace; for until that blessing happiness, I must be deprived the happiness of your agreeable company which is worse than death to me. I hope this will find you and my dear Butty in health and spirits- God Bless you and the children and may you ever enjoy every happiness and pleasure you wish for, and that we may soon meet again- when you write to Caerau make my respects. I continue in tolerable *health which is rather extraordinary considering how uneasy I am in Mental and spirits. Major Jones desires his respects, mine to all as grieving friends and believe me my sweet Dearest Emma.*

Your ever most faithful and affectionate husband.
To command. Hugh Williams'

He was very unhappy and wrote again on June 20th 1762, where he complains that he still has not heard from her. He writes that her father had been kind enough to write and tell him that he had a baby daughter, which pleased him tremendously. That letter was dated April 30th 1762. Again, on June 30th 1762, he complains bitterly that he has not heard from her apart from a letter dated 23rd April 1762, just before the baby was born. He congratulates her on a safe delivery and that she had had a cosy time, and he goes on to give encouragement to try again for a lad. He tells her to take care of her health and her breasts, *'for if I remember with you complaining of a tenderness there, as for the child, send her to any of the Caernarvonshire Cooks to be nursed whether the Tinker or Swine, no great harm'.* On June 30th 1762, he wrote about not having a letter from her which means that he has waited over two months. He goes on about how he thinks of holding her in his arms which is the only thing keeping him together as he complains about his mental stress. He writes:

'Our neighbours the Moors continue stubborn in refusing to supply our garrison with any more provision and we are obliged to live upon salt beef and pork; what Welsh white herring is a feast. If we are not released soon, we shall all be a parrel of scurry fellows. God bless and preserve you from such hardship. My affectionate love and best wishes ever attend you. I hope my dear Butty is jolly and well preparing to visit Mrs Sheeks school soon, assure her of my love although she has not written to me about you. As far as the little child I don't suppose you know how she is for I imagine you have not seen it above twice since she made her appearance, for God's sake write soon. Major Jones desires his respects.

Believe me ever My Dear Lady Bulkley
Yours Truly faithfull & affectionate
Husband & lover
H Williams'

Sir Hugh was thoroughly unhappy with his post, and having spent 11 years out in Gibraltar, felt that he should be allowed to return. This was now more important than ever as Emma had given birth to their daughter. On August the 6th 1762 he wrote:

> 'My Dearest lover most agreeable lady of the glorious June 20th [which was the day they got married] *the first happy day of my life was brought to me yesterday by one packet. I find that I should have had the pleasure by the one before only for the girls' saving stakes of not paying full postage, be it known for the future that only lass is to pay eighteen pence for every cover. This rent charge I hope will not debar me the pleasure of your long letters sooner than you should stop your pen.*
>
> *I will order my agent Mr Ross to pay you twenty pounds a year from my non effective fund. I am happy to find that our letters come now more regular, I hope there is no occasion to expatiate upon real joy I have in receiving and reading your letters which is my only comfort at present, and the delight of my days. I am sorry to say that most of your letters which you sent before March 15th, April 4th and May 22nd and this before me are the only ones I have been honoured with. I am very certain that for the future you will be regular in writing every fortnight.*'

He also informs her that he will be writing to Mr Townshend regarding his release. He has heard somehow that Emma has not been very well and instructs her to see Dr Hayes from Chester. '*If you don't I certainly shall if I find that you continue out of order, I have written to those who will tell me truth about you, for I suspect you will be silent upon the subject*'. He thanks her for her letters and thanks the doctor who has restored her health and compliments her on her letter saying, '*and your letter seems to be wrote with proper spirit*'. He then gives her permission to go anywhere she wants, and he sends his compliments to Caerau.

On November 16th 1762, he talks of the property Friars which he has learnt is to be sold, and that Major Jones is interested in it. Sir Hugh tries his best to persuade Emma to let Major Jones have Friars, and that if she allowed him to have it, he would let her keep houses which belonged to the Friars estate within the borough of Beaumaris. He was doing his best for Major Jones and said that he would be a good neighbour to have. He was pleased to hear that her health had improved and pleased that the two girls were well. He mentions again that he would contact Mr C Townshend regarding his release from the army, and he goes on to suggest that if she went up to town for the winter Emma should see Mrs Young and Lady Dalkeith and ask them to write in support of his request. He asks her about vacating the island for the winter and he tells her that if she does not choose Bath or London, then she should visit her friends and stay with them.

In a letter of November 29th 1762, Sir Hugh tells her the good news that peace has been signed by all the powers at war with England:

> *'... most glorious and pleasing news my sweet dear girl, and I hope it is the same with you and that we shall very soon embrace each other with that natural bliss. To make the principality envy our joy and pleasure.*
>
> *I hope with the letters I have troubled you with this last month are come safe to your hands; and that you approved the contents and taken the Hint of going to London for a few months, and solicit my leave of absence which will be granted you for one word of your asking, it is of that consequence to my happiness that you will not neglect either going or writing to your friends and my relations. But it must be from yourself, not a word of my knowing that you solicit the favour. You are not the only Lady of quality that has got me leave to return to England, from this climate which is reckoned destructive to real felicity. Pray consult Mr Ross our agent of the destination of the 53rd Regiment, he will give the first information of our movement. This agreeable news we have had from the Spanish Commander. In the lines near this garrison, he seems to be more pleased with than we are. Many polite letters have crossed between him and General Cornwall and Sir Charles Saunders, and I hope the peace in*

his packet. I sincerely wish to see him soon and re-affirm what is yet only reported, but we have it from every seaport in this neighbourhood. I assure you my dear Emma, it has given me fresh health, vigour, and spirits. The thought of seeing you soon makes me too impatient for that happiness. - If our regiment is to go to Minorca and that you don't get me leave of absence, I must in that case insist upon your taking bridge. I do assure you it is impossible for me to be another year absent from you. The pleasure of your company will make my place agreeable to me, and I have you too well to be any time absent from you. I hope you and the three children are as well as I wish them to be.

Many thanks for your promise of Butter, Oysters, and Puffin, which will be an agreeable present here. I was so unreasonable as to expect them by the last convoy which arrived here a few weeks since but brought neither letter nor present whilst I am here. I am now very busy with our field days proposing for our review which we are to have next week. I have the honour to command the regiment. Poor Colonel Jonesy is confined to his bed with a fit of gout which attacked him very severe; when the review is over, I intend joining a shooting party to Bariery. The weather is now delightful fine and pleasant, I wish you could give me the same amount from any place where you are. Major Jones desires his respects to your family. Write every fortnight. I am to say sorry to conclude in a hurry. The packet being this moment ordered.

Believe me My Dear Emma most faithful affectionate husband & lover.
Hugh Williams'

Sir Hugh was impatient to leave the army and he would get a little irate with waiting for letters from Emma. It was a difficult situation because he would write and ask her to do something for him but as the letters sometimes took four months to arrive and if Emma had not done what he asked there would be conflict between them. He had asked Emma several times to go to London for the winter and to try and visit Mrs Young and Lady Dalkeith to help her write to

Charles Townshend, the Secretary at War, but she did not do this. He himself had written to the Secretary in August and was still waiting a reply. He had pleaded with Townshend to be allowed an exchange from Gibraltar for a company in the Guards so as 'to get out of this vile climate where I have been eleven years'. On December 12th 1762, Charles Towsend requested Sir Hugh to rejoin his regiment.

On December 22nd 1762, he wrote to Emma quite a long letter. He starts by thanking her for a letter that has just arrived which has been travelling since October 29th 1762. He is still missing her and claims *'nothing to me can be as bad as being separated from you, for I call heaven to witness that I not enjoyed one hours three pleasures since I left the Hill; and one kiss from your sweet dear Ruby lips would be felicity indeed and to me greater value than the riches of Peru'*. He talks of the war and though he has not done anything extraordinary he was a man of honour and believed in doing his duty to his king and country. He talks about the King and tells her that Sir Charles Saunders has been given his flag making him Vice-Admiral, as had his friend Sir Percy Brett who had been made Admiral. This meant there would be a lot of balls for the ladies to attend. He informs her that his body is very tired of that place, and that he hopes she has received all his letters. Then he tells her that they could be sent anywhere in England or Ireland unless they are sent to Minorca, which means it may be some years before he is free to join Emma and be together.

He rebukes her lightly because she has not listened to him and has not gone to London to meet Mrs Young and Lady Dalkeith, who would have written to the Secretary at War, Mr Charles Townshend, in support of his request to leave. He tells her that he is pleased that Mr Rowlands, her father, has made many jolly visits, and hopes that she and her father parted in a fatherly friendship. He then goes on about the borough, and his disapproval of her father's position and those he supports. He informs her that he has heard from Owen Holland whom he says *'is the only person able and honest to give me proper advice upon occasions'*.

He then explains that he may be away from Emma for longer than either of them had expected, and tells her about the terrible weather and the dreadful winds that they have had to endure. He thanks Emma for giving his mother £20 for Christmas.

Then he writes that he was glad that she had taken a jaunt to Pengwern as it was certainly the right thing to do. *'You made them happy. Why did you not, my love, go as far as Porkington and made your peace there? I shall like this acquaintance much admire your account of both old ones and wish to be well with them'.*

He asked about his black mare and whether she had had a foal and wanted to know what horses she had fit for service. He concluded by wishing her and the children many pleasing Christmases, and happy years.

He received a letter dated November 24th 1762. He went on about Emma not having written every fortnight, as he has asked her to do. He wishes her a joyful New Year and hopes it will be the last year of their separation. He begs her to return to the Hill from Penmon as he felt it would be most disagreeable to her. He mentions that no one seems to know what is to happen to his regiment, the 53rd Foot, whether they are to go to Minorca or Ireland. The prospect of going to Ireland would suit him as he would not be far away from home. He goes on to tell her that he had received a letter from Owen Holland informing him that Lady Prendergast must sell every foot of her estate towards paying her debts. He asks Emma if she is going to put in a bid for Marl and its domain. Major Jones had told him to give £1000 more so that he was the highest bidder.

Again, he questions Emma's lack of enthusiasm regarding Marl, which is where Sir Hugh's grandfather used to live. He tells her that as yet, they have not benefited from this declared peace, and no one seems to know anything; but as a field officer he has to stay to look after his regiment.

Emma must have been staying at Penmon as Sir Hugh refers to it. *'I hope to God, this will find you and the little ones in good health and spirits at the Hill, for I hope you would be very soon tired of the Penmon dwelling'.* He thanks her for the butter, oysters and puffin which had arrived safely. He was looking forward to having Major Jones and a few friends to sup with him. He was very interested in Marl which was having to be sold to pay his cousin's debts. Sir Hugh wanted to buy it, then settle it on Emma and her children forever, as he felt it would be much better than £40 a year pension.

Having been away for a month on a shooting trip, Sir Hugh found two letters to the Rock of Gibraltar from Emma. He complained bitterly about them, one letter was from Baron Hill the other from Caerau. He did not like the contents and started by saying *'I am vexed to say that the contents of both are so very extraordinary in their nature as not fitting for me to answer upon any account'*. He told her that it was hardly a letter from an affectionate wife, and goes even further – that he committed them to the fire! This was written on March 4th 1763:

> *'In justice to myself I must assure your Ladyship that what possessions of love and affection I ever made to you before and after marriage are honest, faithful, and from the sincerest heart. If yours are otherwise I am heartily sorry for it and am of all other men most to be pitied, for my happiness depends upon our reciprocal friendship and affection. I find things cannot be properly explained until we meet, therefore, I will not endeavour to comment upon either of yours wishing very sincerely I may forgive and forget content. He describes where he lives and how expensive everything is and writes of saving money that is why he trying to be frugal: if you was with me we should each save money; after all this pray don't be afraid that I shall ever make any demands upon your pocket, you have sufficiently cured me of that, for I shall always be fearful of doing anything that is disagreeable to my dear and most lovely. He tells her that his family out in Gibraltar consists of two dogs, a cat and three pigeons, my house has a parlour, a drawing room upstairs and a bed chamber and a very pretty garden.'*

He then tells her what the men drink at night: claret and other liquors, punch, and Madeira 'sherry'.

The letters which seem to have upset him are probably the results of Emma discussing the possibility of her and Sir Hugh purchasing Marl. It would not suit Thomas to have her move some distance away from Anglesey. On 12th March 1763, Sir Hugh writes:

'With infinite pleasure I am to acquaint my Dearest Emma that this morning General Cornwalis was so kind to give me his leave to go to England by the first opportunity, which I certainly embrace; but at present I cannot hear of any ship, the Man of War Expects their orders to return, but I shall take the first ship that sails whether Man of War or a Merchant Man.

If my love has any business in town, suppose you take that journey. I must make that London my road wherever I land for I have the case of two young lads who are to be educated at Putney Academy; that business will keep me a few days in town therefore I wish you would meet me there if convenient and agreeable and on a very good time to bring Miss Bulkeley to Mrs Sheeks and settle the young Lord, and many other things. The post is going but at this moment which stops my pen, I shall write a longer letter next post.

My affectionate love, Dearest Emma

Affectionate and faithful
H Williams'

Another letter, March 17th 1763:

'This morning a Man of War arrived from Lisburn which brought the very pleasing. Agreeable letter from my dearest Lady Bulkeley. I have not now the time to tell you how happy it has made me- your own faithful man; your professions of the affection and love is a certain cure against all misfortunes to me, indeed, if your letter had not arrived I believe I should now be employing a rope about my neck, but thank god I am much better employed and you have given me resolution to bear the greatest affliction. Last Monday I troubled my love with a short note in the highest spirits telling you of my having obtained General Cornwalis's leave to go to England, and I was so far prepared that I had sold all my household furniture and had sent my baggage in board a Man of War who had orders to sail the first fair wind. We should have been clear of this damned place yesterday had the wind served. This morning an account has *come that our Regiment is to remain here for another year. The same opportunity brought Co Lindsey's leave of absence; therefore, he goes and poor me ordered to remain with the Regiment. If a certain lady had done as I desired, I should be now at home, I hate to think of your neglect of so amiable hope to our happiness.*

God bless you the mainstay for my letters.
I remain your faithful & affectionate husband.
H. Williams'

It was certainly very sad for Sir Hugh, having sold everything, and believing that he was going home. He must have been frustrated having to stay, having built himself up to meeting Emma. He writes another letter dated March 20th, 1763.

'My Dearest Love,

I have now the pleasure to acknowledge the receipt of three extreme and pleasing agreeable letters. Dates now old New Year's Day January 25th and 12th February, which came very expeditious, they were all special. The same day, they were the only things, except your Ladyship's appearance into my arms, could have the least power to give me joy.

That day indeed my love I am pitied by every person in this garrison, and not without reason, I deserve it, for no poor soul so severely hemmed and disappointed of his happiness as I have been lately. In my former letters I had the pleasure to acquaint you of my success with General Cornwalis who very polite and good natured gave me his leave to make my love a visit at the Hill by the first opportunity, which was a point stretched.

In my favour he had refused many other officers in consequence of that indulgence. I wrote you a few lines on the 12th instant acquainting you that I should sail the first fair wind to England; and that we should not lose a moment of our pleasures. I gave my sweet Emma strong hints to meet me in Town; a Man of War was ordered to sail the first spurt of favourable wind, alas I pity those whose happiness depends upon winds.

The captain came and offered me a passage, I prepared and had all my baggage on board, sold all my furniture for a song, emptied any cellar upon the occasion broke bowls and glass in drinking your health. The next morning, we were to sail the wind came foul, but brought a ship from Lisbon with letters and the King's leave of absence for Lt Col. Lindsey. The Governors sent that he designed to speak to me. He told me that he was sorry he was obliged to recall his leave to me for it was not in his power to stop Lindsey from making use of the King's leave nor, could he leave the Regiment without a field officer. I assured him of my grateful thanks to him for his good intentions and that I was ready to submit—Lindsey is now under sail.

Thus, my favourable scheme of returning soon to your arms, is frustrating, and all hopes of seeing old England is now at an end; for it is as certain that our Regiment is to remain on this most agreeable rock perhaps six years longer, ours being the youngest but consequently the senior four Regiments must be relieved before ours.

I will not recall to my memory that contents of my letter in October to a certain lady, had they been obeyed I should now been on my passage home. I do my soul forgiving any neglect to me, and I shall very fervently pray to God for my health, and proper resolution to bear this disappointment which is a severe a stroke as ever felt. I am busy buying furniture to replace those I sold which did not bring me above thirty pounds; I am sure it will cost me above a hundred. I suppose before now Mr Ross has informed you that our Regiment is to remain here, and I am quite at a loss how to advice your coming as you seem to design it. I do upon the honour of all honest soldiers declare that I shall be happy to see you here, and your company will ever make this place agreeable to me. I care very sincerely and return your polite expression that where you are is the Eden for me, I hope you are convinced of this.

I must now inform you of the inconvenience of this place for a family especially one of your Ladyship's titles. In the first place the climate doesn't agree with many constitutions, and should anything happen to obstruct your health and happiness I should be miserable for ever.

The expense of your voyage will be great for there will be no opportunity of a Man of War. You must enquire for the Leghorn Traders what they call the act ships. They are fine large ones and commodious for passengers. Your acquaintance (Gibles) at Portsmouth will inform you all about shipping to this place, it will cost you Ten pounds each servant and Twenty pounds yourself. You must have a companion with you, let her be a smart one and we will snatch her, servants you ought to bring a Housekeeper, a cook, and a butler any others we may endeavour to get here. Linen, plate you must bring the jewels, would make a mighty fine sight.

I must assure you that it will cost above six hundred a year Houskeeping here. I will sign you my income towards it with infinite pleasure, one kiss from my lovely Emma will be worth a year's pay; and if you come you will make me very happy, but if you find the expense a hazard too great, I will endeavour to content myself another dismal year without my love. Your coming or staying I leave to your own discretion and inclination, if my dear does come let it be with the consent of the great lawyers and your father. If I don't write fully upon this subject or anything inconvenient pray excuse me for I am confused and disordered in my mind and spirits that I hardly know what I write and say – consult Mr Ross about destination of the Regiment perhaps they may alter their plan.

I know that the good General Cornwalis has represented the bad consequence of the Keep Bur Regiment abroad, who were raised by County's and the men must be discharged who bound themselves to save only the war.

The fleet here, except four ships, have received orders to go home they are now under sail. This letter goes by one of them, which will go in the afternoon- my last Monday's letter desired you to meet me in town; I hope this will come time enough to stop that hasty journey, for if you should undertake a voyage, there are many things you will want to pack.

I am sorry to hear of Tom Owens death by no means take your father's recommendations, you have given every reasons why you should refuse him; oblige Mrs Owen and let my namesake have it upon his promise to reside in town to do the duty of it, give Mrs Owen the merit.

The Major desires his compliments and gratefull thanks for Fryars, in short, he was determined to have it. Therefore, it is a compliment paid, he assures me that he only wants the house and a few fields for a cow and horse, any houses in town and the tithe my Lord may have, therefore consult with Mr Hughes about it.

I am of your opinion we may repent, but not a word of that, your father bringing the son-in-law obliged you to it- you hear mistakes about Marle for all the other places I should like it. Rent it would freely set out to purchase it, I wish you will write to my vile cousin about the purchase, and if she agrees to it, I will sell out for I am tired of this uncertain service.

My affectionate love attends you my dear Emma and the three dear children, pray write every fortnight, believe me ever and at all places.

Your affectionate and loving husband to command.
H Williams'

He was desperately unhappy and in one letter, believing that Emma was going to join him in Gibraltar, he writes *'I would have but fear of melancholy thoughts',* and in another he laments that because of his sense of duty to king and country, he will not see Emma. In another letter he declares that he can never be happy until he and Emma are together, as it affects his peace of mind. In another letter, dated May 16th 1763, he tells her off, *'I was unreasonable enough to be displeased not receiving a line the last post. I shall be outraged if I don't the next being three weeks since I had one. If we are to be separated some months longer for God's sake comfort me with your agreeable letters, don't fail once a fortnight'.* He believed that she may be in London. He had no idea what was going on in Anglesey and that Emma's father had died.

Sir Hugh is obviously tired of being in the army and writes on May 9th 1763, thanking his lovely Emma for her kind letters of no date, or month, *'but by the London stamp I find it was forwarded from there on April 11th.'* He goes on about her never dating her letters and tells her:

'... whenever you do me the honour of writing again, pray let the date be the first thing you write, then you cannot forget. I assure you; they puzzle me very much for want of knowing the time, besides we are all anxious to know how late our letters are. When I am asked that question it vexes me to say that my friend never dates letters, I beg that my love will never more give me cause to complain of this neglect. Be assured you make me very happy to know that you and the little ones enjoy health and spirits, mine are always indulged whenever you say a great deal of yourself – no other subject half as pleasing to your own faithful man. May our love and affection be ever mutual and be very soon and indulge with each other's embraces. I hope that I guess right of your being now on the road or in London, and that you partook of the diversion of Chester races which begun on the 23rd of April, a good opportunity to make Wilmslow a visit there, I would ask of you to fix on him, for the reason you have given. If the Griffiths family interfered by recommending, it shows how much they depend on their ascendant over a certain person. I hope they are mistaken; your father's view was a reasonable one as to himself, but you have generalised his honour—your account of your gallantry made me laugh and angry the same time, that you have jockeyed the great man is certain. I would not have given 5p for them is certain, but I am angry you should trust yourself to your present issue as you are pleased to call him. I suppose the groom and postilion are in character for god's sake live and have proper servants as you had before you recommended your body to my protection and care. If you go to town provide yourself with proper servants, you know I have been unsuccessful therefore I beg you will try a new butler and your own maid.

You don't mention one word of the park wall, the time you wrote the last letter they had been hard at work, I am afraid Mr. Jones is too busy about his own affairs. I wish my love would give orders to clear the grounds in front of the house and sow it with juniper. I wish to see it in better order than when I left it. Not a word of my black mare and the bay. I hope you have sold them to the backer or sent them where I desired.

The sea Captain's horse is best, and I do wish to have his breed rather his than the master's. It will be very costly to purchase the many horses we shall want when we are blessed with each other's company, you have my dearest made me vain enough to believe that you will be glad I was with you – when you are in London, don't forget to visit her grace of Argyle and our dear good friend Mrs Young; you will most certainly see Lady Prendegast, pray find out in great respect what I have offended her Ladyship. She has declared I should be the very last refusal of the purchase of Marle – you have my dear mistaken me very much about that affair, in one of your letters you hint as if it was indifferent to me to make that purchase; if in my power to have from that, what I would give a hundred more than any other bidder if you could contrive to raise the needfull, do all you can to convince her Ladyship it was neither in my power or inclination to offend her, push her shame about Marle and find the reason why the sale is stopped I have heard old Wynne of Bodysgallen that Marle's domain did belong to the title, perhaps it had stopped their hand – it is worth enquiring into, Mark Evans your friend in this affair, I have employed him about it already, don't quarrel with Tom yet, I have a crow to pick with his honour for a very impertinent letter he wrote, which I shall smother until a proper opportunity. I am afraid that he is very capable of bad advice to the young Lord. I wish my dearest will settle all manner of accounts with him, then we shall be safe; I wish you to consult my Lord's nearest relation about sending him to Eton, or elsewhere, Westminster will certainly not do; I could inform you of things which came from him on the road to town that was a fright.

My Emma – tell my cousin Prendegast that I have wrote her two letters and never see her answer, of all other houses I would prefer Marle. Sir Hugh Williams of Marle will make me proud. Nay, it would induce me to sell out of the army to enable me to make the purchase – I hope my love has received all my letters my last mention the things I have purchased I will send them by the first opportunity of Man-of-War; I have more Barcelona handkerchiefs and nets, yesterday I bought the largest and finest Gally shell I ever did see, it cost me 36 shillings. Don't forget to pay my mother twenty pounds, on 24th June, which you will receive from the Castle money in October next.

We are now vastly crowded here the two Regiments from Portugal makes eight in a town not twice larger than a corporation. We are gay beyond a place I ever did see; there is a garden which makes a very handsome Vauxhall, tonight it is open for the first, the price a dollar, about 3s 4p, some public diversion every night, our commune into Spain is at last opened it is a very pleasant riding there. There are horses to hire at a crown a day, which will be the ruin of many of our youngsters, many of them gone already.

If Holland Williams comes to Wales, pray enquire what he has done with my baggage I left at Plymouth under his care; if we have no certainty of the time that the four old Regiments from here are to be relieved but expect them every day; we have very extraordinary weather for this country, I am now writing by a good roaring fire, cold, raining blowing weather.

I am happy to know that my chill is recovered but of the expose. Pray God continue you all in good health and jollity, write every fortnight and number your letters as I do. God bless and preserve you to your faithful husband.

H Williams'

Sir Hugh knew nothing of Emma's plight and that she had had to travel back from London to Caerau in a hurry, without stopping at Baron Hill. Her grandmother had sent word to Emma's cousin, and he had managed to notify her in London as fast as was possible. Emma packed her things and came back in her chaise and horses hoping to see her father, whom she loved dearly. When she arrived, her grandmother told her that she had seen no change in him since he had been taken ill and that no doctor had been called, but that Emma was two days late as her father had died on April 27th, 1763.

Now she had to look after her grandmother and talk to her about making contact with the vicar and the undertaker and decide on a day of burial. It was a shock to Emma. She managed to write to Sir Hugh explaining everything, and that she could not decide whether to go out to be with him. That letter arrived during May, and he replied on May 30th 1763:

'Dearest Lady Bulkeley,

Two letters of the same date April 20th, 1763, came very safe to hand last Thursday. I am truly sorry to read the enclosed paper on Mr Rowlands being so very ill as to think it necessary to send for you to Caerau. I hope that the sight of my dearest should this old gent drop, it is no more than what you want except he has prepared you for that shock, he declined very much since I had the honour of his acquaintance, but I hope he will recover this illness to be our comfort for years. I think I would freely venture my money on the young ladies' days against it. I beg my dearest will not shock me in complaining of her own health and spirits.

Think of the many joyfull days and nights we shall soon have together. Every hour of my life shall be dedicated to your service and to make happy by day and give you pleasure by night it is very cruel in our being absent a moment from each other.

Dame fortune does her worst at present by separating us – I will not blame anybody, it is now too late to find fault, nor am I ever inclined to blame my dearest Emma who, I know will do everything in her power to bring us together. I am now confined to the 53rd Regiment staying here a few years longer, which is in my opinion a very wrong step in the government to suffer; this day serving. A sloop of War came from England with orders for Admiral Sir Percy Brett with his fleet to conduct the 3rd, 57th, and 67th Regiments to take possession of Minorca. They sail on the 23rd, our governor has likewise received orders to reduce the 53rd & 54th Regiments which are to remain here to the Irish establishment which is twenty men a company & Regiment is nine company. We shall be so few that it is hardly a proper command for a Lieut Colonel; but my dream I have no manner of hopes to get leave from this quarter, do him justice it is hardly in his power to leave a Regiment without a field officer, one must always be with the colours, in the Militia manner puts it out of my power to apply at home for the King's leave which may be easily obtained and then the Governor could not stop my leaving the corps to a certain Captain's commander.

> *These cannot be the least reflection upon you to do all you can to get me home, therefore set upon to work. Write to every fashionable courtier friend you know, Sir William Owen & son, who are dogs if they neglect you- Sir George Young at Escot House Devon, Sir Roger Mostyn and your cousin Sir John Glynne these two are very likely to succeed, all that you are to request is, that they get one. The king's leave of absence for six months only to return to England on business of the uttermost Consequences, enquire my presence at home, which is truly your case for I think getting a lad must be of consequence to us, avoid any application to Sir Nicholas Bailey if you can do without it.*
>
> *I think some of those I have mentioned about pleasing his lovely Emma, the weather here is hot at present Major Jones has gone home through France. Pray pay my mother twenty pounds on June 24th god bless you and family I shall write a longer letter on Monday adieu now in haste I am ever my dearest Emma's faithful husband.*
>
> *H Williams'*

It is June 1763 before he learns of Thomas's death:

> 'My Dearest Love's letter no 1 of no date, by the London mark it left that place the 4th of May. I received it yesterday, it shocked me very much seeing it sealed with black wax being disagreeable account of your former letter; I sincerely console with you for the loss of a tender affectionate father, besides loving you sincerely he had many other perfections well known to his friends and relatives. I wish him to live that we might know each other better and that he might be more reconciled with me for not asking his consent upon a certain affair. I hope he died in peace and friends with me – for god's sake take great care of yourself and the old lady, I beg she may not be left alone, when you tire of Cayrey, take her along with you to the Hill and insist upon her living with you, there it will make me very happy to have her with us, it is my inclination and it shall be my study, to please the good old lady; in my opinion you have buried him rather genteel which

I am glad of. The enclosed is a proper letter for the attorney which empowers you to receive rents and act as you please. A copy of this I shall send by the next post, and I hope they will come safe to you. I went to the Governor and told him the affair and desired his leave to return to England, but it is not in his power to let me stir, being the only field officer with the Regiment, he has given me leave to write to the Secretary of War asking for the King's leave. When that comes, I may set out, I shall write by this post. I would advise you to get your friends to back my solicitations; the next post I shall trouble my love with a long letter, I expect one from you, this cruel separation demolishes my peace of mind.

My love and blessings attend you and yours and believe me my dearest Emma your ever faithful husband.

H Williams'

This news becomes very important to Sir Hugh, and he cannot wait to write to the new Secretary of War to ask him for the King's Leave. He knew that Charles Townshend had been given another post and that Welbore Ellis was now the Secretary at War. He writes a letter on June 6th 1763.

'Sir,

I have the honour to acquaint you that I trouble you with this letter by Cornwallis's approbation, to request the favour of you to get me his Majesty's leave to return to England. Last Post brought me account of the death of my father-in-law, which event puts me in possession of an estate of near a thousand pounds per annum. I find he died with his affairs in disorder and confusion which presses my coming home immediately, to regulate those and some money matters which cannot be done without my being on the spot. Many other reasons require my being soon at home, one in particular (I beg leave to mention to yourself only) ever since the death of the late Lord Bulkeley; My father in law had the management of the Borough of Beaumaris in Wales, which belongs to the Bulkeley family, my father and

I never thought the same in matters of Politics therefore he declined giving me a Seat in Parliament last election, his choice I suppose you know, his name is Price.

The Borough consists of 24 electors I have the honour to be one and if I am at home in August next, I shall have the management of putting in two which is now vacant and will secure my being in Parliament next election. But if I am absent at that time, the present member may establish himself that I may find it difficult to supplant him. Therefore, his Majesty will lose a faithfull servant in Parliament. If I am elected, I hope to keep possession until the present Lord Bulkeley who is my son in law and is now a minor of Westminster school, comes of age.

I have not been 15 months absent upon leave since I have been in the Army, which is 24 years, eleven of which in this hot climate- I hope these reasons [are] enough to induce you to assist me [t]o get his Majesty's indulgence of leave to return to England for six months upon to pressing occasion. If I fail, I must endeavour to make interest to get leave to sell out of the Army or exchange on half pay. Either will be very disagreeable to me. But my affairs are so pressing for my immediate presence that it is impossible to be any time absent. A line to General Cornwallis from you that he may let me go to England will be sufficient, for he wishes to have it in his power to grant my request. I hope soon to be honoured with your favourable answer. Please direct to Sir Hugh Williams Lieut Colonel 53 Regiment at Gibraltar by Madrid Spain.

I am Sir your most obedient, most humble servant

H Williams'

In a letter of June 1763 from Gibraltar, Sir Hugh tells Emma that he has dressed in mourning for her father.

'I have now the honour to acknowledge my dearest, dear and faithfull Emma's letter of the 30th of May which came safe the last post, and I hope mine wrote in a hurry in answer to yours upon the disagreeable subject of your poor Father's death will come safe.

A letter 8th June 1763. This letter which gives me the particulars of the manner of his death makes me truly miserable, for it is very clear to me that if there had been proper assistance in time, his life might be saved, and be as happy with his friendship and company as we shall be upon our additional fortune. Believe me my love that your description of his death brought from me a flood of sincere tears and especially when you assured me that he paid his last respects to me and mine. I now very sincerely regret the loss of him, and I wish to remember him no more, except in honour and respect to his memory which I hope never to forget.

I will not say how much we have to labour to dry upon the tears of his friends and neighbours, and acquaintances for the loss of him who was a father to the poor and darling of the country he lived in. I hope never to be wanting in friendship and good neighbourhood, but I can never merit the love and esteem he had from the highest to the lowest in his country.

I am in the deepest mourning an officer can appear in. Plain hat, black cloth waistcoat and breeches, stockings, sword and buckles, and a drape round the left arm. I have even put my domestic in deep mourning.

Your description of the old and young is very just and true. I am afraid you will have disagreeable business with the former, for god sake avoid a dispute with her, bring her to the Hill and let her be happy the few days she has to live, give everything she can ask, I am heartily glad my dear Bridget is so well taken care of, I shall never begrudge the extraordinary twenty pounds to my dear little girl.

I send you now enclosed a copy of the letter of attorney which I sent in my last letter and I hope my love will act as she pleases and whatever occurs to her may be put into execution for I know that I shall highly approve of everything my Emma does; My dearest love take care of your own health don't let your good and agreeable flow of spirits be lowered upon this occasion, or the absence of a husband who dearly loves you and can have no enjoyment of riches without the agreeable company of my sweet Emma, one kiss from my love would.

Perhaps all the estate father Rowlands left us (which by the by) I think a noble one and shall be improved if your man lives to enjoy some years. Now my dear I will inform you the step I have taken towards my return, In the first place it is not in Cornwallis's power to let me stir before I have the King's leave, being the only field officer with the Regiment. By his approbation I have wrote to Mr Welbore Ellis Secretary of War, desiring him to send me the King's leave. I mentioned to him, my father's death which puts us in possession of an estate near a thousand pounds per annum, we must puff to their courtiers and likewise the necessity of returning to secure the Borough before the present man could get footing, that if I was at home in September next I should fill by two vacancies that is now with my friends which will certainly give me a seat in Parliament next election: I know that parliamentary affairs will have more weight with him than any other concerns of mine. I have written such a letter that I think it impossible for him to refuse my request, I can't have his answer sooner than the latter end of July and if it be favourable I will be out immediately by land to Cadiz and there take shipping, I think you may expect me in your bosom happy about September.

I told him that if the leave could not be obtained that I must sell out of the army or go upon half-pay, either would be disagreeable to me, I wrote to our solicitor Tom to go to the war office to know of my letter coming safe and to know from Mr Ellis of my success and to tell him of the necessity for my speedy presence at home. I have likewise written to Tom Wynn our member to beg my request at the War office which he certainly will and succeed.

This to yourself. I rejoice to hear that our cousin is taken care of, it was not possible she could have kept longer. If he makes a good husband, everything well determined in point of blood; and I beg you will be determined to send Butty to Chester, for really dread the thought of her wanting proper education. I beg you will never be without company to divert you. I am angry my paper will not allow me to proceed, I've ten thousand things to say which I can't here.

God bless & pleasure you to me, long and blessings to you and yours

Being ever your faithfull affectionate husband.
H Williams'

Margaret Griffith of Llanfairisgaer, Emma's aunt, was also shocked at the death of Thomas and wrote to Mrs Owen at Porkington.

> 'May 30th, 1763.
>
> Hon Madam,
> I received the favour of your obliging letter. I was much shocked at the unexpected news having not heard of his illness but few hours before he died, nor do I find they were apprehensive of it. I wished him to be younger to survive me But, I believe, I am the chief mourner and that it made the deeper impression on me. The young may have many views and amusements to mitigate their concern. We are glad that cousin Owen has had a good winter and that his cough is abated, poor Mr Griffith's confinement this 6 month has been a great trouble to me, he is a little better and has been a few times a horse back.
>
> As I always retain and ever shall adjust sense of the civilities and friendship, I received and my great regard for you and cousin Owen invariably your silence gave me the greater uneasiness, accept Dear Madam of our respectfully compliments and thanks for your kind offer, and be so good to give ours to Mr. Owen and to the young ladies who I'm sure say are well pleased with the town and hope the gentlemen are well wherever they are may all happiness attend you is the sincere wishes of
>
> Dear Madam
> Your most obliged servant
> Margaret Griffith'

Emma herself wrote to Mrs Owen on May 30th 1763, telling her that she arrived back too late to see her father and that her grandmother told her that she had seen no change in him for two days and no doctor had been called. Emma must have been in shock at losing her father who had doted on her and had always done his best, travelling to Baron Hill as often as possible, playing with Bridget and babysitting the new baby.

Emma was now an heiress in her own right as she would inherit the Plas-y-Nant estate and all the rents from it. It did however cause a little misunderstanding between her and Sir Hugh which she put in a letter to him. She felt proud and rich. Her grandfather, John Rowlands, who had built Plas-y-Nant in 1671, owned substantial tracts of land around the Betws Garmon and Beddgelert district including land up to the summit of Snowdon, inherited from his ancestors. Whilst at the bank, he also purchased properties in Clynnog, Llanwnda, Llandwrog, Nantlle and Caernarvon. Little wonder that Emma, whom many thought of as a snob, felt rich and powerful. The only matter was that her father's papers and various accounts were in total disarray, and Sir Hugh would have to help her sort them out.

Despite everything that had happened, Emma missed London. Since she was young, she had been taken by the Owens of Porkington to Bath and later, when she became engaged to Lord Bulkeley, had been taken to the Bulkeley House in London, she had well and truly fallen for the place. There was everything a girl could possibly need: fashion, style and different hair-dos, all of which excited her.

Now she would have to buckle down and see to the many debts incurred by her father, besides sorting out all his accounts. She wished Sir Hugh was with her, knowing that he would sort things out quite quickly. She wrote to him, and he answered her on June 20th 1763:

'My dearest and most faithful Emma, you may believe me to be this instant the most miserable of his sex, in being debarred the pleasure of your agreeable company especially now that you are so desirous to have me with you, indeed my Emma is ever I am so happy to meet you again I will give you my hand on heart never to separate more until grim death parts us. We must subscribe patience to each other, I hope in a few months to kiss your fair hand.

I must say that General Cornwallis is so convinced of the necessity of my presence at home that he is truly miserable, it is not in his power to grant my request, he has done all in his power to forward my leave from England, he has wrote to Mr Ellis the secretary at war, but it must be the latter end of July before any answer can possibly come here.

Indeed, my love you are a very slow advocate in business, you should plague every courtier acquaintance you have, it is the last time you I hope will want their assistance or favour therefore you should write free upon the subject. I remember a certain lady of my acquaintance would have soon got me leave, as she often did in my younger days. If you find that my leave is not tomorrow entertain my love with when I have the pleasure to kiss her hand.

I have already made this letter longer than intended, this garrison seemed to me a delightful place after my long stay the other side. Here one may demand law for their life and property, these you are deprived of both without knowing why or even your crimes.

When you see Burges Owen Holland make him my compliments. Tell him I had an excellent shooting at Barbury. I killed near seventy braces of Partridge besides cocks' quail – tell him I have a very fine pointer which I broke there, and I hope to see him on the Hill next summer.

The county abounds with the finest horses I ever did see, but there is no such thing as bringing one out of the country. I have brought with me a bridle which was a present Emperor's and a pair of spurs, the leader gave me, which is all I brought away, except their coin and some galley shells. I could not find anything worth buying poor things. They are deprived of every ornament in dress or otherwise.

Major Jones has this moment left me and desires his compliments, he wishes to know your answer to my letter on his behalf about purchasing of Friars, he seems determined to have the house and domain of it is to be sold what you mention will never satisfy him therefore I have declined the subject, you must not now quarrel with the family if you expect any service from the sons vote, it was a very prudent choice to be sure, he proved it no later than the last contest upon Madam Hughe's account. I am sorry for his disorder along unlucky incidents for the family. The Major snorts at your worse throwing the son joins your opinion of his being a bad horseman, it seems so far, these are bled enough even to carry his weight. When I come your way, I will lend him my Barbury Spurs – you don't mention a word of your horses or how you visit about whether upon occasion *sidesaddle, or as you ought in your chariot and four handsome nags, is your black mare in season? The bay wants refusing this spring pray send them to Captain Edwards horses, Nanhoron. I beg my dearest you will answer this by return of the post. This comes through Spain. The packets are walled therefore direct for me here which is all you must mention. I find by a letter I received from London that my Lord spent Christmas in the country in company with Tom Evans, which I do not like to hear for I believe he is neither our friend nor capable of advising wrong things. I am much inclined to have him removed some which his spirits are too gay for London education, what do you think of Eton?*

I have understood your hints about Emma Lewis and shall do as you please, I am sorry the mother is so high as to reject your offer to her son, would you have me propose it to them, pray keep well with her – blessings and love to your two dear girls. I hope Butty grows, I sincerely long to be with you all, whenever that happens you will find I have been truly faithful to my promise made you at parting, you will in your jockey hide friend me free from all blemishes, sound wind and limbs wishing to be in your dear arms – I am and shall ever remain

*My Dearest Emma's
Faithfull and affectionate
H Williams'*

With this letter he also told Emma about his trip to Tangiers to shoot wild boars and how they killed all Christians. He said the people were very handsome. He goes on, *'They are not by the law allowed to go to any worship. The town of Tangiers is large but very dirty and disagreeable and country around is most delightful but inherited by the meanest brutes and savages'*. He had killed six boars in total and took three with him back to Gibraltar; he said that the meat was as good as any English venison. He went in a boat from Morocco back to Gibraltar. He tells about the colour of the people's skin and how the person who had invited them to go and shoot looked after them quite well, though the Moors kept threatening them with their *durkes,* a large knife. Back on the island he writes again on July 11th, 1763:

> *'My Dearest Lady Bulkeley,*
>
> *Last Thursday's post brought me two obliging letters from the Hill, dated 3rd & 9th June number 5&6. The number 4 never came to hand, I suppose through some mistake in the post house allow this conjecture therefore I could wish you would not give yourself the least trouble to endeavour being methodical for the future, which will lessen my disappointment. Whenever you are inclined to honour me with a letter it will ever give your man infinite pleasure to receive and kiss your fair hand, even without name, date or number. The two later I never expect. I hope all mines are come safe and regular and that you don't compare the expense of them to your Grandmother's jointure. Ten thousand thanks to my own Emma for sending so agreeable news of her health and that you follow Doctor Hayes's prescription.*
>
> *Bathing must certainly be of infinite service to your bad nerves, which is a very disagreeable complaint to your sex; I am pleased to hear that Miss Bulkeley is at Chester. Pray God it may restore her to that state of health and spirits. I wish the dear girl who I know is faithful in loving you can and your choice. I wish to say so much of the youngster – I have the honour to assure Emma that I have read her last letter of June 9th, I believe nine times, and each time equally astonished at your unheard-of generosity to me – in the first place you approve my conduct not consenting to sell out of the Army before your good father's death.*
>
> *In the very next paragraph, you are pleased to assure me that his estate and personality is invested to you. If so, how does it altar my situation if my Emma understands the word invested. I can have no benefit from that estate or personality; I am as I was before the good man's death, therefore I must not sell my commission.*
>
> *I am afraid my Emma, that Monday morning only consulted the God Avarice, for it certainly is the original proposal from a wife to her husband. You wish me to sell out and get £4,000 for my commission then sink the principle to clear your estate, and*

you are generous enough to allow me for life only £200 per Anum. My dear Emma, I can have two hundred pounds a year for the interest of four thousand pounds in exchange alley and reserve the principle for Ann Jane after I am gone. If I agree to this most dearly and generous proposal, would not my Emma hand me about Beaumaris Streets, as your near relation does her brother.

No more of this my dear and believe me not fool enough to sink a principle and lesson the present income a hundred and fifty pounds for Ann, far be it known that my pay as Lieut Colonel to the 53rd Regiment is near twenty shillings a day, and as independent (if I do my duty which I hope always to do) as you allure of £240 pounds for Ann for life unless I am excellent. That is very lucky for me you have wrote this generous letter before I was determined to sell out of the Army; for I really have stopped a contract I had party made with Major Corbett who would give the four thousand pounds, but I now find Emma's apron strings are too tight to support a quarter any weights; indeed my dear Emma I would say a great deal more upon this affair, but I hope never to aggravate this subject and be assured that whenever I pose sixpence, you may freely command and ask and as certain as ever dispute about matter of property.

I lay my sweet Emma upon her back, would to God – it, precise moment you shone all was mine, and rather put in my love; then pull in my love. Indeed my girl you should have enclosed me Sir George's letter or answer it yourself, which you can do much proper than your husband and will please my friend better, for I assume my cousin is a good load; I wish him settle near us, you would like his acquaintance and I am really grieved to hear of Mrs Lloyd's death, we will keep on our acquaintance there. I always in my greatest distress found him friendly and sincere.

I have great hopes of setting out from here the first week in August which I hope will bring me home about Michaelmas Day which is your time of choosing the Borough Officers. If I should not be lucky enough to return by then, I beg you will avoid filling the 3 vacancies, that are Price and Roberts, as they will certainly try their interest in having their friends put in and if they succeed will take upon themselves the full management of the Corporation. I have written to Holland upon this subject to stay all attempts.

Adieu for some time, the cellar is much stacked. I shall order from here, white wines and Minorca wines and now I shall send enough to last some years. It is economy to do that my Dear, you are the proudest Dame in Europe of our Ann Jane. I suppose you think her a martyr for a young fletching. I am now angry with my prospect that I can't proceed and be much in love with my Emma as ever for all her apron strings which her Sampson will crack, God preserve you.

H. Williams'

Again, on July 29th 1763:

'My Dearest Love,

I have just time to inform you that last Wednesday morning I left Gibraltar and arrived here last night. I am lucky enough to find the Gibraltar frigate Captain Griffith who has expressed great pleasure in giving me a passage on board his ship. We sailed this morning, but the wind failed us, and we were obliged to anchor, but we shall sail next tide and I hope to be my dear's arms before this arrives.

However, for fear it should be otherwise I will desire you to favour me with a few lines to Holland at Oxendon Street. If you have any business in town, it will give me infinite pleasure to meet there which will be the proper place to settle any of your family affairs and see my young Lord to settle him proper, for I am very much afraid he will be too ripe where he is- Pray God send the safe and soon into my lovely Emma's arms. I shall not part us again, for I have not words to say how much I have suffered I must conclude my dearest Emma.

Most faithful and affectionate Husband.
H Williams

This is to certify that I make my wife Lady Viscountess Bulkeley Williams my heir and executrix and that I do give to her all my estates & personalities and that I do now revoke all former wills given under my hand in perfect health at Cadiz this 29th July 1763.

H. Williams'

Hugh's will was written at the foot of the letter he wrote informing her that he was sailing home. He may of course be worried that if something happened and that he were to drown, Emma would not benefit without a will.

Chapter Seventeen

Emma was very excited about her husband's return, which, according to him, would be around September 29th, the feast of Michaelmas. St Michael was the patron saint of the sea and maritime lands and of ships. In England it was the custom to eat goose at Michaelmas which was supposed to protect against financial need in the next year. Emma longed to be in London. She always felt excited there with so much going on. The constant influx of ladies who decided to winter there was always interesting and meant that there would be plenty of invitations to tea or to play cards.

She had seen many changes in her life and suffered many losses, which set her on a course to enjoy herself as much as possible. Her love of London had started when she visited Porkington and stayed with her father's cousins, Sir William Owen, and his family. They would take her to Bath where they spent most of the summer. They all spoke well of London and when her father sent her to a finishing school there, her appetite for London grew. Her marriage to Lord Bulkeley also helped as the Bulkeley family had a house in London where various members of the Bulkeley clan spent some time each year. She would make any excuse to be in London when the house was vacant.

She was interested in so many aspects of life. She had heard from her husband that George III had been proclaimed king in 1760. She read about Josiah Wedgewood who created early pottery to be produced at Etruria, Staffordshire. Edmund Hoyle who established the rules of Whist. Matthew Boulton who established a hardware factory. Lawrence Childs who printed the first banker's cheques. And Gainsborough who held his first exhibition of paintings. The practice of numbering houses was introduced in London. The first exhibition of agricultural machines was held. The Literary Club was founded by Dr Samuel Johnson with Edmund Burke, Edward Gibbon, Samuel Goldsmith, and Joshua Reynolds. Emma felt proud of it all. And of course, when Robert Clive returned to London, and she received an invitation for tea, she was ecstatic. This was all a far cry from Anglesey, especially Caerau, which she hated and where she had felt cut off from the real world.

Having received Sir Hugh's letter informing her that he was on his way home from Gibraltar, Emma set about some of the jobs he had complained needed doing. Excited at the prospect of his homecoming, she employed a workman from Beaumaris well-known for his hard work and enthusiasm for building or repairing stone walls. He could go around and check the walls, then repair where needed. She employed another man to clear up around the house itself and the gardens, making Baron Hill look its best for when Sir Hugh arrived back.

Her grandmother had long since returned to Caerau, preferring to be within her own surroundings and Emma employed two girls who would visit five times a week and make sure that Mrs Roberts had food and looked after herself. One would make a fire each day and see that there was plenty of wood and coal ready. Emma noticed that the loss of her father had affected the old lady more than she had anticipated. She was very silent and would not always answer when Emma asked her something. But she was content on leaving her there, knowing that she loved Caerau.

The white entrance gates to Baron Hill.

View of Baron Hill.

Emma had been extremely busy between sorting out Baron Hill, keeping in contact with her grandmother, and writing letters to various members of her family keeping them informed of all that was going on. When she wrote to Mrs Owen of Porkington, she asked advice on paint as she felt it was time to make Baron Hill a home fit for entertaining her husband's friends when he returned. She also acquired recipes from various people, in the hope that when she employed a full-time cook, she would be able to have them served. She would use these wondrous dishes to entertain many visitors. She moved things about in the drawing room and morning room and placed her harp near a window in front of a small chair. She sat and played a few tunes, which she would be able to play for her husband.

The gardens at Baron Hill from the terrace.

The terrace at Baron Hill.

Porkington (later known as 'Brogyntyn').

The next day a letter came to say that Sir Hugh had arrived back in this country and would stay in Portsmouth to sort a few things out, before making his way home. Emma was deliriously happy and walked around everywhere to make sure that he would have a good welcome. Mrs Williams was there with her, checking various things. They went into the kitchen to make sure that there were plenty of vegetables, so that the cook could start preparing the food as it would only be a matter of a few days before Sir Hugh arrived home. She wrote to Bridget and told her about Sir Hugh's return. Bridget thought the world of Sir Hugh and thought of him as her father just as he regarded her as a daughter. She wrote to her son, Lord Bulkeley, and also told him the good news.

    The day Sir Hugh was arriving home, Emma kept walking around the garden making sure that the walls were in good condition and the driveway clean and tidy. She was pleased with herself for having asked her grandmother to get her a goose. It was cooked at Baron Hill not only to celebrate Michaelmas but to welcome Sir Hugh home. When he eventually arrived, there was such a commotion. Having hugged his wife, Sir Hugh could not wait to meet Anne Jane, his own daughter. There were comings and goings that evening with so many people that Sir Hugh felt like a king – though a tired one. He was very pleased when the house emptied of visitors and they were left in peace. Sir Hugh was very tired and looked forward to bed with Emma.

So many celebrations were held with so many visitors that even Emma wondered if she had done the right thing in informing them all of Sir Hugh's return. Sir Hugh felt wonderful spending time with Emma and Anne Jane. It was the first time he had seen his daughter and he loved her and showed her off to the many visitors that called on them. At the end of two weeks frolicking about with his girls, as he called them, it was time for more serious business.

There were many papers relating to Caerau, and Sir Hugh feared that there could be many debts. Every morning after breakfast he would play with Anne Jane, then after lunch he would sit trying to make sense of the vast amount of paperwork Emma had carried from Caerau. It took him some time before he found a map of Caerau Hall with all the properties surrounding it. He wrote to a solicitor at Beaumaris who dealt with the business side of Baron Hill. He made a list of people he would have to visit who were involved in loans with Thomas. Unfortunately, Thomas, when visiting London, spent much time gambling and lost quite a lot of money. Sir Hugh shook his head at the thought of what he was about to face.

He still had to travel down to Portsmouth to see to his men and find out where they were to be sent next. This time he travelled feeling better than ever. He was home, and travelling up and down made him think. He had felt for some time that the army had not been kind to him, and he knew of only a few who had given eleven years to their regiment as he had. He would much prefer to stay at home now and build up Baron Hill and then buy their own place. He must have been away, probably on duty and wanting to get back to Emma. He arrived at Chester, very tired, and the following day wrote to Emma:

'My Dearest Emma,

Will be pleased to hear that I arrived here last night at ten o'clock, but so much fatigued that I was obliged to go to bed immediately after I came into the house. I find myself tolerable now, Butty and Miss Griffith breakfast with me. They are both very fine girls, ours much grown and healthy, very happy with the thought of coming with her brother to Baron Hill. I have bought you a mattress to put on our bed from Harvey's; bespoke a dozen dessert spoons and your oven from Mr Richardson. I find that Mr Briscoe has sent the box to the wrong place, therefore I shall write to him tonight from Nantwich. It is but 30 miles further to Ashborn which I can easily do tomorrow, one day before the fair will be enough there. Write by Thursday post for me at Rinna's where I shall have it safe, and I hope I will bring the agreeable account That you and your King are jolly which shall be my happiness in this life, for God's sake & mine. Tell Hugh Wynn not to go from you more especially as we are not very certain of the critical moment. I hope you have sent the pheasant by Richard your grooms' ship. I have spoken to the Coach maker who promises to fit it to our satisfaction, he is an excellent workman. In your letter mention what quantity of the different sort of paint you will have me bring home and your other commands shall be carefully obeyed.

I have seen George Smith who gives one but indifferent encouragement of Ashborn Fair, he has been there often and never could see anything worth buying, if I can't be thoroughly satisfied, I shall bring the cash home and wait some other opportunity. Have you sent your card to Briscoe about the mine Richardson confirms that he gave the 2 guineas advance for the mine. I shall be very impatient until I see you, my faithful love attends you, blessings to Chit, compliments to Emma, Believe me ever truly, My Dear Emma,

Yours most faithfully and affectionate Husband.
Williams

Chester
Monday 2o'clock.
It is impossible for me to say when you will see me, some thought of going to Winningham, and to see Colonel Widem as I come so near to his house. These will delay me.'

Emma was pregnant and gave birth on July 20th, 1764, to Robert Williams. He later became Sir Robert Williams, who eventually inherited the Plas-y-Nant estate. Sir Hugh, when he realised that they had a son, was ecstatic and opened champagne. He then gathered Ann Jane and took her to see her little brother. He took an interest in making Baron Hill look as homely as he could.

When he went off to look after the men in his regiment, he would stop at a sale sign and see what they had to offer. He was also keen for them to move and, find their own home which did not tie them to Baron Hill, but Emma had just lost her father and was not keen to leave Anglesey. She loved London but it was all too soon after losing her father and then giving birth to her son, Robert. She needed more time to consider all options.

In August, Sir Hugh travelled to Portsmouth to see to his men and then went to London where he stayed in Oxendon Street. He wrote to Emma on Thursday, August 3rd 1764:

'My Dearest Love,

The only pleasure and satisfaction I have had since my arrival here is sitting to write to my lovely Emm, who I sincerely long to be with. I am already tired of this place owing to my being absent from the dear agreeable companionship, which is my only joy. I long for tomorrow to receive some lines from home pray God give me good news of your recovery and the dear little children.

Does Ann Jane enquire about her Papa. I have seen Tom Evans and Jane determined to have nothing to say to the purchase. The nine thousand pounds mortgage is before it, for I find without having them together it can be of no advantage to our scheme.

I shall attend at auction and if it goes very cheap, perhaps I may venture although Tom makes some difficulty to have cash; he declares that five per cent is the last that is given for money. We have made a fine chip in giving ours at four. Don't be surprised to see me return without a lock aid, I do assure my love it is resolved, if I can get leave to sell unless it be disagreeable to my Emm. If it be you must let me know by return of the post my love I expect your sentiment upon this subject sincerely without reassurances. Tell me truly will you love me as well in a brown coat as a red one. I believe that I shall get as fine lads in a brown. My dearest Emm shall I buy the machine agarose will do until we come here to live. I would give the value of this great city for one slap at my dear girl, no other will satisfy thy longing man.

I have seen the buck who is well and hearty very much grown and improved in every respect. He longs for the time to set out for the Hill, little Hauchens is to be of the party. The Viscount will have no refusal; the father has given his consent; he is much smaller than my Lord but very lively and strong.

Yesterday, I dined with many of our officers who are on their way to Gibraltar. They gave me a violent headache this morning. I have been at Briscoe's and settled everything, paid for tea, bought a clock for the hallway, and I can buy a very fine good repeating watch of Atten's make for fifty pounds, it cost new seventy. It was made for an Irish young blood who sold it to Briscoe, it has not been in wear a week, I shall buy it. Tell me in your next, Jack joins me in love and best respects to all at the Hill, I believe ever my dearest Emma.

Yours most faithfully
H. Williams'

Keeping check on his regiment now was easier apart from having to leave Emma. In December 1764, he once again wrote to the newly elected Secretary at War, Welbore Ellis, saying that if he was not released then he would leave on half pay. He had to stay a while until a suitable officer was found to replace him. In January 1765, he wrote to Emma:

'At Mr David Perfumer in Spiez Street, near Leicester Square 24th Jan. 1765.

I was with Trauter today, tomorrow we go to the Mercer – I wish you had given me full power to discharge the bonds you mentioned for I am at a loss as to how to secure the cash. That and servants are the plague of one's life, I find that John was prepared for my parting with him, he had sent all his things here by the same carrier that brought mine. I have little or no news,

I hear there has been high words in the house, but that the majority My Dearest Emma, I hope it's a mutual pleasure to have news from each other. Your son and husband are well as can be expected when absent from those they love most, already longing to return from where they came; Tuesday night we delivered four proud companions safe in Pall Mall, we did not see the family sooner than today at 4 o'clock.

My Lord and I dined there, we were received in a form of civility and politeness at seven my Lord and myself took a coach and visited Madam Potene. I was sincerely rejoiced to see her quality arrive there left my dear good-natured boy. I assure you with equal grief at parting. Davies Thomas, tailor took his measure on Wednesday morning. His clothes are to be finished Saturday night, he has chosen blue with yellow buttons and a gold laced hat.

Now for my own business and I hope you will be happy as I am to know that Hulls commission was signed the seventh of December and is at Mr Roberts waiting my orders for the delivery. This morning, I went to Mr Oldham who offered to pay me the 105 pounds and give Hull and Col Parrs joint note for 50 pounds for a few days. I shall defer delivering the commission and due of the cash until I consult my married friends how I am to secure it from the perils of a London Lodging house which I cannot think safe for that great sum all my military and civil acquaintances approve of my bargain and I find that every thinking person who is past thirty is as desirous to quit all pretensions of a gaudy baton, as your humble servant was before he was made a free English man. I most sincerely congratulate my dearest upon the agreeable event, and I think myself blessed in being once my own master, with the pleasing thought of returning soon to the dear arms of my Emma, there I shall find the agreeable repose and ease of mind flourishes. Miss Warbuton's marriage with Mr Littleton is off, the reasons are not given. I must wish my love a good night- to begin a letter to Mr Lewis the attorney about money to Mr Griffith, love and compliments to all from Dear Emma's faithful lover and husband.

H Williams'

In February 1765 he wrote again, probably the last letter he wrote now that he was a free man, having left the army on half pay.

> 'Tom Evans Middle Temple 14th February 1765.
>
> My Dearest love's most pleasing epistle of the 9th came safely last night. This morning, I was impolitely up at eight and went immediately to Traughtons who assisted to buy an adult negligee, the part is lacy. I have not now the time to expatiate upon, your other fine things are safe at my lodgings and shall be packed tomorrow. They are the finest affairs I ever beheld, genteel and pretty I do assure my love. I am almost a grown as to my extra cash, exclusive of my own principle- Saturday I hope to set out as far Dunstable where there is a fine horse fair Monday as it is in my way I will endeavour to buy a pair of Nags Byson Black. This affair will detain me there until Sunday even Monday morning early. Don't expect me sooner than this day seven nights when I shall be at my dear girls' home.
>
> To be home of all other things, but I am afraid you will be tired of my company, when that unlucky, unhappy hour comes away to the rocks at Nant I will retire. Yesterday I discharged Maples Bonds and paid six hundred and five pounds six shillings. The remainder comes in Bank bills found in different places. I am called to supper excuse hurry and haste; my dear Buck is well – I shall write Saturday from Dunstable.
>
> This seven nights at my dearest until then believe, believe me virtuous and shall ever remain.
>
> Dear Emma
> Most affectionate.
> H. Williams'

Sir Hugh was very pleased to be home and felt that his life would now be good; no more suffering in the heat of Gibraltar, he would enjoy the cool air of Beaumaris. This is what he had dreamt of for so long.

Bridget had not been too well, and Emma went to visit her at Chester. She seemed quite recovered by the time her mother arrived. She told her mother that she had taken her medicine every day and felt that it had done some good. They enjoyed the two-day visit and Emma returned to Baron Hill and Sir Hugh.

March brought better weather and Sir Hugh continued with the many papers belonging to Emma's father. Then matters took a turn for the worse as they were called to Caerau: her grandmother was not well and had taken to her bed. Emma was pregnant again and had been aware for some time of the deterioration of her grandmother, especially after Thomas's death. It was obvious that Mrs Roberts was very tired of life and was preparing herself for her death. Sir Hugh decided that he would stay at Caerau, to be company should the old lady need it and to make sure that nothing went missing as Emma was the only one to inherit anything. He wrote to Emma on Tuesday morning April 2nd, 1765:

> 'Ten thousand thanks to my dearest love for her pleasing agreeable letter. By Will, and before this arrived you will have received my scrawling epistle for not writing by post you have now made ample satisfaction in giving me pleasing account of your health and spirits which is of the first concern to me.
>
> The good old lady is now very bad and, in my opinion, draws near the Harbour of death, that harbour which will secure her from all future storms of this restless world. She seems very delirious to leave it in expectation of a better and wishes sincerely to die soon. Her sense continues but don't choose to speak to anyone since yesterday. Twelve o'clock this morning she made signs to have her bed made and they found her much weaker and altered for the worst; I have this moment paid for her four pounds, nine shillings and eleven pence Land Tax and window tax, which will reduce the poor old lady's capital to a small sum. This moment J Long came in to offer me 6 tumblers of brandy which I shall accept of it and keep.
>
> Will Tom until night which will afford me something new to mention from Bodewryd where I shall dine; adieu now—
>
> I am just come from Bodewryd and find the old lady neither better nor worse, than she was in the morning, your cousin received me politely and asked very kindly for you and the young ones; I find that Mrs Owen has the good old lady's will and one

hundred and eighty pounds which she intends to design to you, or order upon Mrs Roberts's death which I am afraid will be soon.

Sir John and Lady Stanley are expected there daily for a short stay, then to Chester for a long one which looks as if the Anglesey fools don't intend being caught, and he given up all hopes at present of carrying the county; Will Thomas is to bring you a cask of Brandy which cost me £6 pounds, and I have this moment bought 6lbs of Tea which cost two guineas, the soap is sent by Mrs Williams, she's a good woman sits most nights with her old friend and has been here ten days and nights without going home, which will lay me under great and lasting obligation to her, although she is but grateful in her return for innumerable favours from this house.

Just as I was finishing this scrawl word was brought to me that Will Thomas is so drunk that he cannot be trusted to go with the things and I must keep him here until tomorrow night, advice now.

Wednesday twelve o'clock very rainy disagreeable morning the good old lady is alive, but had a very bad restless night and those who sat up with her thought it was the last that she could survive, but rather better now and enquired for me what I should have for dinner complaining that my intention was but homely the only thing that makes my time heavy and disagreeable here, is being so long deprived of your company with pleasure I could finish my days with you my love in this retired retreat, but alas it's not a place you approve of, therefore I must not think of it, except for a chamber, sorry for which I shall never want whilst you are – desire Emm Lewis to inform me the date of the Whitehall paper which is wanting which I can bring to complete mine – my dearest need not for my making any wanton distribution of Miss Bulkeley's property. I hope you cannot accuse my being extravagant of anything belonging to them, therefore that caution was needless. You will allow I have less reason than your ladyship to have the least regard to what the dear cousin would miss report of me, my dear girl is not free from their censures let it be ever such nonsense.

I am under terrible apprehension that Madams Longford and three will be here soon, if they come, I shall give up patience and leave them commanders in chief of this poor place.

This moment I was honoured with the enclosed from Mrs Owen. By the contents you may find how great we are; Sir John and her ladyship is to honour us on Monday next at the Hill – my loves agreeable letter is just arrived. I wish it was now in my power to give you a thousand kisses, for it and five hundred for the good apples which I munch unreasonably. I sincerely long to return although I do assure my dearest we are in this retired hole, all quiet and serene, no thunderstorms or lightning have I seen or heard in this place since I came and convince you how forward we are here, than at Baron Hill, I have sent you a dish of asparagus which I cut this morning. I hope you will receive this vile scrawl tomorrow in bed, pray wish me between thy dear pretty thighs. I would kiss thee out of breath was I there now let the enclosed be delivered Saturday next. John Williams is to excuse my attendance on the Grand Jury, one barrister is too many to afford the tablet.

Love, blessings and compliments to all at the Hill and I remain my dearest Emms ever faithful, affectionate, and thankful husband.

H Williams'

There were constant letters going backwards and forwards and then came the day when he would have to write with the news of the old lady's death.

'Caerau April 4th 1765.
My Dearest love,

This brings you the last account of your poor old Grandmother's. She died this morning about 1 o'clock, her speech left her since yesterday morning, and was quite easy and reposed to resign this troublesome world for a better; pray send me all the instructions and orders you can think of. The burying cannot be sooner than Monday morning by her own request.

I have locked all her drawers and closets; I shall act in a frugal manner as decency will admit it. The two young ladies have offered to stay here until the funeral and manage things in the house. Miss Fowles is rather sensible and clever, the other a good-natured country wench.

Do as your own inclination leads you about Robert's coming, her presence will be agreeable to me, but by no means distress yourself, for we can do without her. If you have killed a Beef send a piece or two, with some veal for certainly there will come a number of people here especially neighbours, send 3or 4 bottles of Port wine for I have non here – give me all instructions you can about the funeral, and the service I am to offer and for whom – write immediately to Miss Bulkeley.

Paying Will Lewis's bill for Brandy tea etc has drained my pocket therefore send me ten guineas by safe hand: I hope to kiss my dear girl and children Wednesday, or sooner if I can for I truly long to be with you, I want you every moment day and night – I hope Will Thomas brought the things safe last night – I beg my dearest will not fret upon this occasion which was so long expected pray take care of your health which is of so much consequence to my happiness in this life – I shall write this moment to Caernarvon for the necessary things. What am I to give Margaret Jones and Mrs Williams for this trouble in being here so long, adieu my love and life.

Love blessings and compliments from all here to all at the Hill, let me hear from you often which is my only pleasure whilst absent, Believe me ever, Dear Emms

Most faithful and affectionate Husband
H Williams'

On 7th April he wrote again hoping that this would be the last time before returning to Baron Hill.

'April 7th, 1765.
My Dear and only Love,

I shall tire you with my scrawl and your writing to me, which is my comfort, but I am certain of forgiveness when I am blessed in thy sweet arms which I now long for; everybody says you look *charming and breeding agrees with you. Sorry my lump is so bad with his feet, but better out than in the little body.*

Thanks for the goods you sent in return you will I hope to have 2lbs of Ceylon Tea, 4lbs common tea and a lobster, which is the first this year.

Check the enclosed correct it and waver it then send it to your cousin's lodgings. I hope you will approve the contents. Desire Mr Hugh Jones to consult with the mayor about the office meeting, I shall be glad it was not sooner than Friday which time I shall be at Baron Hill I hope at eleven o'clock. It will be very inconvenient to leave this hut sooner for I have a great deal to settle with the tenants and servants; but if my Lord's affairs require my presence I will come at a moment's warning I find Nancy intends to go to her Mother and is to be married soon, therefore you must look out for some honest body to take care of this house and furniture. There is an excellent little girl who is father and Motherless, very fit to be your poultry girl. Pray let me send her to Baron Hill, what am I to do with your boy Dick? The two horses and a cow are they to be sold or sent to Baron Hill with the chaise. Pay Hugh Jones the 40 pounds otherwise there is 5% interest on it. I find that Mrs Owen will send me on Wednesday next with the horses comes for Miss Fowles, the hundred and eighty pounds and ten pounds of this is your ladyships, which the good old lady has left you in her will.

You ought to send an invitation to your cousin Jenny Edwards to come to Baron Hill for a week and give her horses to return home. The family of Boderwyd refused her horses, on invitation the house being filled soon by John and Daughter. She is a very quiet good country girl, and you will like her for a few days, and she was at your grandmother's. I think it important upon you to take some notice of her in this strange country. I will send the groom upon-with her home, and I can assure you this is Boderwyd sentiment my Dearest tell Hugh Jones to acquaint my Lord's friends of The Office Meeting and to desire their attendance for fear the Evans's hand be proposed. I shall name your cousin Jack to become if you have no objection; he has truly the right being related to you.

> Let me have the pleasure of Tuesday morning after you have spoken to councillor Williams; I propose to have the old ladies' tenants here Wednesday to make their returns, and show their accounts, sooner is not proper or decent. God Bless and preserve my Dearest Emm take care of yourself and the little ones, now we have them. Madam Ann behaves well and easy, she goes to Boderwyd, they desire their respects.
>
> My love blessings and compliments attend you and your family, I remain ever.
>
> Dear Emms
> Most affectionate and sincere husband
> H. Williams
>
> Send cash as desired in my last
> I am near ground.
>
> - Black silk new cape.
> - Brown collar silk gown old.
> - Grey stuff silk gown new fringed.
> - Grey silk gown very old.
>
> The others given as you desired to Mrs Williams, Magory Jones and Nany. What am I to do with these, I have not given. Jenny Edwards the one you mentioned, for I don't know which you mean her to have, if you mean – collar silk – I will give it to her, the light collar is not worth her acceptance now will I give her so dirty a thing.'

Sir Hugh returned to Baron Hill and went about sorting out more of the paperwork. He made arrangements to visit Caerau again to talk to the tenants and he spoke to Emma about one or two pieces of furniture he felt would help fill a corner at Baron Hill. He told her that until they found someone to look after Caerau, he would visit every week, making sure that things were safe with no break-ins.

He played with Ann Jane and took care of his son, Robert. He was over the moon with how life was going, and he felt very proud. More concern was shown over Bridget who was home for the summer holidays, and had coughing fits and terrible tiredness, though after a day or two it would abate. She loved looking after the younger children and Anne Jane thought the world of her. This was the comfort she had needed, and it made her feel better.

Sir Hugh certainly had his plate full, with all the paperwork to sort out as well as keeping an eye on Caerau and carrying out his duty as Constable of Beaumaris Castle. He was also keen to become a member of parliament, so his time was very occupied.

On October 10th 1765, Emma gave birth to Frances Emma Williams. There were many callers and many celebrations. Sir Hugh was in his element. He had always wanted children. He believed that it was what made a home and a family.

The weather was still warm for the time of year and the farmers had been busy with their usual tending of their lands. Emma seemed more settled now, though she worried about her son Lord Bulkeley. However, Sir Hugh had taken on the role of being a stepfather quite seriously and guided him in various interests which would stand him well once he was of age and standing for the county.

Bridget had been sent home from school in March 1766 as she had not been very well, and her mother loved having her home. She had worked so hard looking after Bridget from the time she was a baby. Bridget had never been strong, but Emma felt that some time at home would put everything right again. At the end of June, however, matters got worse, and Bridget was having difficulty breathing. She had lost weight and the maid made her a special soup, which she enjoyed. Emma was extremely worried, and Sir Hugh was also distressed. He felt that Bridget was his daughter and had taken a great interest in her. He travelled to Chester to the doctor and brought medicine back, which certainly helped with the coughing. Bridget would get up, but then needed to return to bed in the early afternoon. This is how her life went until July 17th 1766, when she closed her eyes in death. Emma was fraught, another death, she thought, all so close, starting with her father then her grandmother and now Bridget.

Sir Hugh did all he could to comfort her and talked with her for hours about life and death, that it was what they all had to accept, however awful it was. He told her a little of how he felt stuck in Gibraltar when he lost some of his men, how hard it was to talk to an officer one day and then have to bury him the next. You could not complain he said, it was expected of you. He comforted her by telling her that she had had Bridget for 16 years and that she could have lived longer but for the consumption that attacked her body taking away her strength. Slowly Emma accepted her daughter's death. She was worried how Lord Bulkeley would react but being young and not having the same understanding about death left him more able to cope.

Life went on and they went to London to meet friends and have a good time. So much was happening and Emma understood now what was meant when people said 'life must go on'. She was happy in London; it was a place she loved with all its constant activity. She met up with friends there for a few months which meant invitations to coffee or afternoon tea. Sir Hugh met with some of his officers home on leave and the time passed very quickly. They took daily walks around London and noticed that footpaths near Westminster had been laid with paving stones, making it easier and cleaner for people to walk. Emma took a great interest in the changes now that she had three young children, they would grow and take an interest in all that was going on.

They returned to Baron Hill ready for the winter months. Plenty of fires would keep them warm and Sir Hugh took a great interest in Beaumaris and its people, which occupied most of his time. He was delighted to learn that Emma was pregnant again and during 1767 she gave birth to a son named Hugh Rowland Williams.

At last, he felt, this was home and with four children he had to be a father. He would take Ann Jane around the gardens at Baron Hill telling her stories about various flowers and bushes. It wasn't long before Robert joined them and he was always trying to climb trees, with many a fall and crying, which his father believed was just wanting attention. Then Frances Emma came along, and Sir Hugh loved to see the three of them running around and watching the boats pretending that they were off somewhere exotic. Returning indoors he found Emma nursing Hugh Rowland, who was a very bonny baby, full of energy, but Emma found it rather hard to keep up with them all.

Emma took an interest in what was happening throughout the country and was pleased to read that the foundation of the Royal

Academy was under way under the patronage of King George III. 1768 saw Captain Cook's first voyage to the Antipodes in *The Endeavour*. Sir J Banks, the naturalist, joined him. He sailed late May on the first circumnavigation. Emma was full of wonder at so many things going on and the excitement of it all.

The first weekly numbers of *Encyclopaedia Britannica* were published; 100 copies were planned, and the *Morning Chronicle* was issued in London. Sir Hugh agreed that they must get copies of the *Encyclopaedia*, there would be much education in it he believed for the children. Life went on outside the household. Emma took an interest in her cousin, Margaret Bold, who became Margaret Owen when her mother married Hugh Owen of Penrhos. She married Sir John Stanley and both Emma and Sir Hugh were very fond of them.

The year 1770 started well, but Emma began feeling unwell and Sir Hugh was constantly worried about her. She would have good days and bad ones but somehow they managed to get along without too much to worry them. Sir Hugh was constantly thinking of ways to invest; that had been his pet scheme for some time. However, late July 1770, Emma showed signs that things were not as they should be, and Sir Hugh called in a doctor who, when he saw her, realised that she was far from well. He diagnosed consumption, but what worried him more than anything else was the fact that Emma was also pregnant. In August 1770, things deteriorated even further and as hard as she tried for the sake of Sir Hugh and her children, she became weaker and eventually became bedridden and died on August 18th. Sir Hugh lost his beloved Emma. He was inconsolable and tried his best to keep it within himself for the sake of his little children.

He found it difficult having loved her so much and wondered how he was going to tell the children. He had four little children deprived of their mother. Also, he would have to tell her eldest son, Thomas James, who was just 18.

Emma was buried on August 27th 1770, at Llanfairynghornwy Church, where a plaque in her memory from Sir Hugh remains today. She was home amongst her family: her mother and father, her grandmother and grandfather and her eldest daughter, her sisters and her brother.

Plaque in memory of Emma's second husband, Sir Hugh Williams, 8th Baronet 'of Penrhyn' (1718–1794), in Llanfairynghornwy Church.

Plaque in memory of Emma in Llanfairynghornwy Church, 1770.

Llanfairynghornwy Church is small and stands on the northwest side of the island. It was built in the 16th century. It is believed that the stone used to erect this extension probably came from the ruins of the old chapel at Cader Mynachdy which was used by the Carmelite monks; hence the name Capel Mynachdy. On the south side of the centre respond is a decorative corbel of a carved Celtic head in stone. It might have been carved by one of the stone masons while building the south chapel. On the eastern respond are the 16th century letters 'SCA MARIA ORA PRO ME DAVID A JACO'.

On the north wall of the chancel is a plaque in memory of Evan Thomas, one of the famous bonesetters of Anglesey. Legend has it that one stormy night there was a shipwreck, two young boys were the only survivors, Evan being one of them. They were taken to Mynachdy, where one of the boys died. Evan survived. It soon became apparent that he had a special gift of bone setting, and he became famous throughout Anglesey. His descendants also had the gift of being able to set bones, the most famous of them was Hugh Owen Thomas, who invented the Thomas splint. The plaque was given by Emma's son, Thomas James, Lord Bulkeley.

This is from a pamphlet about the church by Gwenfron Evans:

Llanfairynghornwy is a medium-sized coastal parish eight miles northeast of Holyhead. The church is the principal monument. According to the *Inventory of Ancient Monuments* for Anglesey, Llanfairynghornwy Church of St Mary stands in the southeast part of the parish. The walls of the nave and the chancel arch are from the 11th to 12th century; The chancel was rebuilt and lengthened in the early 16th century and the south chapel and arcade were added. The west tower was built in the 17th century; the south porch is an addition of uncertain date. Interior memorials listed are:

- To William Roberts of Cayrey. 1715.
- To William Roberts of Cayrey Esq 1714.
- To Ellen wife of Thomas Rowlands of Cayrey and daughter of Wm Roberts and plaque to Emma 1770.
- To Margaret wife of William Williams of Cayrey 1740.
- To Emma wife of William Roberts of Cayrey 1765.
- To Jane Hughes's daughter of Rowland Hughes, A. M., Rector of Llangadwaladr 1766.
- To William Hughes of Mynachdu, 1767.
- To Emma, Viscountess Bulkeley Wm's: daughter of Thomas Rowland as of Nant, Caernarvonshire, and Ellen Roberts of Cayrey 1770.
- To, Sir Hugh Wm's 8th baronet of Penrhyn, 1794, his daughter Anne Jane, 1801.

The commission refers to a large plain silver cup with an inscription and date of 1713. However, in the book on *Church Plate for the Diocese of Bangor* by E. Alfred Jones, we find a reference to the silver cup, as a large plain silver chalice with a deep beaker-like bowl, with a narrow-moulded lip, standing on a tall stem divided by a large plain knob, the base moulded. Inscribed in script lettering in three lines.

*'The gift of Ellen Roberts of
Cayrey to Llanviar church
1713'*

The bowl is also engraved with I.H.S., a cross and nails in glory. London date letter for 1712-13. The maker's almost illegible mark is probably WA with anchor between (TOS WARD). Dimensions: height nine and three-quarter inches, depth five and a quarter inches and a bowl four and three eighths of an inch. The donor, Ellen Roberts, was the daughter and sole heiress of William Roberts Esquire of Caerau and Castellior.

Emma was now safe with her family in her familiar surroundings.

Bibliography

The Wynn family of Bodewryd, Anglesey. *The Dictionary of Welsh Biography.*

Hilary A. Peters, *"Dear Mama": Mrs Owen of Brogyntyn and the Godolphin Family'.* National Library of Wales online.

Llanfair and Brynodol Estate Records. The Garthewin records (BG 0210 LLADOL). The National Library of Wales, Cardiff.

Brogyntyn Estate and Family Records. Letters from Emma Bulkeley-Williams (née Rowlands) to Mary Owen (PEC5/1). National Library of Wales, Cardiff.

Aqua Browser Library LIGC/NLW. John Rowlands's will. Lands for Sir Hugh Williams. National Library of Wales, Cardiff.

Thomas James Warren-Bulkeley, 7th Viscount Bulkeley, by William Say after a portrait by Sir William Beechey, mezzotint (NPG D908). National Portrait Gallery London.

Sir Richard Bulkeley at the House of Commons.

Meyrick family, Bodorgan. *Dictionary of Welsh Biography.*

The Bulkeley family, Anglesey etc. *Dictionary of Welsh Biography.*

Owen family of Peniarth, Llanegryn, Merionethshire. Dictionary of Welsh Biography online.

The Transport Heritage.

History of the Skerris Lighthouse. Trinity House online (www.trinityhouse.co.uk).

'The Bulkeley family', The Peerage.com. John Cardinal's second website.

Helen Ramage, *Portraits of an Island: Eighteenth Century Anglesey*, 1987. In Welsh, *Yr Ardal Wyllt.*

'Lady Bulkeley & et al.', *House of Lords Journal*, Volume 28, January 1756; and Volume 29, January 1757. British History online (www.british-history.ac.uk).

E. Alfred Jones, *The Church Plate of the Diocese of Bangor,* 1906.

Epilogue

Emma did not live long enough to see her son Thomas James become of age as Lord Bulkeley. Her son Robert was only six when she died. She never met her grandson either, who became Richard Bulkeley Williams, a name given to him by his uncle Lord Bulkeley. After Lord Bulkeley's death, instructions to ask the King to be allowed to adopt the name Bulkeley as his surname were allowed, and he became known as Richard Bulkeley Williams Bulkeley. Lord Bulkeley had died without issue.

Her son, Robert, lived mostly at Plas-y-Nant and he became an MP for Caernarvonshire. He died in Nice, and his body was brought back and buried at Llanfairynghornwy.

Both her daughters died without issue, and her youngest son, Hugh Rowland Williams, died in Grenada, in the Caribbean, in 1795, aged 28, in the service of the King. His monument can be seen in the Church of St Mary and St Nicholas in Beaumaris.

Emma's monument hangs in Llanfairynghornwy Church alongside that of her husband, Sir Hugh Williams.

I visit the Llanfairynghornwy occasionally and always feel Emma's presence there. It is a very peaceful church; the feeling of friendliness and tranquillity makes you want to sit in peace. The church is now open for people who would indeed like to sit quietly and perhaps say a prayer to a friend or lost one. That, I believe, is a very healing thing, and I hope that many visitors will enjoy it.

I do believe that to do just that, and leave the many churches around the Island open, would encourage those who are seeking peace and solitude. It is a wonderful idea for those who need it.

Sophia Pari Jones